Y0-BBC-802

The Practical Sailor Library
Volume I • Outfitting

Outfitting

*Equipping a Boat for
Performance, Comfort, and Safety*

Edited by Keith Lawrence

Belvoir Publications, Inc.
Riverside, Connecticut

Copyright © 1988 by Belvoir Publications, Inc.

All rights reserved. No part of this book may be reproduced or utilized in any form or by any means, electronic or mechanical, including photocopying, recording, or by any information storage and retrieval system, without permission in writing from the Publisher. Inquiries should be addressed to Belvoir Publications, Inc., 1111 East Putnam Avenue, Riverside, CT 06878

ISBN: 0-9613139-3-5

Printed in the United States of America
First Edition

Acknowledgments

Over the years, *The Practical Sailor* and *Better Boat* have benefitted from a dedicated staff and knowledgeable contributing editors, from the advice of numerous marine industry professions, and from the input and experience of thousands of loyal readers. In addition to extending our thanks to all of these, we add a special acknowledgment to the following writers for their contribution to this volume:

Ed Adams
Miner Brotherton
Donald DeRolf
Roger F. Duncan
Ron Dwelle
Cathy Dwyer
Bob Gehrman
Don Hubbard
Nick Nicholson
John Pazereskis
Matt Schultz
Larry Shaw
Robert Smith
Jeff Spranger
Sue Weller
Gordon West
R. E. White, Jr.

Contents

Acknowledgements 5

Introduction 9

1 Sails and Sailhandling Equipment 11

2 Reefing and Reefing/Furling Systems 40

3 Winches, Ropes, and Running Rigging 62

4 Awnings, Dodgers, and Custom Canvaswork 79

5 Ground Tackle and Anchor-Handling Equipment 92

6 Navigation Equipment and Electronics 119

7 Safety Equipment 186

8 The Ship's Tender 222

Index 241

Introduction

Most new boats are advertised at "sailaway" prices, and used boats are invariably advertised as "fully equipped." As any sailor who has ever purchased a new boat knows, "sailaway" may mean that the boat includes a suit of working sails and a pair of life jackets, but it hardly means ready to sail away. If you've ever bought (or sold) a used boat, you know that "fully equipped" means complete with whatever odds and ends of gear the seller has decided not to reinstall on his new boat. In these instances, what the terms *sailaway* and *fully equipped* mean is "ready to be outfitted."

Outfitting, however, is not simply a one-time exercise or expense; it is a continual process. As a sailor's knowledge and experience grows—as he reaches for a horizon farther and farther in the distance—his needs in equipment grow with him. In evaluating and selecting that equipment, we trust that you will find the answers to your questions in *Outfitting,* and in the pages of *The Practical Sailor* and *Better Boat*, from which most of this material was edited.

Keith Lawrence

1
Sails and Sailhandling Equipment

A PROPER CRUISING SAIL INVENTORY

Selecting the sail inventory is possibly the most difficult aspect of outfitting a boat. The subject is rife with conflicting opinion. There are no easy to answer questions like, "How many sails should I buy," or "Are fully battened mainsails all they're cracked up to be" and "What about roller furling gear?"

The sailmaker is a good source of information on sail inventories and sailhandling hardware. We determined, as a result, to begin this chapter by interviewing four sailmakers that represent a broad spectrum of opinion.

At the more conservative end, we talked to Tom Clark of Thomas Clark Sailmakers. Toward the more progressive end, we spoke to Herb Hild of Hild Sails, Tom Whitmore of Doyle Sails, and finally, Bill Bergantz of North Sails. Then, just for good measure, we called a well known "free thinker," Garry Hoyt, known for his innovations with the Freedom line of boats.

We asked each of them to describe the proper cruising inventory. "It can't be done," they responded, "because every customer is different. The inventory will depend on the type of boat, the conditions it is sailed in, and the number and ability of the crew."

Not wanting to let these talented professionals off the hook so easily, we divided the question into three categories. The first inventory is for daysailing, defined as daylight sailing in winds under 25 knots. The second inventory is for coastal cruising. This is for the boat that makes an occasional overnight passage in winds of up to 40 knots. The third inventory is for bluewater cruising. That's for the boat that makes long offshore passages and has to be capable of handling any condition the ocean can throw at it.

As the sailmakers felt that the sails must be tailored to suit the boat and its crew, we assumed that all three inventories were for a moderate displacement 32-footer, sailed by a 45-year-old couple whose experience is appropriate to the conditions defined for each category. (In other words, if they are daysailors, they will not use these sails to cross the Atlantic.)

We noticed right away that our guest experts agreed on very little. We had hoped for a consensus, but except on a few items, we didn't get it. The following is a summary of our discussion with the sailmakers. Later in this chapter, we'll cover many of these subjects in greater detail.

The Cruising Rig

In order to chose a sail inventory, we first had to agree on a rig. The choice of a proper cruising rig for a 32-footer is relatively simple. All the sailmakers chose a masthead rig for all three types of cruising. Only Garry Hoyt preferred a fractional rig, citing the advantage of smaller, easier to handle headsails.

Everyone went with a sloop for daysailing and coastal cruising. For bluewater cruising, Clark, Doyle, and Hoyt chose a cutter rig. The separate inner forestay requires a running backstay for support, but allows the use of reaching staysails and provides an alternate stay on which to rig a staysail or storm jib.

To Furl or Not to Furl

All of the experts would put roller furling headsails on the daysailer and the coastal cruiser. For bluewater sailing, the opinions were divided. Even traditionalist Tom Clark, who believes roller furling to be an excuse for poor seamanship, recognizes that there is no squelching the public's demand for carefree sailhandling.

None of the experts saw roller furling as suitable for mainsails on our hypothetical 32-footer. One reason is that the sail is too small to make the advantage worth the cost. Furthermore, some sailmakers have fallen in love with the battened mainsail, which can't be roller reefed.

Roller furling is best suited to the daysailor, as he is likely to carry only one headsail. It becomes less practical with the larger inventories needed for coastal cruising, because of the difficulty of changing sails that feed into a luff groove. It's easiest to leave one sail permanently on the furling gear, and have a second forestay to hank on the remainder of the inventory.

When putting up a smaller headsail, it's easier to control and bag a sail that is secured with hanks to a second forestay. But you can't rig a second forestay to the bow, because it can foul on your furling gear. It has to mount well aft, and that means a cutter rig.

For North, roller furling is always worth the compromise. Bergantz also prefers a sloop with roller furling, even for bluewater cruising. He believes that feeding headsails in and out of furling extrusions can be done shorthanded in any condition. No hanks; he believes they are too old-fashioned.

Doyle also prefers furling gear for all types of sailing, although Whitmore says he would use a cutter rig for bluewater cruising to enable a combination staysail/storm jib to be hanked on. Still, like North, both the genoa and working jib are on luff tapes that are fed into the furling gear.

Hoyt, preferring the fractional rig, uses but a single headsail for all types of sailing, adjusting the sailplan instead by reefing a large mainsail. Because he doesn't have a second sail to change to, hanks are of no use. The only exception is a storm jib for his bluewater cruiser; it's hanked on an inner forestay.

Hild has a unique, if questionable, approach. He recommends a coastal cruising inventory that includes a genoa and a working jib. The genoa is roller furling and the jib is hanked on, but there is no second headstay. He recommends taking a wire halyard to a padeye mounted just behind the stem, winching the halyard tight, and hanking the jib onto it. We question the efficiency of Hild's method, however. It would be tough to control luff sag when using a stretchy, undertensioned halyard as a makeshift headstay.

For bluewater cruising, both Hild and Clark take the conservative approach. Roller furling is left ashore. All headsails are hanked on.

Sail Construction

The difference in construction from one cruising sail to another used to be simple to determine. One simply looked at the handwork, the weight of the cloth, and the way highly stressed parts of the sail were reinforced. Today there are many more variables: roller furling, every sort of panel layout, fully battened mains and cloths like Kevlar and Mylar.

Traditionalists will argue that little of this belongs on the true cruiser, but some of the advances made in racing sail construction deserve to be considered by the cruising sailor. On the other hand, however, there are sailmakers so set on forging new technology that their customers become unwitting guinea pigs. So look for the middle ground.

The first thing to consider is panel layout. All of the sailmakers we interviewed would opt for the good old crosscut panel layout on the mainsail for all applications. Doyle "rotates" the lower part of the mainsail layout to better align cloth strength with stress. Both Doyle and Clark also use radial corner patches on crosscut sails; again, to control sail stretch. North does neither, which may be out of character for the largest racing sailmaker in the world.

As for roller-reefable headsails, crosscut construction is out. Clark and Hild go with the traditional miter cut. Doyle and North use bi-radial (North calls it the C-Cut). Both can control cloth stretch better than crosscut layouts, the bi-radial having the better potential of the two. For the daysailor, North prefers a less expensive leech-cut layout for the furling genoa.

One of the advantages of these new genoa layouts is that it allows "step-up" construction; in other words, successively heavier cloth weights from luff to leech. It also allows the final foot and leech panels to be of ultraviolet-resistant cloth, which avoids having to sew on a separate layer of heavy canvas for protection from the sun. At least, that is what we were told when these layouts were first introduced a few years ago.

Now there is no consensus. Only Hild uses step-up construction on their furling genoas; all the others are of a single weight.

Doyle uses two layers of cloth on the leech. Clark uses 4-inch, 4-layer leech tabling, with an added "overlay" along the leech and foot where the sail would bear on the furling gear when reefed.

Leech and foot reinforcement often incorporate ultraviolet radiation protection. Only Doyle and Hild are using UV-coated cloth on the outer panels. North has sworn off it in favor of old-fashioned canvas, claiming "bad luck" with coated materials. Canvas may block out the sun, but it's also heavy and does little to limit sail stretch.

There is a general agreement that padding the luff of a roller furling genoa will make the sail roll up flatter. However, Clark says it doesn't work quite as well as some sailmakers would have you believe. He says many photographs in advertisements look airbrushed, and many sails with padding are severely wrinkled when they come in for repair.

North doesn't pad the luff of furling genoas for daysailing, because the benefit in winds under 25 knots doesn't justify the expense. And North doesn't pad the luff of a roller furling headsail of the bluewater cruiser. Luff padding adds considerable bulk and makes the sail more difficult to bag, and with two luff-tape sails in the bluewater inventory, one of them will always be in a sailbag. North uses foam for padding coastal cruising sails, as do Doyle and Hild. Clark uses layers of sailcloth to build up thickness.

A final consideration in sail construction is the type of cloth. This never used to be a question. Until recently, there were Dacron "white" sails and nylon spinnakers; Mylar, for all it's superior stretch characteristics, was for racing. Not any more, says North, who now uses a Mylar called "soft Norlam" for all genoas. Even the bluewater cruiser, to whom some sailmakers wouldn't even give furling gear, gets two Mylar genoas from North. One, for furling, is of soft Norlam; the other, a non-furling 150-percent genoa, is of racing Norlam.

Soft Norlam, says North, is easier to stuff than most Dacrons. This is especially true now that traditional sailmakers like Clark have gone to firmer, more stretch-resistant Dacrons. Soft Norlam is a thin layer of Mylar sandwiched between layers of Dacron, so the sail is white and actually has very little Mylar in it.

How Many Headsails?

This question is a tough one for most sailmakers, not because they don't know the answer, but because they have to resist the temptation to recommend more inventory than the customer can afford. So to further define our hypothetical situation, we told the sailmakers that our imaginary sailor wasn't pinching pennies, but he didn't want to waste money on sails that will see little use, either.

It's no surprise that the recommended inventory grows with the aspirations of the sailor. The daysailor is going to sail in a limited range of conditions and, hence, can make do with a single roller furling headsail, say all the sailmakers. The most recommended size is a 135-percent overlap; only Hild would go with a full 150-percent overlap, and Hoyt, with his fractional rig, feels he can get away with just a 110.

There seems to be some disagreement as to how small this single headsail can be roller reefed and remain effective. The more sail you have rolled up, the less perfect the sail shape tends to be. It wasn't long ago that any amount of roller reefing would make the sail so baggy that going to weather became a frustrating experience.

Now, with improved sail construction, padded luffs, and advanced furling gear, a sail can be roller reefed more effectively. Whitmore says that Doyle's 135-percent genoa can be rolled to as small as 60-percent (storm jib size) and still be effective. Hild is almost as bold, saying that his 150 genoa can be rolled to 95-percent overlap. Clark is a bit more conservative; his 135 can be rolled to 90.

In contrast, Bergantz doesn't recommend rolling North's 135-percent genoa for the daysailor to smaller than 110 percent. One reason may be that North doesn't use foam luff padding in that particular sail, so the sail doesn't roll up quite as smoothly. However, even on the 150-percent furling genoa for coastal cruising, North only recommends reefing to 120 percent. Either North isn't building furling genoas equal to the competition, or is just more fussy about sail shape. We suspect it's the latter, as there's no denying that the more you roll up a sail, be it North's or the competition's, the poorer the shape is going to be.

As mentioned before, the size of the inventory grows with the range of conditions the boat is likely to encounter. All sailmakers recommend at least two headsails for the coastal cruiser. Both North and Doyle stick with a simple inventory of two furling jibs. Hild hanks on the working jib and adds a storm jib. Clark takes the traditional route in recommending four jibs from a 150-percent overlap down to 60.

For the bluewater cruiser, the pattern is much the same. North and Doyle have a three-headsail inventory with the addition of a storm jib. Doyle has the storm jib double as a staysail. Hild goes to five sails with the addition of twin 115-percent jibs, which can be set wing-and-wing downwind. Clark again comes up with the biggest inventory with the addition of a separate staysail and storm jib.

It's obvious that one loft's idea of the practical size for an inventory is not the same as another's. It's interesting to note that Garry Hoyt, who is not a sailmaker, recommends the smallest inventory yet, adding only a 110-percent furling genoa and a storm jib for the bluewater cruiser. He insists that with a large fractional main and a spinnaker, you can adjust the sail plan for just about any condition.

Clew height is another way of gauging a sailmaker's philosophy. The higher the clew, the less efficient the sail is upwind, but the more durable and easier to trim it will be. Again, Clark is the most conservative. All his clews are high; many of his sails lead to the transom. Hild is bit more moderate; only his bluewater cruiser sails have extreme clew height. Doyle and North are the most racy, with their clews at or just above lifeline height. Even so, they're still a foot or two above racing clew height.

Mainsails

The big decision when ordering a mainsail is what kind of batten design to choose. There's a great deal of difference between a battenless mainsail and one with full battens. Unfortunately, sailmakers don't agree on which one is best.

Clark and Hild don't believe in full battens. As reasons, they cite added weight, added cost, and frequency of repair mostly due to broken battens and batten pockets that tend to chafe and

Most sailmakers would agree that the storm jib should use hanks for luff attachment, either to the headstay, or to an inner forestay.

tear. Hild adds that he thinks full batten mains are "hazardous to your health" because the boom tends to swing through such a great radius as the sail luffs.

Hild goes so far as to recommend a battenless mainsail for the bluewater cruiser. Both Clark and Hild admit, however, that a fully battened mainsail is easier to reef and tends to have better sail shape.

The North loft stands on the middle ground. Bergantz points out that a fully battened cruising main doesn't have the excessive roach seen in the mainsail of a racing multihull. Instead the roach is moderate; a little more than a traditional main, but not so much that it will hang up on the backstay. With moderate roach, the common problems associated with full battens—broken battens and torn pockets—are greatly reduced. Once these problems are licked, a fully battened main should have a longer life than a traditional mainsail because the battens dampen the luffing of the sail.

Bergantz also points out that a fully battened main is quieter when motoring with the sail up. However, he admits that the primary advantage of such a sail—ease of handling—is largely lost on our hypothetical 32-footer. Therefore, North recommends a traditional mainsail. Only if performance were of primary importance would he recommend a fully battened main for a 32-footer.

Doyle, on the other hand, has completely embraced the fully battened main, recommending it for all types of cruising, from bluewater to daysailing. Doyle has even trademarked its mainsail; it's called "Stack Pack" because it uses lazy jacks attached to a sailcover to help "stack" the sail on top of the boom. To combat chafe, Doyle uses zippered batten pockets with the ends reinforced with leather. Doyle isn't the only full batten proponent; Garry Hoyt has long been a believer, too.

As for the traditional mainsails offered by North, Clark and Hild, they all use battens of a length that is legal under the IOR rule (which PHRF follows for sail measurements). Why not make the battens longer to better support the roach? Because, say the sailmakers, the customer may want to enter an occasional race. To avoid a rating penalty, the battens must be short.

The irony is that there is no longer any reason for the IOR rule to limit batten length. In past versions of the rule, the width (girth) of a sail was not measured. The IOR controlled sail girth by limiting batten length; if you made a sail too wide, the leech would hinge on the battens. Now the IOR measures mainsail girth, but they haven't gotten around to discarding the old batten limitations. As soon as that happens, all current mainsails are going to be obsolete.

Downwind Sails

About the only aspect of downwind sails that the sailmakers agree on is that the coastal cruiser needs to have a poleless spinnaker. As for the daysailor, only North thinks that he needs, or can handle, a poleless spinnaker. Hild and Doyle both recommend a free-flying drifter/reacher, a sail that is a bit more conservative, and more closewinded than a poleless spinnaker.

Poleless spinnakers do take some skill to fly. Clark doesn't recommend them, or any downwind sails for the daysailor. They can wrap around the headstay and they need to be poled out when running downwind. It's expected that the coastal cruiser will be experienced enough to handle a poleless spinnaker.

By the time you attempt bluewater cruising, you should be able to handle a traditional spinnaker, say Doyle, North and Clark. This kind of sail offers the best performance of the downwind sails. Doyle would also add a free-flying reacher to the bluewater inventory.

Only Hild shies away from the traditional spinnaker for any kind of cruising. For the bluewater cruiser, Hild goes to separate 115-percent twin jibs, with twin poles, for downwind sailing. Twin jibs offer manageability at the expense of performance.

When it comes to downwind sails, Garry Hoyt is again out on a limb. He feels that everyone, even the daysailor, needs performance downwind. He also believes that his "Gun Mount," a bow-mounted, balanced spinnaker pole, combined with a furling spinnaker, is easy enough for the novice to handle and sturdy enough to take whatever bluewater is thrown at it.

Hoyt's original Gun Mount design incorporated a spinnaker that furled into a sock on deck. The current design uses a fully battened spinnaker that roller reefs like a window shade. The sailmakers also recommend being able to furl both a poleless or a traditional spinnaker; the most practical way is in a sock.

Talking to the experts has helped us to firm up a few of our own opinions. For example, we like fractional rigs, or at least masthead rigs with big mainsails and small headsails. We think that fully battened mainsails are the thing of the future, as are Mylar, radial corners and radial panel layouts. We suspect that sailmakers like Doyle and North are very close to working all the bugs out of these innovations, if they are not already there.

We like roller furling on headsails, but we think that any boat attempting shorthanded coastal or bluewater cruising should be cutter rigged so as to be able to hank a small jib on the inner forestay. We don't like to see shorthanded sailors trying to change headsails on the furling gear. We like robust furling gear for pure cruising.

We don't like poleless spinnakers. We're intrigued by Hoyt's

Gun Mount, but we think its time is still a few years away. We like traditional spinnakers for coastal and bluewater cruising, doused in a sock.

So where does that leave us? Here's our own, admittedly biased, idea of the proper inventory.

For the Daysailer:
- Mainsail with oversize battens (longer than IOR rule allows) and one reef
- 130-percent furling genoa with an oversized whisker pole to enable it to be set wing-and-wing on a broad reach

For the Coastal Cruiser:
- Cutter rig
- Fully battened mainsail with 2 reefs
- 140-percent Mylar furling genoa
- Full size staysail hanked onto an inner forestay
- Traditional spinnaker with a sock

For the Bluewater Cruiser:
- Cutter rig
- Fully battened mainsail with 2 reefs
- 140-percent Mylar furling genoa
- Full-size staysail hanked to an inner forestay
- Storm jib
- Storm trysail on a separate track
- Traditional spinnaker with a sock
- 165-percent free-flying reacher

CHOOSING A SAILMAKER

Getting quotes from several sailmakers when you're shopping for new sails is part of being a smart consumer. Choosing a sailmaker merely because he offers a sail of heavier weight cloth isn't smart, however. That's because there's a lot more to the cloth game than the number of ounces per square yard. It's a game that, if the sailmaker plays to win, you're bound to loose.

When you ask for a quote on a sail, the response you get will reflect your query. If you're vague about what you want in a new sail, the sailmaker's response can be equally vague. If you emphasize price without asking about quality, the sailmaker will make you a cheap sail. If you think that quality can be determined by asking for the weight of sailcloth to be used, you're wrong.

The unsophisticated customer is likely to be treated with more indifference than the sailor who asks intelligent questions. Sailmakers know that most sailors can't identify the cloth used in a sail. There are different types of cloths for different applications, and there are cheap and expensive cloths for the same application. The cloth weight quoted is often an approximation; the sailmaker may use whatever he happens to have on hand.

There are several ways to let the sailmaker know that you care about your sails, ways to get him to take more than cursory notice of your order. But first, you should understand more about the materials with which he works.

Sailcloth Basics

First, familiarize yourself with the names of the cloth manufacturers. It helps to know one brand from another, especially if you want to buy American. The big name in U.S. sailcloth is Bainbridge; lesser, but not necessarily inferior, U.S. suppliers are Dimension and Aquino.

Toray and Teigin are the big names in Japanese cloth. Windmaster, Carrington, Hayward, and Vectus are top British sailcloth companies. In Spain, the big name is Sattimar and in Germany, Polyant.

Sailcloth weight is labeled in ounces per sailmaker's yard, not per square yard. A sailmaker's yard is only 28-1/2 inches wide—the width of early Dacron and cotton sailcloth. Modern Dacron is produced in a width of 36 inches, so the actual weight of a modern yard-long piece of cloth is about 25 percent more than the stated weight per yard.

This is fine as long as everyone follows the same measurement system. However, we have heard rumors of foreign lofts occasionally quoting cloth weight per square yard instead of per sailmaker's yard. This gives the customer the impression he is getting a heavier sail than he actually is.

A properly labeled sailcloth still may not weigh what the label says it does, says Jim Linville of Dimension Sailcloth. He claims that the cheaper cloths from foreign suppliers often weigh 10 percent less than the stated weight. Conversely some expensive fabrics tend to weigh more than their labels would indicate.

Even a U.S.-made cloth is not likely to match it's label exactly. Part of the problem stems from a lack of precise control of the finishing process, which allows the weight to vary by 5 percent from it's assigned label. Another reason is that arbitrary labels are sometimes assigned to help organize the multitude of cloths available. For example, Dimension has a series of specialized mainsail fabrics in a variety of weights. They label them 4.55-ounce, 6.55-ounce, 8.55-ounce, and so on, to make it easier for the sailmaker. The actual weight doesn't agree with the label, however. The 4.55-ounce weighs 4.7 ounces in a soft finish, and 5.0 ounces in a hard racing finish.

Each cloth manufacturer offers different types of cloth for different applications, and each type is often available in a variety of finishes. You have to trust your sailmaker to know which type to use for your sails. Dimension divides its Dacron fabrics into three types: all purpose, high aspect, and warp oriented. Bainbridge divides its fabrics into five types: balanced, blade, mainsail, warp oriented, and Bermuda.

A balanced weave has similar strength in both the "warp" (the length of the cloth roll) and the "fill" (across the roll). It provides the best tear strength, but unless given a very firm finish, it may not provide the stretch resistance to support the heavy loading along a sail's leech. Because it needs a hard finish, its application is limited to racing.

Blade, or all-purpose fabrics, have more strength in the fill than the warp, so can better support leech loads without sacrificing too much tear strength. This is the type of cloth used on most cruising boats, as they have relatively low-aspect sailplans that minimize leech loads. Low-aspect rigs may have increased loads on the "bias" (diagonally across the panel). The most effective method of controlling bias stretch is through a harder finish. Better yet is Mylar. As the resin breaks down, however, the bias support will depend increasingly on the tightness of the weave. Domestic cloth manufacturers complain that their foreign competitors rely too heavily on resination, and that their resin is less durable than the U.S. counterpart.

They also point out that most cruising sailors shouldn't shy away from firm finishes (on U.S. cloth) for roller furling sails. Since those sails aren't handled, they needn't be soft. They already suffer from other performance compromises; it makes no sense to further burden them with a soft, stretchy finish.

A high aspect, or mainsail fabric is used in crosscut Dacron performance sails. It is much stronger in the fill than the warp, so it best supports leech loads. It provides better sail performance to weather, at the further expense of tear strength.

Warp-oriented fabrics are stronger in the warp, the greatest strength running in a direction perpendicular to that of other fabrics. Consequently, they are used for panels in sails with vertical and radial panel layouts.

While most people associate radial sails with grand prix racers, there is no reason why the loads of a cruising sail couldn't be better controlled with radial Dacron construction. However, warp-oriented Dacrons are still in the development process, says Fran Charles, of Bainbridge. The problem is maintaining enough tension on the warp yarns to remove the "crimp" while weaving.

Bermuda cloth is Bainbridge's answer to cheap foreign competition. While it costs more than foreign cloths, Bainbridge says it is of higher quality. Bermuda has been around for several years, but has recently been improved with a harder finish and stronger fill threads. It's not the equal, though, of the Bainbridge blade fabrics of which the higher quality cruising sails are built. Bermuda still isn't available in quite as firm a finish, nor does it have the same number of "high tenacity" (low stretch) yarns in its construction.

With Bermuda, as with any of the cheaper cloths, you pay less but you get less. It's possible to have a heavier cloth be much cheaper than a lighter quality fabric, and for that lighter fabric to make a better-setting sail. Going heavy doesn't always get you more. For example, 6-ounce Bermuda costs only $3.90 a yard, compared to $5.43 a yard for Bainbridge's 5.43-ounce fabric. Yet the 5.43-ounce has higher tenacity yarns and and will hold its shape better.

So where does that leave the consumer? Should he insist on

U.S.-made cloth; should he avoid Bainbridge's Bermuda? Not necessarily. Bermuda is an adequate cloth for the non-performance-oriented cruiser, and is probably superior to the cheapest foreign alternatives. As for the foreign cloth manufacturers, they also offer a variety of fabrics, some of high quality, and all at attractive prices. Remember that you get what you pay for.

Ultimately, you have to trust your sailmaker, but it helps if you let him know that you know exactly what you want. Here's some of the things you should ask:

Tips on Ordering a Sail

Now that you know a little bit about Dacron sailcloth, you can begin an intelligent dialogue with the sailmaker. (It helps to let him know that you're smarter than the average sailor.)

Order in the fall. Not only will you get a discount, but the sailmaker will have more time to design and construct your sails. Don't get lost in the spring rush.

Avoid blind inquiries. Don't send a note to a series of sail lofts asking for a quick quote. You'll either get a lot of telephone calls from loft salesman, or worse, the loft will assume that price is your prime criterion. You'll get a dirt cheap quote, and sails that no one would be proud of.

Get a variety of opinions. Remember that a sailmaker who specializes in cruising sails has a different outlook than a sailmaker known for his racing sails. High performance to one may be tortoise-like to the other; what one sailmaker considers to be soft cloth may mean something else to another. Color the opinions you get with what you know about the sailmaker's professional views.

Articulate your needs. What are the predominant conditions in your sailing area? Do you want to enter an occasional race? If so, will it bother you if you're off the pace because of your sails? Do you harbor any fantasies beyond daysailing; an occasional coastal cruise, or maybe a once-in-a-lifetime offshore cruise? Don't make your sails do work for which they are not designed.

How long do you plan to keep your boat? Do you expect your sails to be an asset when you put it on the market? Do you like to claw to windward, or ghost downwind (both require refined sails), or would you be just as happy turning on the engine?

Are you happy with the way your boat handles? Does she need more horsepower or better balance? Are you aware of all the modern sailhandling conveniences like roller furling? Would you go sailing more often if you could do it shorthanded? Are you contemplating any changes in the rig? A sailmaker can help you with all aspects of your boat's performance. Think about it.

Develop a dialogue and pick the sailmaker's brain. Ask him what he's doing that's new and creative. If you've heard about a certain technique or piece of sailhandling hardware, ask him if he's had good or bad experience with it. Throw your own ideas at him. Get his reaction. Don't be shy.

Remember that most sailmakers can build a work of art just as easily as they can make a dishrag. It all depends on what you're willing to pay for. Ask the sailmaker what improvements more money would buy, and vice versa. That will help you get a handle on what you are ordering.

Ask about cloth. Now that your familiar with some of the terminology, ask about the cloth the loft will use. Ask about the cloth manufacturer, the specific type and the weight. You may want to ask the fill-to-warp stretch ratio. It's about 2:1 for all-purpose or blade cloths, and 3:1 for high aspect mainsail cloths. How hard is the finish? Is the cloth made entirely of high tenacity yarn? That's a question that may send the sailmaker scurrying to the cloth supplier for the answer.

Ask for a cloth sample. This can't hurt. It makes the sailmaker think you know what your talking about, and makes it unlikely you'll get a sail made of a cloth different from what you were quoted. The sailmaker won't grab any convenient roll of cloth when he knows you've got a sample to compare it to. Don't be surprised if the sample seems to have too firm a finish—cloth always seems firm in small swatches.

Ask about the accessories. The extras that go into a sail have a lot to do with the price. How many reefs will the main have? Will the main and jibs have leech lines? How far apart are the hanks spaced? Are the hanks bronze or plastic; what size are they (you may want a sample)? Are they webbed on or held with shackles? (Webbing is better.) Is the webbing stitched or merely fastened with a grommet?

Sails and Sailhandling Equipment

Does the headboard have a stainless steel insert for the halyard shackle? Are the corner grommets strapped with webbing? Unless they're hand-sewn, or the new super-toothed Harken grommets, they should be strapped.

Ask about construction. Determining the quality of construction used to be a simple matter. You'd ask about the size of the corner patches, whether the main has a shelf foot, if the batten pockets were "plaqued" with extra layers of cloth, and so forth.

Now, with the advent of improved "stress mapping" of sail loads (thanks to the racers) you have to get more technical. Are there radial corner overlays or inlays? How big? Are the panels rocked to line up with the leech loads? Is the fill strength of the cloth sufficient to support the roach? For how long? What is done to make a roller furled sail set better? Is the luff padded? What about ultraviolet protection?

And finally, get the dimensions right. Sailors tend to think sailmakers are omniscient when it comes to sailplans. It's true that most lofts keep extensive files on boat dimensions, but it's still smart to make sure that your sail measurements are correct. Many builders make changes to the rigs of their boats—not to mention owner modifications. The sailmakers don't always find out about them until they've made a costly mistake.

If you've got a custom boat, get a sailplan from the designer. If you've got a production boat, it can't hurt to dig up a sailplan from the boat show brochures you collected before you bought it. To be safe, you can always take a tape measure to your spars.

Providing sail measurements, and asking for written confirmation of those measurements from the sail loft, helps to ensure that you will get all the sail you paid for. (Making a sail smaller than quoted is a favorite ploy of some bargain basement lofts.)

You also need some detailed measurements. Find out the distance from the mast to your tack pin. If you have an outhaul car, the sailmaker needs to know the height of the clew pin and the length of the track. If you have roller furling, the height of the tack off the deck is important. If your headsail halyards don't exit close below the tip of the headstay, make a note of that, too. A quality sailmaker will ask you all these questions; maybe more. If he doesn't ask, beware.

HIGH TECH RACING SAILS

It's hard to miss the latest marvels of sailmaking. Just glance at any magazine that covers grand prix sailboat racing. With the exception of the nylon in spinnakers, all the top boats are equipped with sails made exclusively of Mylar and Kevlar, arranged in unusual layouts, with equally unusual names like Bi-Star, C-Cut, Wedge Cut, Quilt Cut, Spidercut, or Tape-Drive.

How does all this new technology apply to the average club racer—the sailor who races in his local PHRF fleet or in the weeknight yacht club series? Will the latest in high-technology sailmaking do much to improve his race results? Probably not as much as most sailmakers would have you believe.

The world of high-tech sailmaking is, almost by definition, hard to define. It encompasses the experimental cutting edge of what is known about the materials used in making sails and the ways they are put together. Because it is labor intensive, it is expensive. As soon as all the bugs are worked out of a new idea, it goes into production, moves out of the realm of high tech and becomes mainstream.

Mylar is no longer high tech. It's a proven material that's no more expensive than the Dacron used in comparable applications. A simple, crosscut sail of Mylar will be about the same price and the same shape as a Dacron sail, yet it will stretch less and be lighter.

Kevlar, however, is high tech. Although there are inexpensive varieties intended for the PHRF racer now on the market, you can expect an all-Kevlar number 3 jib to cost about 25 percent more than a Dacron sail of similar crosscut construction.

Radial construction is high tech, too. Because it's so labor intensive, it increases the cost of a sail. Simple radial corners, used in an otherwise crosscut sail, add about 15 percent to the cost of a sail.

Full radial, all-Mylar construction adds about 30 percent to the cost. Kevlar/Mylar radial construction adds anywhere from 40 percent to 80 percent to the cost depending on the quality of materials used. The sailmaker may be pushing high tech on the PHRF racer, but the materials used are sometimes cheaper than on a all-out IOR racer.

Sails and Sailhandling Equipment

The principal advantage that high technology aims to achieve is lighter, stronger sails. Lighter sails fly better in light air. In heavy air, they reduce weight aloft and, hence, reduce the boat's tendency to pitch and heel. To the PHRF racer who may seldom race in heavy air and large waves, the advantage of lighter sails is minimal.

Reduced cloth stretch is commonly cited as another advantage of high tech sails. While it's true that high tech sails do stretch less, the reduction in stretch is not as much as sailmakers would have you believe, because the sails are built to be so light. Moreover, on smaller boats with bendy rigs, some stretch in the mainsail can be advantageous. There have been many reports of one-design fleets changing back to their stock Dacron mainsails because they were faster.

The casual racer should not be mislead into thinking that high tech means a faster sail shape. In fact, high tech often means a slower sail shape. There has been little refinement in the perception of a fast shape in the past few years. The accepted shapes are easily created with crosscut sail design. Duplicating that shape in radial construction is not so easy. Sailmakers have had to relearn the shaping process, as the panels are now run in different directions. At first they cut a couple of horizontal seams across the radials to try to recreate the shape proven fast in crosscut sails. Only recently have sailmakers begun putting shape into the radials themselves.

Because of the breathtaking pace at which high tech sailmaking has advanced, new techniques are often introduced before they are properly tested. And just as they get the bugs out of one type of panel layout, the sailmaker comes out with a new one. Not only are the chances of getting a poorly shaped sail greater with high tech construction, but problems are also more difficult to correct once they are discovered.

Again, Mylar is no longer considered high tech. The PHRF racer of 25 feet or larger should consider a Mylar genoa. We think a sail of crosscut construction with radial corners will likely be as fast, if not faster than a high tech genoa, and cost less to boot. The Mylar/Kevlar high tech genoa would be overkill on anything smaller than about 36 feet. With a fractional rig, consider staying away from high tech headsails until about 41 feet LOA.

The place for high tech is on big, all-out racers. The smaller the boat, the more diminished the value. High tech headsails are more valuable in smaller boats than high tech mainsails, but the value of a high tech headsail is still dubious in smaller PHRF racers. It's not until the leech loads begin to exceed the strength of the common Mylars that Kevlar is needed. Again, you're looking at a 40-foot boat for a noticeable advantage.

If you do go high tech, make sure you're not a guinea pig. Ask the sailmaker how many sails he has made for boats with rigs of similar size, using the panel layout and specific cloth he is planning for your sail. If the sail hasn't had at least a season of refinement, we'd be wary.

MYLAR SAILS

If winning means everything to you, buy a Mylar jib. However, if you plan to use it for carefree or shorthanded cruising, or if you expect to keep your genoa for daysailing after its competitive life is over, forget it. A Mylar sail is faster and will hold its shape over a couple of seasons of normal use. It will be competitive longer than a Dacron sail, so if you're the type who replaces your Dacron racing sails as soon as they lose their shape, Mylar is better for you. You will have to buy new sails less often, and until a Mylar sail falls apart, it will probably be nearly as fast as the day you bought it (which contrasts to a Dacron sail which gets slower with every day of use).

There are two catches with a Mylar sail, however. True, it will be faster for longer; but because the end of its competitive life is signaled by the disintegration of the Mylar film, the sail cannot be retired for daysailing. In fact, it will not even make a very good paint tarpaulin.

The second catch is that Mylar is always more fragile than Dacron, so you have to be careful when using it. You must take a Mylar genoa down when the wind increases above the sail's capacity. Because a Mylar sail doesn't stretch, your boat won't get overpowered like it would with a Dacron sail, so it is easy to talk yourself into being lazy and leaving a Mylar sail up.

Once the Mylar film becomes overloaded it will develop permanent stress marks. Dacron sails can recover, but Mylar sails do not forgive errors.

You also must learn not to crank up the halyard as you would with a Dacron sail when the wind pipes up. Because Mylar doesn't stretch, it holds its shape; if you overtension the halyard, you can rip the head off the sail. All pressure points of a Mylar sail must be reinforced. Being rigid, Mylar won't distribute the load of any sharp object such as a spreader pressing against it. Stickyback number fabric is good for this purpose. Even if you have spreader patches, if you have the habit of releasing the sheet late during a tack and backing the headsail into the spreader, you will probably puncture the sail.

While it is never a good idea to let any sail flog rather than reefing or taking it down, this rule is doubly important with Mylar. Flailing will destroy a Mylar sail much sooner than one of Dacron. Because of the fragility of Mylar, you have to inspect it whenever it is used in winds approaching its maximum range. Look closely at the seams in the vicinity of the clew, head and tack. If you see stitching holes that are torn or elongating, or glued seams that are slipping, you may be able to repair it with sticky-back cloth. And then again, it may be too late.

LUFF GROOVE DEVICES

Just 15 years ago, one of the hardest jobs on the foredeck of a racing boat was to make a quick headsail change. Unless the boat was equipped with two headstays, which adds considerable windage, a headsail change meant releasing the lowest hanks on the headsail in use, tacking down the new sail, hanking it on below the headsail already up, taking a deep breath, letting the jib halyard run, then going like mad to get the hanks open on the old jib, all the time listening to the skipper scream to hurry up. No wonder it was a lousy job.

Then in 1969, Hood introduced the Sea Stay, a grooved rod headstay that reduced windage by eliminating jib hanks. The concept was further refined by other manufacturers, and a variety of modifications on the basic Hood principle followed. These include grooved aluminum extrusions which replace the headstay, and plastic extrusions which fit over the headstay.

While luff-groove devices were developed for racing, they have been incorporated in modern headsail roller furling gear to eliminate some of the problems associated with the old-style roller furling; most notably, the almost uncontrollable headstay sag which reduces windward performance, and the difficulty of handling sails with heavy luff wires. If you already have a luff groove device, you probably won't be able to adapt it to a roller furling system if you decide to go cruising rather than racing.

For racing, there are two primary advantages to a luff-groove device. First, it will make the leading edge of the headsail aerodynamically cleaner. There will be no wrinkles radiating from hanks, as the halyard load is evenly distributed along the luff of the sail. The "spoiler" effect of jib hanks protruding into the windstream is eliminated, as is the turbulence created by the open slot between the headstay and the leading edge of the sail.

In addition, it is not necessary to lower one jib before setting another. While this doesn't mean that the foredeck crew can get lazy (when two jibs are up simultaneously on the same tack, both are quite inefficient), but it does relieve a little of the hurried fumbling on the foredeck that can put the bowman in danger. A bowman being yelled at to hurry up with getting the new jib on is likely to ignore, or forget about "one hand for the ship, and one for yourself" in the effort to speed up the headsail change.

For the racer, then, the luff-groove device is practically essential. In fact, the advantages of the luff groove device are recognized by the two major rating rules, IOR and MHS, which add twice the fore and aft dimension of the luff groove device to the LP of the largest genoa to determine the boat's headsail area. This provides powerful evidence of the efficiency of the luff-groove device.

But does the device offer advantages to the sailor who doesn't race? Unless the luff-groove device is incorporated in the headsail furling system, the primary advantage for the cruising sailor is the ability to set two headsails at once for downward sailing without a spinnaker. If you have two jib halyards, two jibs can be fed into the twin grooves of the luff-groove device, and sheeted to opposite sides of the boat. This eliminates the twin headstays, with the excess windage and difficulty of tensioning, that are frequently seen on far-ranging cruising boats.

In most other ways, however, the luff-groove device is a questionable luxury for the cruiser, particularly if shorthanded sailing is on the menu. With a hanked-on jib, releasing the halyard usually results in the jib falling to the deck, still attached to the stay for the full length of the luff. If the boat is equipped with lifeline nets, and the boat is brought head to wind or nearly head to wind before the halyard is released, the jib may stay completely on deck in a relatively docile bundle.

Releasing the halyard of a sail set in a luff-groove device is another matter. Usually, there is enough friction in the system that the sail doesn't fall to the deck. For the shorthanded sailor, it's a good thing that the sail stays put, for a lowered jib set in a luff-groove device is attached to the boat only by the halyard, the sheet, and the tack fitting. Handling a genoa in heavy weather, alone on the foredeck when the luff is entirely free, is a character-building experience most of us can do without.

If you are converting from hanked-on sails to a luff tape for a grooved device, most sailmakers will charge about $2.50 per foot of luff length to make the alteration, or about $110 per sail for a masthead 34-footer. In addition, the luff-groove device itself will cost $400 to $450 for the same boat. (The prices of the various devices are quite competitive despite the differences in design and materials.)

If you are having new sails built, the prices of hank-on jibs and luff-groove jibs are usually about the same, given the same specifications, so there will be no additional cost of converting from one system to the other.

* * *

While there is little doubt that racing improves the breed, not all racing innovations are practical for the cruiser. Mainsheet travelers, efficient winches, blocks, and deck hardware have a racing heritage, as does the luff-groove device. When incorporated in a modern roller furling system, the luff-groove device has a place on the cruising sailboat or even the daysailer. For the sailor who is more than casual about racing, and who always has plenty of crew available, the luff-groove device (without roller furling gear) is an essential piece of equipment.

For the rest of us, there are dozens of better places to spend a significant sum of money; better navigation or safety equipment, the down payment on a new genoa, or even hiring someone to help put a good bottom on the boat.

SPINNAKER POLE OR WHISKER POLE?

To the question we commonly receive as to what make of whisker pole to buy, our question in reply may be disarming or, worse, seem evasive: "Do you want a whisker pole or should you be considering a spinnaker pole?" The answer does not always depend on whether the boat has a spinnaker.

For the typical 30-footer, a whisker or spinnaker pole represents an outlay of about $300. At that price, it is worth investigating the quality, value, and usefulness of your purchase.

There is no reason why a pole to be used for winging out a jib cannot be made exactly like a spinnaker pole. As a matter of fact, any spinnaker pole can be a satisfactory whisker pole. The reverse is not true.

A whisker pole is designed to wing out a jib (or perhaps the clew of a "poleless" spinnaker) on the side of the boat opposite the main boom when running before the wind, to more effectively keep the sail full.

A spinnaker pole is designed to withstand the greater forces encountered in supporting the tack of a spinnaker. Its outboard end may be positioned as far forward as the headstay (when the wind is forward of the beam) or as far aft as the shrouds will permit (when the wind is from astern, or even leeward of astern). Its length is usually limited, not by physical considerations, but by rating rules which impose a penalty on a boat with a pole longer than the distance between the forward side of the mast and the attachment point of the headstay (the measurement commonly called *J* in rating rules). As we wish to discuss the relative advantages of whisker and spinnaker poles for cruising, we will likewise disregard the dictates of the J dimension.

From these definitions you can see that a whisker pole is generally designed for lighter duty than a spinnaker pole. They are found in sizes and types to cover a wide range of applications. Small boats use whisker poles with a "spike" or lug fitting on the outboard end that fits into the jib's clew cringle, and with a jaw or latching inboard fitting that affixes it to an eye on the mast. This type of pole should never be considered for any boat much over the size of a dinghy, and is not the type of pole we will discuss here. For our purposes, a whisker pole refers to a pole with latching end fittings that holds the jib sheet on one end and latches on the forward side of the mast at the other.

You may want the pole to be adaptable to headsails of different foot length (LP measurement). For this reason, sparmakers have devised adjustable whisker poles, usually in the form of telescoping devices whereby one length of tubing slides into another of a greater diameter. Some lock in position with a twist, like "extendable" boathooks, and others with finger-activated button latches. The twist-type gives infinite positioning within the retracted and extended limits, and the latch type have finite adjustments.

With the capability of being extended, the adjustable whisker pole can be stowed in a shorter length than it would be in use, typically up to 40 percent shorter. Therefore, a pole that might be 15 feet long when in use could retract to as short as 9 feet, far easier to stow and maneuver around than at the extended length.

For that convenience there is a price, both in money and strength. A whisker pole is intended to be used only with modest-sized headsails (a genoa with an overlap of 150 percent typically has only half the area of a spinnaker designed to the same J dimension). Moreover, a whisker pole is never intended to resist the heavy compression loading a spinnaker pole must (such as when the pole is near the headstay and the guy is nearly parallel to it). Nor must a whisker pole be expected to resist the point loading a spinnaker pole typically suffers when it is allowed to swing against the headstay (whisker poles should never be permitted to hit the headstay).

Because the loads a whisker pole must withstand are less than those of a spinnaker pole, the tubing used is typically smaller in diameter, particularly the inside tube in a telescoping pole. The end fittings too may be lighter and smaller. Lighter fittings, smaller diameter, and lighter weight tubing are among the reasons why a boat's whisker pole should never be used as a spinnaker pole.

The extra strength of a spinnaker pole can, however, work to its disadvantage. A spinnaker pole much in excess of J in length can be unwieldy and, in stronger winds, dangerous. Also, as the length is increased, so must the diameter of the tubing.

The twist-type adjustable whisker pole is suited only to boats under about 27 feet. On larger boats, the length of the extended pole quickly approaches unwieldy limits. If you want the extra length when you pole out your jib, the problems of stowing and maneuvering an oversize spinnaker pole may justify the choice of an adjustable whisker pole for your boat.

In shopping for either type of pole, a buyer is going to have a jolly time trying to decide what to buy. Typically, sparmakers offer a plethora of options in end fittings, features and prices—ranging from the simple (and expensive) to the exotic (and expensive). Some offer spinnaker poles in "kit" forms at a minor savings in cost.

Most sailors looking for a whisker pole for a boat in the 25- to 35-foot range will find simple piston ends perfectly satisfactory. If it is desirable to have a self-latching trigger, which would be handy for short- or single-handed sailing, add about 10 percent to the cost. (The self-latching fitting is a spring-loaded device which is set open, and automatically closes when the sheet or mast fitting is inserted into the end fitting on the pole.)

The price difference between a conventional spinnaker pole and a typical whisker pole, with the same end fittings on each, is about 10 percent. A 13-foot spinnaker pole will run just over $300, and a whisker pole extendable from about 10 to 16 feet will cost just under $300.

In figuring your costs, do not forget to add in the cost of a mast fitting. In this size range, a simple track and sliding carriage with a loop, or a fixed bracket should be adequate. You may also want to add a topping lift or pole lift, or you may prefer to use a lazy (unused) genoa halyard or staysail halyard, either of which would save rigging a separate lift. Any pole is easier to handle when the end is supported by a lift.

When considering price, do not overlook a possibly crucial factor. If you buy a whisker pole and later decide to add a conventional spinnaker, the cost of the addition will have to include the whole package—the sail, the rigging, and the pole.

Conversely, if you opt for a spinnaker pole from the outset, the cost of the spinnaker package is reduced by about 30 percent. Many owners spread the cost over time by buying a spinnaker pole one year and buying the spinnaker the next year.

If you are considering a spinnaker pole as opposed to an extendable whisker pole, apart from room on deck for stowage, there is no reason for a cruising boat not to have the maximum length pole available in an appropriate diameter. Racing boats may pay in the way of rating for an over-length pole, but cruising boats are under no such restraints. Besides, such poles may be readily shortened in the future simply by removing the fitting on one end, sawing off tubing, and reattaching the fitting.

Any boat sailing with the wind from nearly astern will be livelier and faster if it can add sail area either by hoisting a spinnaker or using the jib more efficiently. Winging the jib, in terms of performance, is worth the effort. Whether such performance is worth the price of the pole is an individual decision which will have to be shoehorned in between the other priorities on your list.

If you decide in favor of a pole, we recommend a spinnaker pole of a diameter suitable for the J dimension of the boat as a better investment than a whisker pole. This opinion is based on the lesser versatility of the whisker pole, as well as the fact that a pole longer than the J dimension of the boat contributes little efficiency to a poled-out genoa, even one as large as a 150-percent overlap.

Although the spinnaker pole may have a larger diameter (perhaps 3 inches instead of 2-1/2 for a 13-foot pole) and a longer stowed length (say 13 feet versus 11), we think it is just as easy to rig, trim and handle as the more complex extendable whisker pole, with it's small increase in performance, if any. A properly sized spinnaker pole will be stronger than a whisker pole, and the difference in price is minor.

TELLTALES

Telltales make us all look like better sailors. Without the reminder of telltales on the shrouds, it's all too easy to starve your boat's reaching performance with overtrimmed sails. Most sailors just tie a 6-inch piece of knitting yarn to the upper shroud about 5 feet above deck. For areas where extremely light air or drizzle is prevalent, plastic cassette tape is more effective.

Most chandleries also offer overpriced nylon cloth telltales which clip onto the shrouds with plastic rings. These rings allow the telltale to rotate as you turn the boat, so the telltale cannot wrap itself around the shroud. While this is a convenient feature, we still prefer to save our money and use yarn, even if it means walking forward now and then to unwrap the telltale.

All light-to-medium-air headsails should have telltales on their luffs. Without them, you cannot be sure you are hard on the wind unless the luff of the sail is breaking. When the luff is constantly breaking in light or medium air, you are usually pinching the boat and going slower. With a telltale on each side of the sail, you can sail her in the fine groove between pinching and excessive footing. You want to steer so that both telltales are streaming aft; when the leeward one stalls you are sailing too low, when the weather one stalls you are beginning to sail too high (although it will stall before the luff breaks).

Yarn is almost universally used for headsail telltales. The most permanent ones are made with a single piece of yarn pushed through the sail with a sailmaker's needle so that half of the yarn sticks out of each side of the sail. Telltales can also be stuck to each side of the sail with sticky-back cloth "dots." While they tend to fall off, these telltales can be a different color on each side of the sail, and of staggered height to make it easy to distinguish the leeward from the windward ones. The best place to attach a set of telltales is a quarter of the way up the luff, and 10 percent of the width of the sail (at that height) aft.

Racing sails often have small windows for the telltales. This makes it easier to read the leeward telltale when the sun is shining brightly on the weather side. However they do add $10 to $20 to the price of the sail, and require more care (you must not wrinkle a window).

Wet weather presents a problem for headsail telltales, especially when the wind is light. Yarn telltales get soaked and refuse to fly; cloth or cassette tape telltales stick to the sail. The best solution is to ask your sailmaker to run a 12 inch long "three-throw stitch" onto a piece of 3/4-ounce nylon spinnaker cloth.

This will make two light waterproof telltales with a corrugated surface to keep them from sticking to the sail when wet.

Some sailmakers are beginning to put telltales on the leech of the mainsail. These telltales stall when you have the mainsheet trimmed in too hard. We have found they work in medium air, but often refuse to fly in a light breeze and refuse to stall in heavy air. If you want a mainsail telltale, it's best to use a half-inch wide piece of spinnaker cloth, 10 inches long and attached to the leech between the first and second batten down from the top of the sail.

* * *

Sails for the cruising boat are different from sails for the racing boat, but the requirements for their construction are no less exacting, and the materials and workmanship no less significant and expensive. The cruising sailor owes a debt of gratitude to the racing man for financing the tremendous cost of modern sailmaking technology, much of which has been usefully applied to cruising sail construction.

For the cruising sailor, concerns about ounces of weight and tenths of points of rating can be neglected. However, the days when a cruising sail was less carefully built, heavier, smaller, and less efficient are far behind us.

2

Reefing and Reefing/Furling Systems

Shortening sail can be a trying task. You're always faced with it at the worst time—when the wind is strong, the boat rail-down, the sails flogging, and the crew cowering. The task of reefing the mainsail has, however, become a lot easier since the days of cotton sails. Prior to World War II, the use of cotton for sailcloth made reefing a monumental chore. To reef a sail in those days, first the sail had to be lowered onto the deck, then the luff and leech reef patches secured to the boom, then each of a long row of "reef ties" painstakingly lashed around the boom, and finally, the sail raised back off the deck—not what you'd call a fun task.

Roller Reefing

The postwar years brought the first innovation to mainsail reefing in the form of roller reefing booms. This method incorporates a boom with a swiveling gooseneck and mainsheet-block attachment, which allow the boom to be rotated so that the mainsail rolls up around it like a window shade. Roller reefing proved easier than the traditional method of reefing cotton sails, as no reef ties were needed. However, it has a serious drawback in that the foot of the sail inevitably rolls up too loosely. With the foot slack, the sail sets too fully and performance suffers greatly. Roller reefing booms are rarely seen today.

Slab Reefing

It wasn't until the arrival of Dacron sailcloth that slab reefing (also called jiffy reefing) was developed. Slab reefing is similar to the traditional method of reefing cotton sails, except that far fewer reef ties are used, and those reef ties are more cosmetic than functional.

On cotton sails the reef ties bear a great deal of the load, because the reef patches on the luff and leech cannot be constructed as strong as Dacron reef patches. On a Dacron sail, the reef ties are only used to gather the excess cloth along the foot. The reef patches carry most of the load. The significance of this difference is that the sail does not have to be lowered onto the deck to be reefed.

The procedure for slab reefing is as follows: Lower the halyard just enough to secure the reef point at the tack—this means lashing it to the boom on older boats; on newer boats the reef cringle (grommet) is usually slipped over a hook at the gooseneck. Then the halyard is retensioned. Finally, the reef patch on the leech is winched down to the boom by a line which is led from the boom, up through the cringle, back down to the boom and forward to a winch. The boom's topping lift keeps the boom off the deck, and the reef ties, because they bear little load, can be tied in at your leisure.

A slab-reefed sail sets much smoother and flatter than one that has been roller reefed around a boom. Theoretically, the task of slab reefing can be done by a single crewmember standing at the mast. However, because it is a multi-step maneuver, in the interest of expediency, slab reefing usually occupies two or more crew. In short, it's still a lot of work.

Continuous Reefing

Continuous reefing, a term coined by Kenyon Spars, is a more sophisticated version of slab reefing. Like slab reefing, it is simple and inexpensive to fit to your boat. Also like slab reefing, it allows you to use a full-roached, powerful mainsail, uncompromised by the inefficiencies of roller furling mainsails, which we'll discuss later in this chapter. Best of all, it can easily be operated by one person without leaving the cockpit.

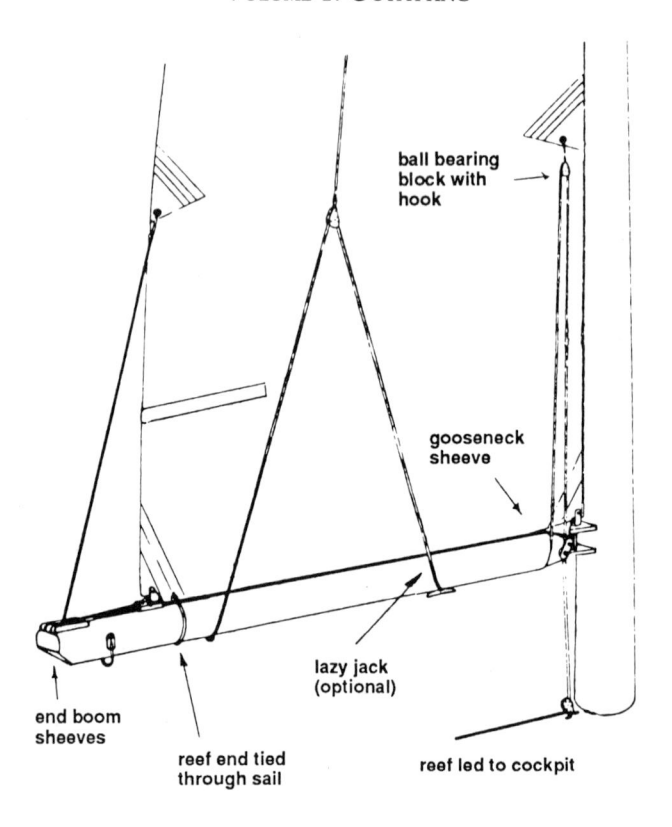

The Kenyon continuous reefing boom.

A continuous reef begins at the after end of the boom exactly like a slab reef. The end of the reefing line is tied around the boom, then led up through the cringle on the leech and back down to a sheave on the boom. It's important to tie the reefing line around the boom (or attach it to an eyestrap on the side of the boom) at the proper place: 6 inches aft of an imaginary line dropped straight down from the grommet on the reef patch.

Many modern boats have a boom end cap with reef sheaves built in. On older boats fitted only with an outhaul, you will have to mount a cheek block on each side of the boom. This will allow you to run two continuous reefs.

After the reef is led through the leech and then into (or along) the boom, the similarity to slab reefing stops. A slab reef exits the boom at the gooseneck and leads directly to a winch (or to a

Reefing and Reefing/Furling Systems

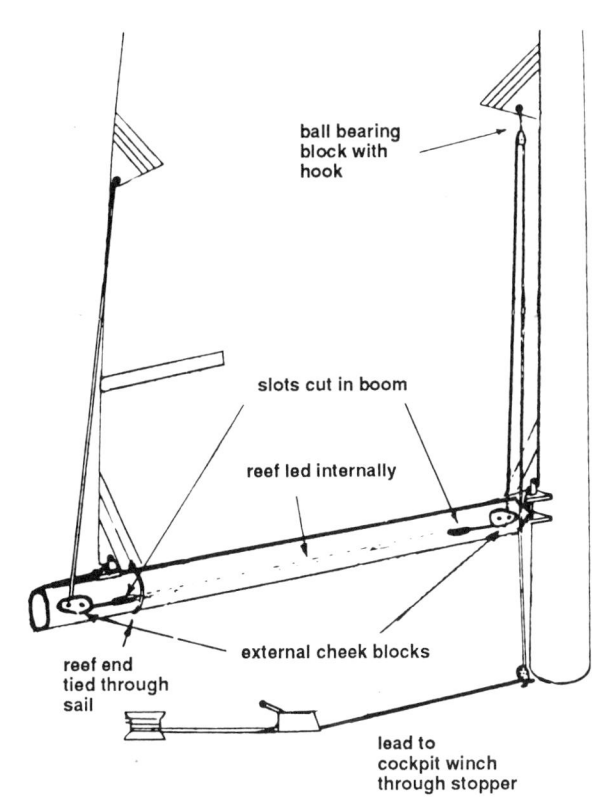

A "do-it-yourself" continuous reefing system.

simple jam cleat on smaller boats). On a continuous system, the reef turns through another sheave at the gooseneck, runs up to a block which is hooked into the appropriate cringle on the luff of the sail, then back down to a block at the base of the mast and aft to a cockpit winch via a stopper.

This single reef line pulls both the leech and the luff down to the boom. Unlike a jiffy reefing system, you do not have to send a crew forward to the mast to hook the luff onto a tack horn or lash it to the gooseneck.

You can either rig your own continuous system for the price of a few blocks and a stopper, or you can buy a new boom from Kenyon Marine which is prerigged with the system. Kenyon says typical prices would be in the range of $300 for a typical 24-foot boat to $800 for a 32-footer. The Kenyon boom is fitted with internal sheaves at both ends of the spar. If you retrofit your present boom, you must install cheek blocks at both ends of the boom. It's important to place the cheek blocks as close to the ends as possible. The aft cheek block should be fixed behind the boom's black band (the point to which the clew is pulled), and the forward cheek block should be mounted within 6 inches of the back of the mast.

It is also important to use a low friction, ball-bearing block mounted on a hook to lead the reef line up the luff and back. If you lead the reef through the luff grommet without a block, friction will cause the luff to be pulled down before the leech, causing the reef to bind. The reef will also bind at the gooseneck if you let the halyard down too far. It's best to mark the halyard so that you ease it just enough to let the reef down to within a few inches above the gooseneck. The luff is tensioned as you winch in the reef—you don't have to touch the halyard again.

The aft end of the reef can be led through any reef patch in the leech, and the forward end can be hooked into any reef patch in the luff, so you're not limited to just two reefs. You cannot, however, rig a continuous reef through a flattening reef (a reef patch positioned a few inches above the clew and used as a super-outhaul).

As with slab reefing, you must have a topping lift or lazy jacks to hold the boom up as you reef. A lazy jack is similar to a topping lift that is bridled to the center of the boom, rather than attached to the end. A lazy jack rigged to both sides of the boom will neatly gather the mainsail as it is lowered or reefed.

ROLLER FURLING HEADSAIL GEAR

To many sailors, roller furling ranks with other great labor saving inventions like the vacuum cleaner and the dishwasher. "I don't know how I ever survived without it," they say. To others, roller furling is recognized as a concept with both merits and disadvantages. However, for all sailors who elect to put roller furling on their boats, choosing new roller furling gear or evaluating used furling gear can be a trying decision.

To help sift through the myriad of headsail furling gear on the market, we conducted a survey of boatowners and talked to eight successful riggers familiar with a variety of gear. Here is what we learned:

Furling

The main reason sailors buy roller furling gear is to save themselves the trouble of clambering about the foredeck, manhandling sails in and out of bags, and hanking them on and off the forestay. When you're sailing for relaxation, you want to eliminate as much work as possible. Roller furling means you don't have to go forward to take down the headsail should the weather become rough.

The ease with which a system furls a sail depends on the amount of friction in the system. Most of the friction occurs in the swivels used at the top and bottom of furling gear. Most types of furling gear incorporate roller bearings in the swivels. The effectiveness of the bearings not only depends on their design and construction, but also on how heavily they are loaded and how well they are lubricated.

The load on the swivels varies from system to system. Some systems use solid, one-piece aluminum extrusions to support the luff of the headsail—there is no wire headstay, inside or outside the extrusion. These solid extrusions have roller bearing swivels at each end, as well as a separate halyard swivel. The swivels on each end of the extrusion bear the entire load on the extrusion. Unless they are well lubricated, considerable friction can develop because of the high loads these swivels encounter.

Some other systems use segmented, hollow extrusions, with the headstay run inside the extrusion. On these systems the headstay bears a good deal of the load and does not turn as the sail is furled. Because the load is less, the bearings in the halyard and tack swivels of these systems are more likely to operate with less friction.

In addition, there are several variations on these two basic types, some which use bearings in their furling drums and some which do not, and new systems seem to be coming on the market with increased frequency.

Whether a system uses bearings or not, it is important to keep all moving parts well lubricated and free of dirt and salt. In recent years, several systems have changed from plain steel to more corrosion-resistant bearings of stainless steel or plastic. Plastic or stainless steel bearings need only to be flushed with fresh water to be kept in smooth working order.

Just because a system has plain steel bearings, however, doesn't mean that it is doomed to corrode into a pile of rust. Bearings will only freeze if they are neglected. Steel bearings must be packed in a quality marine grease so that no moisture can get to them. Most roller furling manufacturers advise against using a Teflon-based grease because they have found that it doesn't stick to the bearings well enough to prevent moisture from attacking them. Steel bearings that are well sealed will need to be repacked with grease less often, and therefore tend to work longer with less friction.

Reefing

Some sailors get roller furling confused with roller reefing. Furling is the act of rolling up the sail completely; reefing is the act of partially rolling to reduce sail area. All furling systems are intended to furl. Not all are intended to reef.

For example, a typical furling brochure says, "You can reef with your furling system. But...it's better to remove the jib entirely and use a smaller headsail." No roller reefed sail will set as well as a smaller headsail specifically designed for heavier air, but some systems do better than others.

Furling systems where the headsail rolls around a wire sewn into its luff are the least effective for reefing. In these systems, the sail rolls about itself, as it is not attached to the headstay. Wire has very little torsional rigidity. In other words, when you twist one end of a long piece of wire, the other end may not turn at the same rate. When the furling drum turns the bottom of a wire luff, the top of the wire may lag behind . The longer the wire and the smaller the wire's diameter, the greater the problem. Sailmakers rarely install a wire luff of the same diameter as the boat's headstay. Also, if the sailmaker should neglect to use 1x19 *counterlaid* wire, the "lag" will be severe because the wire will tend to unlay itself as you furl the sail.

Because of the lag in these systems, in a strong breeze the bottom of the sail will tend to roll up before the top. This can leave the sail with the bottom furled, the center badly creased and wrinkled, and the top exposed and flapping in the breeze. If you sail downwind to blanket the sail, pressure is reduced and the sail will roll up more evenly. However, when you head upwind again with your sail "reefed," the chances are good that the top will unroll itself. Also, care is required when rolling the sail downwind, to prevent the headstay from getting wrapped inside the luff.

Other systems incorporate a wire that is turned with a drum at the bottom, however, the wire that turns is the headstay, so it is likely to be of greater diameter than a wire sewn into a jib luff. Hence it is likely to be more torsionally rigid, so lag will be less of a problem.

The roller furling systems that do the most effective job of reefing use some sort of grooved aluminum extrusion, also called a headfoil, to support the luff of the jib. An extrusion is inherently more torsionally rigid than wire. The bigger in diameter, and (for sectional systems) the less sloppy the joints, the greater the rigidity. It is possible, under extreme conditions, however, to put a permanent twist into a solid extrusion or to break the joints in a sectional system. One should also remember to proceed carefully whenever using a winch to assist the furling of a sail.

Sail Set

Roller furling and roller reefing involve a number of performance compromises. The presence of a furling drum means the tack of the jib must sit from 6 inches to 18 inches above the deck. The clew must be cut high, too, so that the foot and leech of the sail will roll up evenly. The higher the foot of the sail is off the deck, the less windward efficiency the sail has. We expect to see cruising boats of the future with recessed "troughs" molded into the bow so the top of the furling drum will lie flush with the deck.

As a sail is roller reefed, the cloth will slide slightly toward the center of the sail. When a sail is unfurled, the jib halyard gives adequate luff tension. When a sail is reefed, however, the effective "head" and "tack" of the sail, which are somewhere along the leech and foot, are not tensioned. This allows the sail shape to get fuller as it is reefed, This problem is aggravated by the heavy leech and foot covers installed for ultraviolet protection.

It's obvious that some sort of protection from the sun is necessary for a furled headsail, especially in southern climates. Most sailmakers accomplish this by sewing dark-colored acrylic cloth along the leech and foot. When the sail is furled, the acrylic shields the sail from the sun. Not only do these ultraviolet covers encourage a sail to set poorly when it is roller reefed, but they hurt sail shape when the sail is completely unfurled, as well. Because of their weight and stretch characteristics, the covers can make the leech and foot flutter violently.

In order to set better when roller reefed, a genoa is often cut flat and made of heavy sailcloth, neither of which does much for light air performance. We think there might be a better way to make a roller furling and reefing headsail. Instead of putting leech covers on a flat, heavy crosscut sail (horizontal panels), make the sail leechcut or mitercut and vary the type of cloth used throughout the sail. The panels nearest the luff would be made of lighter cloth, with the panels in the center of medium weight cloth, and the panels on the leech and foot of heavier ultraviolet-resistant cloth. Although UV-resistant cloth will not last as long as acrylic covers, one sailmaker told us he can replace worn-out UV panels for less money than the original cost of installing a cover. And the sail will set better, too.

Sailmakers have also come up with an innovative way to make a roller furling headsail that is full enough for a modicum of light air performance, yet rolls up flat for a decent heavy air shape. They pad the midsection of the luff of the sail, so that when the sail is rolled, the fullness in the center of the sail is taken up around the padding.

Although a leechcut sail with a padded luff should set better when reefed, one must remember that roller reefing puts a great deal of strain on both the sail and the furling gear. A roller-reefed sail will never set as well when sailing upwind as a hanked-on working jib. Many of the riggers we talked to advised against roller reefing a sail upwind for a prolonged period of time, especially if the sail is reefed to smaller than 70 percent of its original size. While sailing off the wind with a roller-reefed headsail does no harm to the sail or furling gear, if you plan to sail any distance upwind in a strong breeze, it is smarter to change to a working jib.

Reefing and Reefing/Furling Systems

One "breakthrough" in roller reefing that nearly all riggers condemned as of dubious worth is the patented double tack-swivel. This feature, used on a couple of systems, allows the tack to swivel independently from the furling drum. The manufacturer claims that the double swivel action permits the luff extrusion to turn independently from the tack and head, allowing a full cut sail's luff-round to be rolled first, flattening the sail as it is reefed. The only part of the sail which is not fed into the extrusion is a short, several-foot section just above the tack. That is the only part of the sail affected by the double swivel action. Riggers say it has an unnoticeable effect on sail shape.

It should be noted that most of the discussion on sail set is not applicable to systems set up independent of the headstay, because roller reefing should be out of the question with these systems. Because the sails in these systems are not attached to the headstay with hanks or with an extrusion, the only thing that keeps them from sagging off to leeward is halyard tension. It was quite obvious from talking to owners that this type of "unsupported" furling system will always suffer from poor upwind performance because of excessive luff sag.

The manufacturers of these systems recommend rigging the jib halyard with a 2:1 or 3:1 purchase in order to be able to create more tension and cut down on sag. Although most riggers also recommend a purchased halyard, most owners don't elect to pay for mounting extra blocks, or installing and stowing a halyard two to three times longer than the original halyard. Consequently, most boats with these systems have such sag problems that they cannot point within 10 degrees of similar boats in a moderate breeze. Even when using a halyard with a proper purchase, riggers report that they can not achieve the same tension as on a fixed headstay without "breaking something."

Another reason for poor upwind performance is the restriction on luff-tension adjustments. These systems use a wire luff. In order for the sail to furl, the wire should be seized to the luff, thereby making adjustments in luff tension impossible.

Changing Sails

With all roller furling systems, there will be times when you want to change sails. With a free-standing, unsupported system, this simply means releasing the halyard and letting the furled jib fall to the deck. However, even this easy task is unnecessary if you have a spare halyard, because with these systems the headstay remains available so you can hank on and hoist a working jib without removing your furled genoa. This advantage is the only redeeming value of this type of furling system.

Changing a sail that is fed into an extrusion can be a great deal more difficult. With a hanked-on sail, you can stuff most of it into a bag before you unhank the luff. A "headfoil" sail can't be stowed until it is taken out of the extrusion. In strong winds, there are two problems. As you pull the sail down and out of the extrusion, it can blow out of your hands and overboard. In addition, the luff tape can tear if the sail gets away from you.

The same is true when putting the sail back up. With a hanked-on sail, hoisting is a one man operation—first hank it, then hoist it. With a headfoil, though, the ease in hoisting depends on the wind velocity and the quality of the "feeder," which guides the sail into the extrusion. Even in light air, a poor feeder can require that one person be on hand to guide the sail, while another crew handles the halyard.

Extrusion systems with internal halyards are by far the most difficult when it comes to changing sails. You can't sit in the cockpit and tail a halyard winch with this type of furling gear; you must feed the sail into the extrusion and painstakingly tail a thin internal halyard while standing on the bow. Owners report that changing a sail is next to impossible unless the boat is at the dock and the wind is calm.

The difficulty in changing sails can present a safety problem when sailing offshore. Should you want to put up a smaller jib, or even if you should want to roll up your genoa but the system jams, you will be faced with taking the sail down and out of the headfoil. In this respect, the safest systems use hanked-on sails. These systems lack the convenience of reefability, though, due to the fact that the hanks cannot be rolled up inside a reefed sail without the danger of tearing the sail.

Installation

Some roller furling systems can be installed by amateurs; others must be installed by professionals. Some require special tools for assembly, and some use solid extrusions which cannot be rolled up for shipping, requiring special, extra-long trailers for transportation. These systems should be installed by professionals.

Other furling systems made of sectional extrusions conceivably could be installed by an amateur, but not without a certain amount of difficulty. Not only is assembly of the mechanics usually complex, but in some cases you must cut the swage fitting off the headstay, then slide the extrusions over it, and finally fit the headstay with a Norseman-type end terminal.

A few systems are somewhat easier to install, because the unit can be ordered practically preassembled from the factory, and there is no need for the owner to install an end terminal.

The unsupported furling systems are the easiest for an amateur to install. There are a few steps, though, that many sailors forget about. First, you usually have to install a padeye on the deck as an attachment for the furling drum because the drum might not clear the headstay if you attach it to the existing stemhead fitting. Second, you should use at least a 2:1 halyard in order to be able to apply enough halyard tension to limit luff sag. The dead end of a 2:1 halyard should be fixed to a tang mounted several inches below the halyard block. A halyard rigged in this manner has less tendency to twist than one rigged solely to a halyard block and becket. To rig it properly you must climb the mast to bolt the new tang in place.

Climbing the mast and attaching a fitting is not a chore unique to unsupported furling systems. On all furling systems, the halyard may wrap around the headstay when furling, if the halyard enters the mast or turns on a block which is fixed in close proximity to the headstay. The remedy is to mount a fairlead several inches down the mast to slightly deflect the halyard away from the headstay.

Racing

A surprising number of boatowners with roller furling gear occasionally race their boats. Those who use their furling gear during the race are sailing with a big disadvantage. As pointed out earlier, roller-furling headsails sacrifice a great deal of windward efficiency to their flat shape and high clewed, high-off-the-deck configuration. No popular handicapping rule gives credit for using a roller furling headsail; all rules assume that you have a proper inventory of special-purpose headsails and the most modern twin-groove headfoil system.

If you don't want to be at a disadvantage when racing, you should purchase a furling system that is easily removed before a race. The easiest to remove are the unsupported systems; you just lower the sail to the deck and unshackle the drum from its padeye. Then you can hank your racing headsails onto the headstay. For club racing, most sailors can live without the convenience of a headfoil for sail changes; a hanked on sail will suffice.

The extruded headfoil furling systems offer the best prospects for racing, as some systems allow you to remove the furling drum. In the case of the simplest systems, the drum splits in half for removal, in other cases the headstay must be detached and the drum slipped over the end. However, detaching the headstay may be impractical unless you have a backstay adjuster with a long throw. Also, for true sail-changing ability while racing, an extruded headfoil with two aft-facing grooves is needed.

Some furling systems are currently offering a continuous line drive in place of the more common furling drum. The line drive uses a "drum" of much smaller diameter than normal. Because it does not distort the sail as a conventional drum, it does not have to be removed for racing.

Some Cautions with Roller Furling

Overrides on the furling drum can occur when the furling line is cast off to unfurl the sail. The trick to preventing overrides is to keep some tension on the furling line as you pay it out. In a strong breeze on larger boats this tension can be maintained with one wrap around a winch.

You must be careful, however, when using a winch to roll a sail up. It is sometimes hard to tell when a furling system is jammed if you are using a winch, and if the system does jam, you stand a good chance of breaking something if you try to force it. Forcing a frozen bearing can put a permanent twist in an extrusion on a foil system and forcing a twisted halyard can break the halyard.

When stepping or unstepping the mast with an extruded foil system, you must be very careful not to bend the foil. First you

Reefing and Reefing/Furling Systems 53

Due to the presence of the furling drum, the tack of the jib is located as much as 18 inches above the deck.

should disconnect the system from the stem fitting, then lash it to the mast as it is hauled out of the boat. For sailors who trailer their boats, an extruded foil system may prove to be too much of a hassle. Sailors who trailer their boats would probably be happier with an unsupported furling system.

With any system you install, you are bound to come across some hidden costs. For example, your sailmaker might have given you a reasonable quote on converting your present genoa to fit your new furling system. However, he might have neglected to tell you that the sail should have ultraviolet protection. Or he might discover that the luff is too long for the headfoil, so the foot must be recut. Or your might find that your sail will no longer trim to your present genoa track when you tack it to the top of the furling drum (as you raise the height of the sail, the lead moves aft). This could require moving the genoa track or recutting the clew of the sail.

Unsupported systems require a longer halyard and frequent

halyard replacements as they wear more quickly than the halyards in supported systems. Some systems require that the headstay be cut to install the headfoil. If you don't want a short headstay or the drum sitting an absurd distance off the deck, then a new headstay is needed.

The real purpose of twin aft-facing grooves in a headfoil system is for racing. Many daysailers don't even have a second halyard to hoist a second sail, nor do they have twin poles to use two genoas wing-and-wing. Also, they forget that no system has more than one halyard swivel, so they cannot furl if two sails are set without wrapping the second halyard.

MAINSAIL ROLLER FURLING

When sailors think of roller furling, they usually think of genoas, not mainsails. Why hasn't mainsail roller furling caught on? Perhaps it's because of the cost, which ranges from two to five times the cost of headsail furling; or the fact that many people think it's ungainly in appearance. It could also be that it is too great a detriment to performance.

It also has competition from the traditional forms of mainsail handling—slab reefing and lazy jacks. Many sailors consider it a sign that seamanship has "gone soft." Traditionalists like sailmaker Tom Clark say, "If you spent the cost of mainsail furling on time learning to sail better, you wouldn't think you couldn't handle your sails."

There is one segment of the market, however, that needs mainsail furling. That's the sailor who, due to advanced years or the sheer size of his boat, hasn't the strength to wrestle with traditional systems, yet does have the money to afford the luxury of roller furling. The limitations of size and budget make mainsail furling of dubious value for any boat smaller than 40 feet.

Evaluating Furling Gear

Mainsail and headsail furling use many of the same components, so you'd think it would be just as easy to come to conclusions about specific brands of mainsail gear. Not so. That's because mainsail systems are customized to fit the boat. This customization can be done by the original manufacturer, as it is in the case of the Hood Stoway. In most cases, though, it is done by the individual rigger.

In the case of headsail furling, the rigger simply assembles and installs the system straight out of the box. The only customization is the positioning of leads, halyards and control lines. With mainsail furling, the mast may be replaced or extensively modified with new brackets, shrouds, and so forth. The rigger may construct a system with a spar and furling gear from different manufacturers. Or he may take a headsail furling system and modify it to work behind the mast.

Whether you have success with your mainsail gear is likely to be just as dependant on the skill of your rigger as it is on the quality of the materials used. Consider the reputation of both the gear and the rigger. Because of the skill involved in putting together mainsail furling, it's installation is not a task to be tackled by most boatowners.

This requirement for specific skills translates into more labor costs. Compared to headsail furling, mainsail furling can be as much as two to four times more expensive to install.

Behind or In the Mast?

Mainsail furling operates on the same principles, and with much of the same equipment, as headsail furling. The mainsail luff is fed into a grooved aluminum extrusion, which may be either solid or hollow. If it is hollow, it will usually have a separate "stay" run inside. The sail is furled or reefed by rolling it around the extrusion.

That extrusion can be mounted either behind an existing mast on brackets, or inside of a new mast built with a special cavity to encase it. Each system has its pros and cons. Let's take a look at some of them:

COST. In-the-mast furling is much more expensive than a system that retrofits behind an existing mast. That's because you have to buy a new mast and boom. Let's take an average 40-foot cruising boat, for example. An in-the-mast system will cost at least $7000 for a "cheap" system, up to as much as $20,000 for a custom fabrication.

The prices mentioned above don't include the labor for installation (about $500), or the cost of a new mainsail (at least $2000). Don't forget to add the cost of shipping the spars, which can add another $500 to $800 for a cross-country trip.

While a behind-the-mast system can be shipped economically, the savings is likely to be eaten up by the increase in labor costs to install it. Installation is likely to be double the cost for an in-the-mast system. The total cost, however, will be much cheaper. For example, on our hypothetical 40-footer, the "do-it-yourself" price from the manufacturer is likely to be about $2500. That may or may not include the cleats, control lines, and the relocation of other hardware necessary to complete the job.

If you have a professional rigger do the job, add $700-$1000 for his time and materials. Again, if you want to minimize the loss in performance, you would be wise to purchase a new sail. Even if you opt to recut the old main, you're still looking at a $700-plus retrofit.

There can be hidden costs with behind-the-mast furling. If you don't have aft lower shrouds on your mast, you'll have to add them. That's because a behind-the-mast stay acts like the string of an archer's bow to induce compression bend. The lowers are needed to restrict that bend. If you plan any bluewater cruising, you'll have to add running backstays with a behind-the-mast system. Otherwise, the mast will pump in a seaway.

If you have a wooden mast, a thin walled or a bendy aluminum mast, it might not be able to withstand the extra compression, even with aft lowers. Then you will need a new mast, which makes the cost comparable to in-the-mast furling. Double spreader rigs are also hard to retrofit, both because they tend to be bendy, and because the aft lowers have to be anchored "mid-panel" between the spreaders.

SERVICE. Behind-the-mast systems are easier to service because all of the hardware is exposed. Most in-the-mast systems are captured inside the mast, which makes their inner workings more difficult to get at. While access plates may allow you to service the drive unit, you may have to unstep the mast to work on the furling extrusion or it's swivels.

There are two other aspects of service to consider—that of the rigger/dealer and of the manufacturer. With a big name manu-

Reefing and Reefing/Furling Systems

Behind-the-mast furling systems need to have UV-resistant leech and foot covers, which can adversely affect sail shape.

facturer, you're more likely to find parts and service when cruising far from home. You're also likely to get better service from a rigger/dealer who has made more of a profit from his dealer discount. Riggers tell us that some manufacturers offer much smaller dealer discounts than others. That means the rigger makes less profit off of a sale, and hence has less incentive to go out of his way to service the customer.

PERFORMANCE. Your boat's performance will be hurt no matter which type of system you choose. With both systems, you're adding weight and windage aloft. This is especially significant with in-the-mast furling.

You will also lose sail area from the roach and foot, as the mainsail must be made battenless, and the clew must be raised. More area is lost if the luff has to be shortened to accommodate the halyard swivel and furling drum. This is less of a problem with in-the-mast systems, although behind-the-mast systems can sometimes be modified to mount the furling drum below the fixed gooseneck.

Don't plan on maintaining your sail area by simply choosing a taller mast. In-the-mast systems are already heavier than the boat was designed to handle. The increase in the weight of the section alone is typically 10 to 20 percent. If you increase the rig height, you will sacrifice even more of your boat's stability, and increase the strain on the hull as well.

Another factor which decreases performance is loss of proper sail shape. The sail must be made flat to roll up smoothly, and the leech may not be as smooth without battens.

Finally, with behind-the-mast systems, the furling extrusion will sag more and more as the breeze builds, making the sail fuller and fuller. This problem can be acute on systems that are supported by a wire inside of a hollow furling extrusion, but not on systems that use a solid aluminum extrusion.

Some riggers are convinced that a good behind-the-mast system is actually more efficient than the typical in-the-mast system. They reason that with controlled sag, airflow over the leeward side of the sail is less disturbed than it would be behind the large-section mast needed for internal furling.

While the disadvantages of sag are subject to debate, it's safe to assume that a reefed sail will set even better with the use of a padded luff tape, similar to that used in headsail furling. This padding makes the middle of the sail roll around a greater diameter and helps keep the sail flat as it is reefed. Padding would not fit in most in-the-mast cavities.

Reefed sails also set more smoothly when rolled on furling extrusions of larger diameter. Hood, for instance, puts a plastic sleeve over its extrusion to increase its effective diameter.

The significance of lost performance will depend on how optimized your boat was before the conversion to furling. It also depends on how much value you place on performance. To a majority of daysailing and cruising sailors, the loss of a few tenths of a knot of boat speed is unlikely to be noticed.

OPERATION. How easily a system operates depends, for the most part, on the quality of the original hardware and the skill of the rigger who installs it. However, occasional jamming is one problem not uncommon with in-the-mast systems. Another consideration with in-the-mast furling is sail chafe. One sailmaker we talked to insisted that in-the-mast furling cut the life of a sail by half or even two-thirds. The chafe occurs when the sail is dragged across the mast cavity slot during furling and unfurling. Behind-the-mast systems do not have that problem.

Whether you're using an internal or external furling system, it's important to keep tension on the outhaul as you roll up the sail. This helps the sail roll smoothly. A sloppy furling job causes the sail to gather in the center of the system. With a behind-the-mast system, a baggy sail set is the worst result. With an internal system, however, the sail can gather enough to bind in the mast cavity. Then you have to unroll and start over.

Worse things can happen with an in-the-mast system if the furling extrusion isn't tensioned enough. The beauty of being inside the mast is that the sag of the furling extrusion is controlled. With some in-the mast systems, however, a sagging extrusion can be pulled out of the mast through the slot. This problem can cause a jam that is very difficult to free, and can be a genuine hazard when trying to shorten sail. Even if it doesn't come out of the mast, a sagging extrusion can add considerable friction. This problem can usually be prevented by proper tensioning of the furling extrusion. But remember, more tension means more compression on the mast, and compression increases a mast's tendency to bend.

You might wonder why all furling manufacturers don't offer masts that contain their furling extrusions. The main reason is that Hood has a patent on the "mast-captured furling device." Some in-the-mast manufacturers have simply ignored Hood's patent. Others have tried to work around the patent by using extrusions that can slip out of the mast's sail slot, and so are not "captured." These are likely to cause problems.

Some manufacturers use a wide open mast cavity that makes no pretense about capturing the extrusion. Forespar imports a system, called the Easyfurl, which is a furling system contained in a cavity which fastens to the aft side of your existing rig. Hood says that it has sent letters complaining of patent infringement to a number of other furling gear manufacturers. Whether they are able to change their competitor's products remains to be seen.

WHISTLING. Another problem with in-the-mast furling systems is that the furling cavity acts as a flute in a cross wind. The resultant whistling can be loud enough to drive you bonkers. This is a problem mostly when docked, as a moored boat will swing to the breeze. Only by using a wide open cavity, as Metalmast does, is the problem completely solved. Most other manufacturers provide a cloth "flute stopper" that must be hoisted inside the mast's sail slot to seal the furling cavity.

ANOTHER ALTERNATIVE: THE STOW-AWAY BOOM

The Hood Stoway Boom is a refined version of the roller reefing booms of the 1960s. Those old booms got a bad reputation for being hard to operate and giving poor sail shape when reefed. Today, they've all but disappeared in favor of slab reefing and roller furling masts.

The Stoway Boom is, in some ways, a throwback to an earlier era in sailboat hardware. Yet some of the riggers we talked to were convinced that it's the way of the future. The Stoway Boom was designed by a French company; Hood bought the rights to build the system. Hood reasons that it will sell to the small boat and retrofit market—the market they been unable to capture with the Stoway Mast, because of its cost.

The Stoway Boom comes equipped with a new mainsail; you can't buy one without it. That makes the price tag (about $5000 for a typical 40-footer) seem fairly reasonable. Mast furling systems are rarely quoted with new sails, although in many cases the owner will want to purchase one.

The best point of the Stoway Boom is its reefing performance. We sailed a boat equipped with one in 25-knot winds and found the reefed shape nearly the equal of slab reefing, and superior to mast furling. Part of the reason is that the sail is rolled around an extrusion of relatively large diameter. Also, the luff is fed onto the furling gear.

According to Hood, the mainsail doesn't have to be built "super flat," as it would with mast furling. You can also keep the sail's roach, as battens can be rolled on a boom. On the boat we sailed, the mainsail was fairly flat, and the leech a little short, but it had adequate shape for cruising.

Achieving a smooth furled shape does take a bit of skill, however. You must keep tension on the halyard as the sail is rolled. The boat must be nearly head to wind for the gooseneck universal to rotate. The furling system can be operated two ways, either with the line drive mounted at the gooseneck, or with the through-the-mast direct drive which works with a winch handle.

The Stoway's furling device is enclosed in a canvas cover, which is hung on a frame of three separate extrusions. All three extrusions "float" inside the canvas cover, their only common anchorage being a strap around the center of the boom and a cap at the end of the boom. A mainsheet hung from the end of the boom is well supported by the cap. However, the farther forward a fitting is mounted, the more the load is carried by the canvas. For that reason, Hood doesn't push the system for boats with mid-boom sheeting or powerful boom vangs. Converting from mid-boom to end-boom sheeting might not be practical, and we'd miss being able to vang properly in a strong breeze.

The Stoway Boom is recommended only for boats of about 40 feet or less. For small boats with end-boom sheeting and plans limited to coastal cruising, its probably a reasonable choice.

3

Winches, Ropes, and Running Rigging

WHICH WINCH?

As overlooked as winches are, they play a large part in determining how much you enjoy sailing your boat. A big genoa can be a real bear to handle. That's why sailhandling hardware like roller furling is so popular. It's a shame that more boatbuilders don't give us rigs with more manageable proportions—bigger mainsails and smaller jibs—but until they do, your choice of winch may be more important than you realize.

You'd expect that choosing a new winch for your boat, or evaluating a winch already installed on a boat, would be a simple task. For most people, the brand isn't crucial; price is. Ease of maintenance and quality of mechanics are generally ignored.

Price shopping is easy. You just look in the discount catalogs. Deciding what size to buy isn't so easy, although you'd think it should be with all the charts available in the brochures of the winch manufacturers. The brochures are sometimes oversimplified and sometimes recommend winches on the small size. They don't take into consideration the friction of your sheet blocks, the strength of your crew, or how much of the winch's mechanical advantage is lost to internal friction.

Determining Sheet Loading

To properly size a winch, you have to determine the load it has to move. The first step is to determine the maximum pull that any of your headsails is going to exert. Most sailors assume that their biggest genoa pulls the hardest, and size their winches for that headsail. Winch manufacturers also seem to use this standard in their brochures.

However, the headsail that pulls the hardest isn't the number 1 genoa; it's the number 3, also called the 100-percent genoa or working jib. That's because the number 3 is used in heavier wind than your larger headsails, and the force on the sheet increases by a factor of the *square* of the wind velocity. It just doesn't seem that way because there is so much less sheet to tail with a number 3, compared to a number 1.

Harken Yacht Fittings, a manufacturer of high quality sail-handling hardware, uses this formula to determine how hard a sail pulls on its sheet:

$$\text{Force} = .004 \times \text{Sail Area (sq. ft.)} \times \text{Apparent Wind Velocity}^2 \text{ (MPH)}$$

The .004 variable represents what Harken has found to be an average value for wind density, the angle of attack, and the sail's coefficient of lift. Note that the variable for wind velocity in the equation is squared. That's why a number 3 genoa pulls harder than a number 1.

For example, lets look at a typical 40-footer. The 150-percent genoa (number 1) is 525 square feet. Its "top end" is 20 knots of apparent wind, a typical figure for most 150-percent genoas. Using the Harken formula, the number 1 will be pulling at 840 pounds when closehauled in 20 knots apparent.

The working jib for the same boat is only 325 square feet. However, it can be carried in wind up to 32 knots apparent, also a typical "top end" for a number 3 on any boat other than an IOR racer (IOR boats carry number 4 jibs for this wind strength). Using the Harken formula, the number 3 will be pulling 1330 pounds in 32 knots apparent.

The next smallest jib on our typical boat, and on most coastal cruisers, is the storm jib. The top end of a storm jib is about 45 knots apparent, and its area is 100 square feet. The formula puts it's maximum pull at only 810 pounds. You'd have to leave the sail up in almost 60 knots before the pull would exceed that of the working jib.

This means that you only need to consider one sail—the number 3—when sizing a winch. Most number 3s are 100 percent of the area of the foretriangle. Even if you don't know the area of your number 3, you can easily find the size of your foretriangle from old boat brochures, your sailmaker, or with a tape measure.

Take that area and plug it into the Harken formula, using 32 knots as the sail's top end. Because 32 knots, squared and multiplied by .004 gives you 4.096, you can make a simple approximation by just multiplying the foretriangle area by 4.1. That's the hardest any of your sails will pull. It is not, however, the maximum load your winch will have to handle.

Friction

The way you sheet your jib to the winch makes a big difference in the load the winch has to move. The friction from a poor lead can add significantly to the total load.

First, let's assume that you are using jib lead blocks of the proper size. If your sheets are braided Dacron, the sheave diameter of the block should be six times that of the sheet. For example, a 1/2-inch sheet requires a sheet lead block with a 3-inch sheave diameter. If you have Kevlar sheets, the sheave should be 12 times the sheet diameter.

When you use a sheave that is undersized, you add to the friction in the system. When rope is forced around too sharp a curve, the fibers on the outside of the curve are stretched, while the fibers on the inside are compressed. This takes energy, and where does that energy come from? It comes from the guy sweating over the winch handle.

The quality of the block is also important. No block is friction-free; you always lose some of the force you apply to the sheet to friction. The poorer the block's bearing system, and the greater the load applied, the greater the friction.

Let's say you are using a block at or near its maximum recommended safe working load. If the sheave runs on ball bearings, Harken says that you only lose 2 percent to friction. With low-friction bushings, the loss is 3 percent to 5 percent. With no bushings—just a sheave riding on a pin—the loss can be 7 percent to 10 percent.

To find out if you are approaching the safe working load of your sheeting blocks, first check the specifications of your blocks in the hardware catalogs in your local chandlery. Then figure out how hard your number 3 will pull (sail area x 4.1).

Finally, look at how the sheet runs through the block on its way to the winch. If it takes only a 60-degree turn, the load on the block equals the load on the sheet. When the turn is 90 degrees, the load on the block is 140 percent of the sheet load. At 180 degrees, the load is 200 percent. When using a second block to lead the sheet to the winch, you are adding even more friction.

When trying to figure friction loss, the best you can do is to approximate. On our typical 40-footer, the jib sheet first turns 60 degrees through a block with bushed bearings on a jib track. At a top load of 1330 pounds for the number 3 jib, we guess that friction loss through the first jib block is about 2 percent. The force needed to move the load is now 1357 pounds.

Then the jib sheet is turned 180 degrees through a deck-mounted turning block with an unbushed bearing. Because the block is poor and the load is doubled, figure a 6 percent friction loss. That brings the force that the winch needs to exert to 1438 pounds. As bad as this sounds, the friction of the sheeting system is almost insignificant compared to the friction inside the winch.

Power Ratio

The most common method of sizing winches is by power ratio, sometimes called velocity ratio. Power ratios are usually given for a 10-inch handle, although some manufacturers give power ratios for 8-, 10- and 12-inch handles. Power ratios are the theoretical mechanical advantage that you have when you push against a winch handle. The word "theoretical" is important, because no winch is 100 percent efficient. All winches lose efficiency to internal friction. Typically from 15 percent to 35 percent of the theoretical mechanical advantage of the winch is used up in overcoming its internal friction.

In addition to winch efficiency, you must consider how hard you can comfortably push or pull on a winch handle. Winching involves as much technique as it does brute strength. It's hard to maintain constant force on a handle for the full rotation around a winch. Unless you squat directly over the winch, you're not going to push as hard when the handle is on the outboard side of the winch. With good timing and body position, you can really boost your output.

Rather than making exotic measurements, we will use an estimate. It seems that a safe, comfortable force for a smallish man or a medium-size woman is about 35 pounds when winching home a headsail in second gear. When the friction of the winch itself is considered, that reduces this figure to between 23 and 28 pounds.

We calculated the theoretical winch-handle loading for a sampling of boats in the 29- to 37-foot range. For each boat, we determined the maximum load of the number 3 headsail. Then, using the power ratio of their standard equipment winches, we determined the theoretical load on a 10-inch winch handle.

On the boats we sampled, the handle load varies from 22 pounds to 39 pounds. Twenty-two pounds seems reasonable; 39 does not. Remember, these handle loads are derived from winch power ratios, which are theoretical figures. Because of internal friction, actual loads are much higher.

We have estimated that a comfortable handle load should be no more than 35 pounds. When you figure in the friction of the winch, and toss in another 5 percent for friction due to blocks in the sheeting system, you come up with a realistic handle loading of no more than 22 to 25 pounds. That leaves the winches on many of the boats in our survey looking somewhat underpowered for their application.

They are underpowered only in heavy air, however, because the loads represent a worst case situation: sheeting home a number 3 jib in heavy air. A sail as small as a number 3 doesn't have so much sheet to be hauled in, nor is it the most commonly used sail for the typical fair weather weekend sailor.

For the sailor who cruises often in heavy air, the standard winches on most boats will be underpowered. Before changing to larger winches, however, consider a 12-inch winch handle. Longer handles give more leverage, although they cut proportionately into your sheeting speed. A 12-inch handle adds about 20 percent more than a 10-inch handle to your effective power.

In the brochure of each winch manufacturer you will find a chart to help you size their winches to your boat. The categories are usually divided by the size of the 150-percent genoa; divisions are every hundred square feet or so of sail area. As a rule, the recommended winches seem to be on the small side. You can, however, use the sizing charts with a fair degree of confidence by following some rules of thumb in making your selections. First, if your boat's sail area falls near the end of its size range, opt for the larger size winch.

Likewise, you should select the larger winch if the brochure recommends two different sizes—a larger one for racing and a smaller one for cruising. It makes little sense to us to use a smaller winch for cruising. If anything, it should be the other way around. You need all the mechanical advantage you can muster for cruising, because often you're shorthanded. Racers have plenty of muscle onboard; what they can't afford is the extra weight of a larger winch on deck.

And finally, don't place too much faith in the advice of a clerk in the marine hardware store. Try, if possible, to talk to owners of boats similar to your own and learn from their experiences.

ROPES FOR MARINE APPLICATIONS

Sailors can't exist without rope. A properly outfitted 24-footer could easily go through a full spool of rope in order to make up an anchor rode, and a set of bow, stern, breast and spring lines, plus fender pennants, fenderboard hangers, flag halyards, dinghy painter, warps, and so forth; you know how the list goes on and on.

Rope is raw material. That's the stuff that comes on a spool or in a carton; a full spool is usually 600 feet. When a piece of rope is removed from the spool, cut, spliced or otherwise made up for a specially designated use, it then becomes a *line*. Thus we have dock lines, anchor rodes, sheets, halyards, lifelines, and so on; all of them lines, no longer ropes. The exception is the bolt rope on a sail's luff or foot, which remains a rope.

Incidentally, when removing rope from a spool, put a pipe or rod through the hole in the center of the spool and support it off the ground so the spool can rotate smoothly. Then pull the rope off slowly as the spool turns. Never slip one turn at a time over the end of the spool, and don't let a clerk selling you a piece of rope do it to you either. Each one of those turns may develop a kink or hockle.

If rope or a line becomes twisted or tangled, it should be carefully untangled and then "overhauled" by pulling the entire length through your hand while maintaining a slight tension on it. If you watch the remaining part of the line, you'll see the twists unwinding as you pull it through. If it still looks twisted, haul it back the other way. Another solution is to tow the line behind your boat for a while, but only after the ends have been secured so they can't unlay themselves; otherwise, you'll end up with a bunch of spaghetti instead of rope.

Laid Ropes

All ropes, whether natural or synthetic, laid, braided or plaited, are made up from much smaller fibers. Three-strand laid rope, commonly used for docklines and anchor rodes, is usually produced as "right-lay" rope. If we were to look toward the end of a piece of right-lay rope, the strands would be twisted in a clockwise direction. Practically all fiber rope is made this way. The fibers are twisted together to make yarns, and several yarns are twisted to make each of the strands. While the final twist of the strands is right lay, the strands themselves are made with left-lay yarns, and the fibers are spun into yarns with right lay. This alternating twist helps to bind the rope together internally, reducing its tendency to come apart, or unlay. It works well with natural fibers, such as manila (hemp), but most synthetics are so slippery that they fall apart unless the ends are secured by whipping, dipping, melting or taping.

The tension with which the rope is spun determines its degree of stiffness or hardness. There are three grades; soft lay, medium lay, and hard lay. Medium lay is the only one to consider buying. Soft lay is so limp that it's almost impossible to splice, and it will unlay and kink at the slightest provocation. Hard lay is like a rock; even with a marlinspike or a fid, you can't pry the strands apart enough to get a smooth looking splice, and it's so stiff that knots are not only difficult to tie, but they won't hold very well either.

Medium lay lines are beautiful. They are soft enough to tie a knot easily and hold the knot, and yet firm enough to splice smoothly. They run through a block without binding, as long as the sheave diameter is sufficient.

Braided Ropes

The most commonly used braided rope for boat use is double braid. It consists of a rope within a rope, a braided outer cover over a braided core. The great advantage of braided rope is its flexibility and softness. Unlike laid rope, it does not have a memory of being twisted, so it can be coiled in any direction, and it resists abrasion well because of the great number of surface strands. It can be spliced, but with difficulty, and it requires several special tools—more than one set if you splice a couple of different sizes.

Braided or plaited rope can be either of "solid" construction, or have two parts—a cover and a core. The smaller diameters, one-quarter-inch or less, are often of solid construction and cannot be spliced. The larger diameters are usually two-part, and all two-part ropes have a braided cover.

The core can be braided, twisted, or have straight, parallel fibers. Ropes with braided cores are called double-braid or braid-on-braid. Ropes with parallel cores cannot be spliced, and those with twisted cores are much more difficult to splice than a double-braid. Parallel cores offer greater strength and less stretch than twisted or braided cores, but when turned around a radius like a halyard sheave, the fibers on the outside of the core can be overloaded. Parallel-cored line is also more likely to knot up or kink than double-braid, so despite its superior stretch characteristics, most manufacturers have opted for spliceable braided rope in the diameters commonly used on keelboats. Small boats continue to use non-spliceable, low-stretch line, especially for control lines like cunninghams and outhauls.

While a manufacturer can't make a line with a parallel core if he wants it to be spliceable, he can, by investing in advanced machinery, weave a braided core and braided cover that keeps all of the individual fibers running parallel to the direction of the rope, rather than with the direction of the weave. This technique improves the abrasion resistance of the rope and allows it to approach the stretch-resistance of non-woven cores.

Fibers

After deciding which style of rope you will use for a given application, the next decision will be the type of fiber. Natural fibers have been used aboard vessels since time immemorial. These have included flax, cotton, hemp or manila, and coconut fiber. These will all mildew and rot if not thoroughly dried before stowing, and they all swell up and get shorter when wet.

If not natural fiber, then the choice must be synthetic. Which one? That all depends on its use. Each of the synthetic fibers has its own set of good and bad points. For the recreational sailor, the choices are pretty well limited to four: nylon, Dacron or polyester, polypropylene, and Kevlar-reinforced Dacron. If you shop where the fishing fleet does, you'll come across some other varieties, often combinations of the above, usually selling at reasonable prices. Check them out. These are special-purpose ropes made for hard work and wear. If you find one suitable for your purposes, don't be afraid to use it.

Now let's look at the possible choices one at a time and see what their good and bad points are. Nylon was the first synthetic fiber rope that came on the market for the boating public shortly after World War II. Nylon's first appeal was its strength; it is more than twice as strong as comparably sized manila rope. Also, it won't rot or mildew; it has great resistance to chemical attack; and it is lighter than the same size manila rope. But its greatest attraction for sailors was its elasticity, making it the ideal choice for anchor rodes, mooring pennants and dock lines. However, this same elasticity eliminates the choice of nylon fiber for some other uses.

How would you like it if after you got your sails hauled up and set just right, the halyards stretched by half a foot? Probably about as much as you would enjoy seeing your genoa sheet stretch out just after getting it cranked in hard for a tough slog to weather. So, nylon is not ideal for every job on a boat. In both these cases—halyards and sheets—we need a fiber that resists stretching, and we'd like to keep as many of the other admirable features of synthetics as possible.

Polyester or Dacron rope is the choice for sheets. It is also known as *Terylene* (its original name) in England and *Teteron* in the Orient. Some newer trade names for the product include

Kodel, Fortrel and *Duron*. In general, it is strong, but not quite as strong as nylon; and it weighs more than either nylon or manila. It is not easy to recognize Dacron rope by appearance, because the manufacturer can give it various surface-finish textures.

For halyards, the new Kevlar-reinforced ropes provide the next best thing to wire. Although expensive, Kevlar halyards won't stretch, are tough, and will last longer than Dacron. The rope has found a permanent home in the racing fleets and many cruising folk are gradually learning its merits.

Polypropylene rates at the end of the list for most boat uses. It is weaker than either nylon or Dacron, it is more susceptible to chafe and abrasion than either, and it is the most seriously attacked by ultraviolet radiation in sunlight. The better grades will include an ultraviolet-light inhibitor, but the cheap stuff ends up looking woolly as the surface fibers degrade and break, and it constantly scratches you every time you handle it. It has one good feature—it floats—making it a good choice for a dinghy painter, for water-ski towlines, and also for heaving lines that are not usually exposed to sunlight for extended periods. Polypropylene has a slippery surface feel, and it will not hold a knot very well.

Breaking Strength

When discussing the relative strengths of the various types of rope, a word of caution is needed. Just because a chart lists the breaking strength of a given size of rope as 6,000 pounds, don't try to pick up your 5,000 pound boat with an old piece of it you find lying around the boatyard. A new sample of the rope may have been tested to 6,000 pounds, but it was never intended to be used under that load. Overloads can severely damage a line without breaking it, especially if they are shock loads. The plastic fibers will actually cold-flow like they had been melted, and the line will attain a permanent set that does not go away when the load is removed. It may not look too bad, but it will never be the same. The clue to look for in detecting this kind of serious damage is that the line will be thinner in the weakened spots.

How do we cope with all this uncertainty? The best way is by relying on safety factors, and building them into our estimates of how much strength is needed for any given line. As a rule of thumb, a safety factor of five is usually used. The selected rope should have a breaking strength equal to at least five times the expected maximum working load.

What if you don't know what working loads will be imposed upon a line in normal operations? That's a good point. Most of us don't have the foggiest idea of their magnitude. But naval architects and boat designers do; that's how they earn their pay, by making all those complicated mathematical calculations (and a few educated guesses) in order to select a specified size and type of line for each purpose. If you have a stock boat, replace each line with only the same size and type as the original; and if in doubt, contact the builder.

Strength Versus Size

Strength is one criterion we must consider when selecting a rope, but it's not the only one. Size is another factor to consider. We know that it is intimately related to strength, but there is a little more to it than that. We call this usability.

Five-sixteenths-inch nylon rope has a breaking strength of 2,650 pounds. That should be adequate as an anchor rode for a 26-footer with a 13-pound lightweight anchor and six feet of chain. It is, but when you anchor in a blow, the anchor buries itself in the bottom, as it is supposed to. You safely ride out the storm, and now it is time to get under way. When you start pulling on that skinny anchor rode, you'll see what we mean by the term "usability." *Adequate* and *useful* are two different things. Five-sixteenths-inch rope will cut grooves in your hide while you're struggling to break the anchor out. Three-eighths or 7/16-inch rope would be overkill as far as strength is concerned, but much easier on the hands.

Extending Rope Life

What can you do to extend the life of your lines? Try to eliminate their enemies—kinks, nicks, abrasion and dirt. If lines are always kept coiled and hung up, and not left lying about in a heap where they can be walked on and dragged over, their life should be nearly doubled. When coiling a line, remember that its original twisting in manufacture has given it a memory. Right-lay line will coil only in a clockwise direction. Do it the other way and it will kink every time.

Abrasion, especially on anchor rodes, can be avoided by careful use of chafing gear where the rode passes through the hawsehole or chock. All running rigging should be turned end-for-end every year or so to distribute the wear over the entire length of the line. This is especially important for sheets.

When transferring fuel, be careful of spills on and around your cordage. Petroleum products can deteriorate synthetic fibers, and so can paint thinners and strippers, fiberglass solvents, and the new epoxy and polyurethane paint catalysts and solvents. Be careful of tar and other substances on pilings and docks. When it gets on your dock lines, clean them up thoroughly as soon as you find it. When securing a mooring line or anchor rode, be careful to avoid sharp bends and kinks when you make the line fast around pilings and cleats. All these things will help to extend the useful life of your cordage. Just remember, as with most other parts of the boat, neglect is your worst enemy.

No matter how careful you are, eventually you're going to have to replace some of your lines. It's not uncommon for sailors to throw whole lengths of line away just because they had a bad spot or two in them. An anchor rode might not be serviceable anymore because of some bad chafing, but you probably can cut out the defects and make a couple of good dock lines from it, or a nice long dinghy painter, which you'll need for towing in heavy weather.

Where should you buy rope? ...Not at your local discount hardware store, bargain auto parts store, mill outlet or flea market. Your family's lives may depend upon that piece of rope. Stick with quality and name brands. Patronize your local marine store, but still look around for the best price. When you go in to buy 67 feet of 3/8-inch braided Dacron for a new jib sheet, expect to pay through the nose for it. But during the off-season, especially just before the inventory taxes are calculated, many marine stores have big sales. That's the time to stock up on replacement items you will need sooner or later. And always ask about quantity discounts, even if it means buying a whole spool. Those per-foot prices often are up to double the per-spool price.

MAINSHEET AND MAINSHEET TRAVELER SYSTEMS

The mainsail is a big part of the motive power of almost every sailboat. The art of mainsail control, however, is a relatively modern one. One tool that greatly facilitates mainsail control is the traveler.

Traditionally, the mainsheet traveler was a heavy bronze or iron rod that allowed some control over the position of the boom relative to the centerline of the boat. In heavy air, the main could be eased down to leeward without easing the sheet, helping to keep the boat on her feet with the main still sheeted down. Compared to modern travelers, this is a primitive system, but it can be made to work.

Without some form of traveler, the main is frequently sheeted to a single point on the boat's centerline. When the sheet is eased, the boom tends to rise, as well as move to leeward. To offset the rise in the boom, a vang is fitted, which tends to hold the boom down, albeit at the expense of placing considerable load on the boom. In extreme cases, the entire sheeting load of the boom is borne by the vang in the attempt to keep the boom low while the sheet is eased. A broken boom is sometimes the result.

The next stage in mainsail control is a traveler made from a section of T-track, just like that used for headsail leads. A car similar to the slider used for a genoa lead is used on the track, and adjustable stops allow the primary sheeting position to be adjusted to windward or leeward as necessary. The genoa-type slider, however, is difficult to move under a load, making the repositioning of the slider tedious, if not impossible, without easing the mainsheet. The friction is simply too great.

The solution is the modern ball-bearing or roller-bearing traveler. By reducing friction between the car and the track, bearings make it possible to adjust the position of the lead under the heaviest loads. The traveler car is fitted with control lines on both ends to allow constant adjustment of the lead position if necessary. It's far easier to depower the main in puffy conditions by dropping the traveler down to leeward momentarily, than it is to ease the sheet, then struggle to retrim it.

Winches, Ropes, and Running Rigging 75

This is a good mainsheet installation for a boat without a traveler. The lower block is within reach of the helmsman, and the rest of the cockpit is left relatively clear. The pedestal guard should be beefed up to take the mainsheet loads.

Without control lines, a roller-bearing traveler is only a little better than its predecessors. The primary advantage of the roller bearing traveler is its adjustability under load, yet without control lines this is virtually impossible.

The position of the traveler is often a problem. Almost anywhere in the cockpit, it will interfere with either movement through the cockpit (if for example, it bridges the seats just forward of the helmsman) or with seating in the cockpit.

With the short boom of a modern rig, the bridgedeck at the forward end of the cockpit is frequently the ideal place to mount the traveler, since it provides a strong mounting position close to the end of the boom for maximum leverage. This location can, however, interfere with seating for those times spent relaxing in the cockpit in port. Another common problem with this installation is that the mainsheet may chafe on the cockpit coaming if the traveler car is well to leeward and the mainsheet eased.

The location of this traveler at the aft end of the bridgedeck is just about perfect for sailhandling. However, it reduces the comfort of the cockpit in port, preventing anyone from sitting against the aft end of the deckhouse.

Mounting the traveler at the aft end of the cockpit is another possibility, but the main boom often ends several feet forward of this position. This means that the sheet leads forward at an awkward angle, reducing leverage, and perhaps interfering with the person at the helm.

Mounting the traveler atop the coachroof has both advantages and disadvantages. The cockpit is kept clear (a real advantage), but a forward position usually means mid-boom sheeting is necessary. The disadvantages of mid-boom sheeting can be significant. In order to exert the same trimming force on the sail, more force is required on the mainsheet. The tendency of the leech to pull the end of the boom upward is not directly offset. Instead, the downward force is exerted in the middle of the boom. The resulting lever-arm between the two loads tends to bend the boom, and can result in the boom breaking, particularly if the mainsheet runs to a single bail in the middle of the boom. This problem is usually offset by spreading mainsheet blocks

Winches, Ropes, and Running Rigging

A good solution for mid-boom sheeting. The traveler is bolted to the top of the seahood as well as to molded end supports. The mainsheet leads aft through an opening in the support molding.

along the boom, which unfortunately reduces their efficiency somewhat. Often, the designer will specify a larger boom section for mid-boom sheeting than that of a comparable end-of-boom sheeting arrangement.

Almost inevitably, a mid-boom traveler must bridge the companionway hatch cover when it slides into its forward position, or it must bridge the seahood. This usually means a long unsupported span of traveler, necessitating a strong support system. This also can put substantial point loading on the top of the coachroof, which must be suitably reinforced. It's not uncommon to see travelers bridging the middle of the main companionway hatch opening. The disadvantage of this installation will become painfully obvious the first time you crack your head.

The traveler should be far enough forward to allow the fitting of a companionway dodger. You may not want one now, but someone who owns your boat someday will. In the best arrangement, a wood or fiberglass breakwater is part of the cabintop aft of the traveler. Try to minimize the number of lines piercing the breakwater. Even with a dodger up, holes in the breakwater will let a lot of water through if you take a solid green one over the bow.

Be sure that the position of the aftermost boom block doesn't interfere with the dodger. Even though the front of the dodger slopes forward, the mainsheet could chafe on the dodger if not properly led.

A traveler is not absolutely essential on a cruising sailboat. Without one, however, the mainsail will never deliver the sort of performance it was designed and built to provide.

4

Awnings, Dodgers, and Custom Canvaswork

Some boats are eye-catchers, others are not. It's not surprising if our heads snap around for a second look at the hundred-foot motoryacht with the helicopter on the deckhouse pad; or the brine-encrusted double-ender with the battered vane steering, baggywrinkled shrouds, and the South African hailing port.

What makes the difference? Why do some boats from our own cruising area, of a size and price similar to our own, stand out and catch our eye? One practice that can produce an aura of greater quality and care, is the capping off our outfitting with a fine dusting of well designed and well finished canvaswork.

We're not talking about sails. We mean folding tops; cockpit awnings; dodgers; cockpit covers; winch covers; sail bags; sail covers; binnacle, compass and electronics covers. In fact, you name it, and chances are that a well designed and well tailored cover will improve not only the longevity and performance of the item to be covered, but the cosmetic impression of the entire boat as well.

Unfortunately, department stores and fabric stores have notoriously poor selections of boat canvases, which means a trip to your local canvas shop is in order here. But, whatever the source, the more you know about today's materials, hardware and design, the better your chances for satisfaction when you finally take delivery. Let's, therefore, briefly examine the whole field of boat "canvasing."

THE FABRICS

There are, basically, four fabrics that have application in the boat canvas field. These are natural-fiber canvases, acrylics (many marketed under the tradename Acrilan), polyesters (often marketed under the tradename Dacron), and nylons.

Natural Fiber Canvas

Old-fashioned, natural-fiber canvas, while still valuable in certain applications, has been largely supplanted by modern synthetics. But the replacement of true canvas by synthetics has created a great deal of confusion. Which material is best for which application; which is most economical; and which is most attractive? These are all logical questions.

To begin with, why was cotton, jute, hemp or flax (linen) canvas so popular for so long? Because all these natural fibers exhibit a property no man-made fiber has yet been able to duplicate. When they become moist, they swell, which tightens the weave and renders them watertight. Then, as they dry, shrinkage loosens the weave, allowing the passage of air, causing the fabric to "breathe" again.

With such a miracle fabric available, why did we ever turn away from natural-fiber canvas? Because, unfortunately, each time it becomes damp, in addition to swelling and becoming watertight, it also deteriorates a little. Anyone old enough to have lived with natural canvas will recall clearly the day he grabbed the boat cover (or the Bimini top, dodger, or what-have-you) to remove it, and had it disintegrate in his hands. Lamentably, this often occurred a year or two after purchase if the item was routinely exposed to the elements.

On the other hand, it's not unusual for dacron folding tops to last for ten or twelve years, even when stored out in the weather. A natural-fiber canvas top might have to be replaced three, and probably four times during this same period.

The Synthetics

While rating gold stars for durability, where do the synthetic fabrics fall in terms of "breathability?" Not too bad, actually, because most can be engineered to offer adequate air passage,

The full awning helps to protect brightwork from the sun while keeping the interior of the boat cooler. The matching jib and staysail covers allow the sails to be stowed on deck, for convenience, and to save space down below.

although at some loss in waterproofness. (This is usually remedied with a "moisture-resistant" compound sprayed on the finished fabric.) So let's look at the individual qualities of the three most popular synthetics, so that specific materials can be assigned to specific jobs.

Nylon is an extremely strong material and resists abrasion well, even in lightweight fabrics made up of extremely fine threads. It takes dye easily, allowing a wide selection of colors. Unfortunately, it deteriorates rapidly when exposed to ultraviolet rays, rendering it a poor choice for such routinely exposed items as sail covers or dodgers. Another characteristic that would disqualify nylon as a dodger or top material is the fact that it stretches readily and easily. Any item that should retain its tautness over a period of time should *not* be constructed of nylon. Nylon would, however, be a premier choice for a cockpit awning that is used infrequently and stored below.

Unlike nylon, acrylic fabrics are almost impervious to sunlight and to ambient chemical pollution in the air. They can be dyed to offer a selection of colors, seemingly making them a wise choice for all exposed items. Unfortunately, the acrylics are vulnerable to chafing, and while better than nylon where tautness is required, the acrylics do stretch more than the polyesters. Balancing all these factors, the majority of dodgers and folding tops are probably made of acrylic, with dacron a close second. Acrylic items should definitely have leather or polyester patches at points of potential wear.

Most sailors will probably find the bulk of their covers made of dacron. What are its advantages and disadvantages? Its ultraviolet resistance is good, and it is the strongest and most stretch-resistant of the synthetics. It's overwhelming shortcoming is its resistance to dying. Colors don't take well to polyester fibers, so they're not as colorfast as acrylics or nylons. This is why most dacron items are produced in any color you want—as long as it's white.

FINDING QUALITY CANVAS ITEMS

There are four ways to acquire canvas covers: sew them yourself, find and order them through mail order catalogs, purchase them with your new boat as "original equipment," or have them custom-built locally.

If your budget is badly bruised after over-indulgence at the "optional-items" trough, the first alternative will obviously appeal as a money-saver, although in reality, making your own canvas items may cost more in the long run. The second alternative will require a little higher original expenditure; the third could provide some satisfaction, as well as saving money; and the fourth option should produce the highest quality products— *if* you shop intelligently. Let's look briefly at each alternative.

Do-it-Yourself
A talented and well equipped seamstress (or seamster) can certainly do an adequate job on covers. But, as in most do-it-yourself projects, you will probably be frustrated initially by lack of experience, so try to start with the simpler projects like hatch,

Awnings, Dodgers, and Custom Canvaswork 83

These hatch and windshield covers protect brightwork from the weather and help to keep interior upholstery fabrics from fading.

winch, and instrument covers. A book such as *The Complete Canvasworker's Guide* by Jim Grant would be helpful if you choose to do your own canvaswork. Still, as the materials amount to significant percentage of the cost of canvaswork (and if you put a value on your own labor) making more than one item, before you come up with a usable one, does tend to erode any anticipated savings.

Mail Order
This is a notch above do-it-yourself, but not a very big notch. Half the battle in obtaining really good-looking and functional canvaswork is in the detail work and the placement of the fasteners. Very few mailorder companies send experienced installers via United Parcel Service.

Original Equipment
The best thing to be said about original equipment canvas is that it comes with the fasteners installed. Beyond that, it's sometimes hard to tell from homemade. More often than not, the fit is

The dodger allows the companionway hatch to remain open in rough or rainy weather, while the Bimini top shades the occupants of the cockpit from the sun.

terrible; items that should be taut gather rainwater by the gallon; and materials are often not of very good quality. Which lead us, naturally, to the final alternative:

Custom Canvaswork
Every small town, it seems, has at least three listings in the Yellow Pages under "Boat Covers, Tops and Upholstery," and any town within driving distance of saltwater will have thirty. Unfortunately, a visit to most of these may reveal more chintz and taffeta than canvas. In fact, many won't even know where to order marine fabrics.

The fact of the matter is that many self-proclaimed "Boat Cover" experts have little experience with custom canvaswork. Given a Naugahyde cushion to be recovered, about half will return it in usable shape. But, if you ask them what they know about dodgers, don't be surprised if they tell you that they don't follow baseball.

Given this low percentage of truly professional boat tailors, how do you find the one who will come up with the exquisite *objects d'arte* you picture in your mind? Probably the best starting point is your local marina. Spend a few minutes walking up and down the dock and decide which boats exhibit truly superior (or at least satisfactory) canvas accessories. A little detective work should soon reveal the names of the owners of these boats.

Then talk with the owners. What about price, reliability (of the shop, not the cover), installation, knowledgeability, and so forth? The fact is, unfortunately, that some of the best cover men are the most independent, and can be hard to work with. The reason is, of course, that good craftsmen are in demand, and can afford to be independent.

Assuming, however, that you're fortunate enough to find that gifted young artisan who hasn't as yet become preeminent in his field, you'll want to start with the matter of design.

DESIGN

Covers are covers and folding tops are folding tops. If you've seen one wheel and binnacle cover, you've seen them all. Well...yes and no.

If you have an aesthetic sense, you should have considerable input into fine tuning the appearance of the accessories you're considering. (If you don't, throw yourself on the mercy of the canvas man.) But practical considerations intrude too; "form follows function." Too much emphasis on aesthetics (an overly rakish dodger, for instance) can produce striking, but totally unworkable, final products.

The really competent canvas artist will have some strong opinions on materials and design that could drastically alter your prejudices and opinions—if you'll listen to him. One of the best ideas we've seen recently, for example, is a dodger with an extra bow attached just behind the after bow (the one that stretches the top open). When the dodger is up, crewmembers leaving the cockpit to go forward, invariably grab the after edge of the dodger to hoist themselves on deck. This practice does two things. First, it offers them an excellent chance to fall overboard, because folding dodgers (and Bimini tops) are notoriously poor handholds. Secondly, it causes unnecessary wear on the fabric, drastically shortening the life of an expensive item.

That supplemental bow extending aft from the dodger provides a super handhold, not only for exit from the cockpit, but for any movement about the cockpit in dirty weather—a logical and ingenious addition that can make life aboard easier and safer.

FASTENERS

If you are fortunate enough to find a superior craftsman to do your canvas work, you can probably trust him to use appropriate fasteners. But the more you know while discussing the project with him, the more he'll respect your knowledge, thus the better chance you have of your getting what you really want.

Among the fastening devices you might want (or require) are: Velcro strips, ties, straps, zippers, snaps, studs, rings, grommets, sail hooks and drawstrings.

Velcro

While offering little resistance to displacement, Velcro is an excellent material where applicable. One of the mating surfaces can be attached to the hull or deck with adhesives or screws, and the companion strip sewn to the fabric (or both mating surfaces sewn to the joining fabric). For applications where security or watertight integrity aren't involved (for example, for securing seldom used straps out of the way), Velcro can sometimes solve seemingly insoluble problems.

Zippers

Zippers and saltwater are congenitally incompatible. But, by using zippers with extra large plastic teeth, some of the inevitable problems can be postponed. Zippers are commonly used for inserting clear vinyl windows in dodgers, and for access openings in full-cockpit enclosures.

As a general rule, zippers tend to fail long before the synthetic material of most dodgers and sail covers; metal ones corrode, and plastic zippers wear out quickly. If after studying the other alternative, you conclude that a zipper is an absolute necessity, try to plan the work so that replacing the zipper is as simple as possible.

The drawstring closure, where applicable, is the simplest and most maintenance-free means of securing a canvas cover.

Drawstrings

Drawstrings are one of the most rudimentary of attaching devices, and probably date back to prehistory. They also have no moving mechanical parts, which tends to make them durable and irritation-proof.

Drawstrings consist of lengths of nylon cord passed through an open-ended hem, just like that in the top of a sail bag. Depending on the shape of the particular item to be covered, drawstrings might be considered first, as an alternative to more complicated attaching methods.

Straps, Rings, Ties, and Grommets

Basically, all of these are means of tying two fabric parts together, or of tying a fabric part to the hull or deck. The more years you spend around boats and saltwater, the more respect you'll probably develop for a simple cord and a few basic knots. While the various "patented" fasteners are impressive in their ingenuity and complexity, they do offer more room for breakdowns. Don't arbitrarily reject your canvas man's advice if he feels that

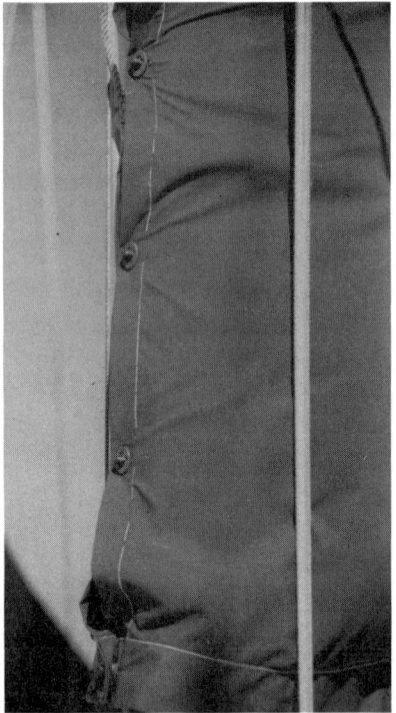

Two approaches to closing a mainsail cover; sail hooks on the left; twist studs on the right.

certain applications will be best served by a length of cord and some reinforced openings to tie it in.

Sail Hooks

Sail hooks are little bent pieces of wire that are sewn or riveted to one side of adjoining fabrics, around which loops of cord are passed, joining the two sides. They can also be used on the base of equipment to be topped with a cover employing a drawstring, thus anchoring the cover. Sail hooks are commonly used along the foot and in front of the mast on canvas mainsail covers.

Snaps

Snaps are the basic nutrient of the marine cover business. Snaps come in two primary parts: the round base that is attached (usually via the integral screw) to the hull or deck, and a round cap which is fastened to the fabric by means of an internal retaining ring.

Snaps are unconditionally guaranteed, if not properly maintaind, to corrode and fail during the first year of use. On the other hand, when maintained, they go on practically forever and provide a quick and efficient means of attaching removable accessories to hull or deck. Snaps are not the preferred means of attaching fabric part to fabric part as pressure is required, which means a hand both inside and outside the joined structure, which is often difficult or impossible.

What is involved in snap maintenance? Once a year (or at the beginning and end of each season) insert a dab of petroleum jelly (Vaseline) in the head of each snap. Five minutes, once a year, will service all the snaps on a boat and render them docile and cooperative for a whole season. For some reason, most boatowners fail to perform this ritual, resulting in endless hours of tugging and wrestling.

A superior piece of canvas will include canvas tabs at each snap to facilitate the removal of the item. Parts not so equipped make for difficult removal as it's hard to gain a purchase point using two fingers along the edge of the cover.

Lift-the-Dot Fasteners

Lift-the-dot fasteners will serve in many of the same areas where snaps are commonly used, and are a step up from snaps. They consist of grooved studs which fasten to the hull or deck, and grommets (with internal retaining springs) which attach to the fabric. By "lifting the dot" (at the external perimeter of the grommet on the fabric part) these remove easily. At the same time, a straight upward pull will *not* free the grommet, making this a very tenacious fitting.

In use, lift-the-dot fasteners seem to last for a long time. Their one disadvantage is that the studs do protrude higher than a snap base, making them inappropriate for use in traffic areas where someone could trip on them. As most covers are fastened to vertical surfaces, this seldom prevents the use of lift-the-dot fasteners.

A hemmed square of canvas protects the teak caprail from dirt and wear: a novel use of custom canvaswork, and a simple do-it-yourself project.

Twist Studs

Twist type fasteners are sometimes called "commonsense fasteners" and are another excellent fitting. These consist of an oblong (in cross section) stud of which the top half can be twisted at right angles to its base. An oblong grommet fits over the aligned stud, onto its oblong base, and the top is then twisted to a right angle, locking the grommet to the stud base.

These are excellent fasteners but do have two disadvantages. First, they are even longer than the lift-the-dot studs, making them inappropriate for use in traffic areas. Secondly, the rotating top can be bent out of alignment by a kick, or by the tension of an improperly attached piece of fabric. Both the grommets and studs are easily replaced, however, so this problem is obviated if you obtain a few replacement grommets and studs when you buy your covers.

* * *

Take two boats of the same size and type, clean and polish them optimally, and put them up for sale in adjoining slips. The one with an attractive (albeit aging) set of quality canvas accessories will sell faster and probably at a better price than its bare-bones sister. Canvas is, therefore, an investment rather than an expense. Add to this the fact that the equipment and areas protected by the canvas will be in better condition (and with a history of less repairs), and you wonder why anyone would skimp on covers.

When you buy your covers, track down the best "top man" in your area and spend some time discussing your wants and needs. Listen to his advice and hope that he'll listen to you. Where appropriate, go for the heavier (and more expensive) weights of fabrics, and don't skimp on reinforcing at points of strain or potential abrasion. At any sign of wear, remove the cover and take it in for additional reinforcing. It's much easier to prevent problems than to repair them.

Many excellent canvas shops consist of a large van or a converted school bus, which the operator brings to your boat, and from which he does his work (or at least the initial cutting, pinning, and the final installation).

Although your first contact with such an operator will no doubt be via an answering machine, don't hang up and look elsewhere. Give your name and number and wait for him to return your call. Then rejoice. You've probably found a bona fide boat tailor—not an upholsterer who occasionally makes something for a boat.

5

Ground Tackle and Anchor-Handling Equipment

GROUND TACKLE SELECTION AND USE

The recovered artifacts of ancient civilizations, from the stock-in-crown anchors of ancient China to the wood-stocked and lead-stocked anchors of the Greeks and Romans, indicate that for centuries sailors have known that an anchor's friction against the sea bottom contributes very little to its holding power. One has only to drag a smooth, ski-shaped heavy object along the bottom to discover that the pull required to drag it is less than half of its weight.

To have any useful amount of holding power, an anchor must have projections—flukes of some sort—that will engage an obstruction or probe into the bottom soil deeply enough to develop the necessary resistance to being dragged.

For an anchor to engage the bottom, it must be designed so that when lowered, it will turn to the proper attitude for the fluke to probe into the soil. Some types of anchors, such as the kedge, Northill, and lightweight, are fitted with a "stock" to effect the correct positioning. Stockless anchors, such as the plow or Bruce, depend upon the shape or the pivoting action of their flukes to position them for digging into the bottom.

Once the flukes have begun digging into a penetrable bottom, their holding power depends on the internal friction or shear resistance of the bottom material and upon the total area of material that is subject to stress. The stressed area depends on the depth of penetration, the shape and area of the flukes, and the angle at which the flukes are held. For some anchors, the stock also becomes buried, so that its projected area is also a factor.

Anchor Selection

When outfitting a yacht, the sailor needs to consider the suitability of the ground tackle for the anchoring conditions that the yacht may encounter. First considerations will include the stress of weather, available protection from wind and sea, and the character of the bottom in likely anchorages. Information regarding these can be acquired from charts, coast pilots, books, and magazine articles, as well as from other sailors. With this information at hand, one can begin an assessment of the types and sizes of anchors that will be appropriate.

The characteristics that influence an anchor's suitability in order of importance are:
1) suitability for the expected bottom conditions (whether sand, mud, shingle, rocks, weeds, or kelp);
2) stowability aboard the boat;
3) probability of fouling (will the parts of the anchor that project above the bottom foul the cable if it is dragged over the anchor by a change of wind or tide);
4) readiness for use (must the stock or flukes be prepared before use); and
5) recoverability (can the anchor be broken out readily by a near vertical pull; if raised under way will it kite about as it is being raised; threatening damage to the boat).

The following is a general summary of a series of tests conducted by naval architect Robert Smith on the suitability of various anchors. General anchor types are shown in the sketch on the next page.

Choosing Anchors for Sand or Mud

Bottoms of sand or mud that are free of weeds, kelp, and stones provide the most suitable holding ground for anchoring. All anchors will hold on bottoms of this type.

LIGHTWEIGHT. Because of the high ratio of holding power to weight, the lightweight type (such as the Danforth) makes it the

Northill
stock in crown

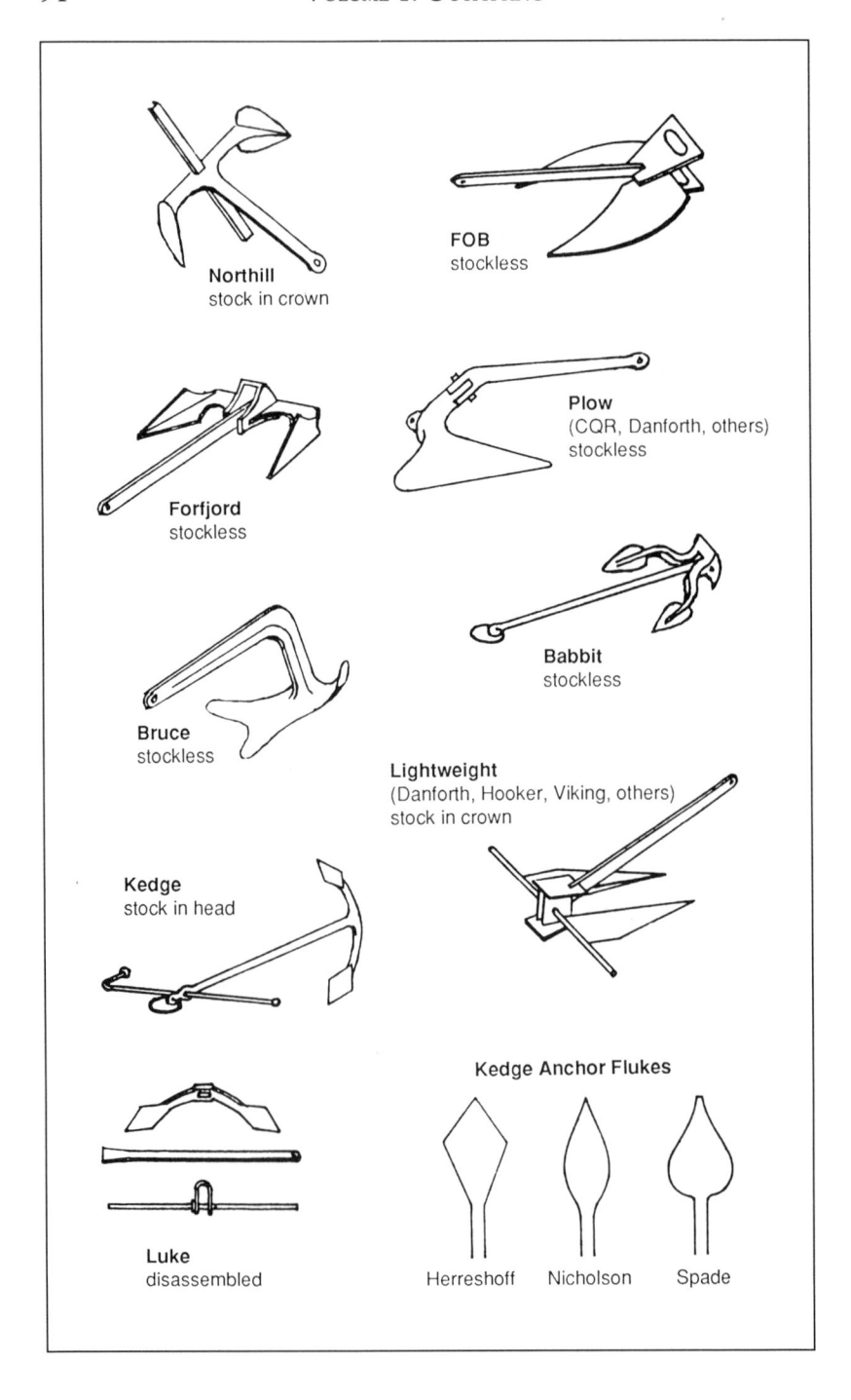

FOB
stockless

Forfjord
stockless

Plow
(CQR, Danforth, others)
stockless

Bruce
stockless

Babbit
stockless

Kedge
stock in head

Lightweight
(Danforth, Hooker, Viking, others)
stock in crown

Luke
disassembled

Kedge Anchor Flukes

Herreshoff   Nicholson   Spade

clear favorite for sand or mud, especially on large boats and as a "storm" anchor on all boats. In some of our tests, the smaller sizes of lightweight anchors were difficult to get started in hard sand, but this was not a problem with the larger sizes or in bottoms of softer sand and mud.

FOB. In the area of our final testing, the FOB anchors, when seeming to have taken hold, would often break out as soon as any significant load was applied. Two or three attempts were often necessary before the FOB anchors held well enough to complete the tests.

CQR, BRUCE, and NORTHILL. All three anchors took hold immediately in either hard or soft sand. When dragged but a short distance, the Bruce anchors would break out and not take a new hold until raised and freed of the accumulation of sand that had adhered to the three-lobed, spade-like fluke.

KEDGE and BABBIT. On hard sand, the Kedge and Babbit anchors did not completely bury their flukes and were dragged with their crowns clear of the bottom.

Mud With Clay

The above tests were all conducted on a sand bottom which the anchors were able to penetrate satisfactorily. On a bottom of mud having a high content of clay, tests of the small Northill and Babbit anchors indicated holding powers greater than on sand, 30 percent more for the Northill and 46 percent more for the Babbit. It is expected that holding powers for the other anchor types would be increased in similar mud bottoms, although tests were not conducted.

Gravel, Pebbles, and Shingle

Bottoms of gravel, pebbles, or shingle are poor for anchoring. The pivoted fluke anchors—lightweight, CQR, Benson, Babbit, Forfjord, and FOB—are unable to start the tips of their flukes into this kind of bottom, so the anchor slides over it with a minimum of resistance.

The kedge, Bruce, and Northill-types offer the best prospect of holding. Of these, the kedge assumes the best posture for digging in. One having Nicholson-type flukes (see diagram) would be most suitable. The Bruce will engage one side lobe of its fluke; however, only in very loose, small material could it bury sufficiently to right itself. The Northill rests initially on the side of one fluke and one end of its stock so the fluke does not point directly into the bottom, and the stock is susceptible to damage as the anchor is dragged.

Rock and Coral

On bottoms of rock and coral, an anchor can hold only by hooking on to a projection or by getting a fluke between two rocks or into a hole or crevice. The kedge type of anchor is best suited to this condition. Other types—notably the Bruce and CQR—will also work, but somewhat less effectively.

When hooking into rock or coral, holding power is limited only by the structural strength of the anchor. For example, a typical 20-pound kedge will have a maximum safe load of 540 pounds; a 40-pound kedge will have a maximum safe load of 840 pounds; a 60-pounder will have 1080 pounds. When anchoring in rocks or coral, a buoyed trip line should always be secured to the crown of the anchor and used for raising it. Anchoring on rock or coral bottoms should be avoided whenever possible.

Kelp and Weeds

Kelp grows on rocks that do not dry at low tide. There will be foul bottom underneath should the anchor find a way down through the kelp. In moderate winds, an anchor may hold to the kelp alone, but anchoring on kelp is to be avoided. When necessary to do so, a trip line should be used to assist in disengaging the anchor from the kelp or underlying rocks.

A heavy cover of weeds will tend to keep an anchor from the bottom and quickly foul it as it is dragged. The CQR and kedge types are the most suitable anchors for use on weed-covered bottoms. The flat anchors—lightweight, Benson, and FOB—are the least suitable, especially in the smaller sizes. Although it can be difficult to get any anchor started in a grassy bottom, the roots of weeds do increase the holding power of the bottom once the anchor has taken hold.

Size and Holding Power

When the types of anchors to be carried have been decided upon, it will be necessary to determine suitable sizes. These will depend on the size and type of boat and the force of the winds in which the anchors will be used. Together the boat and the wind force determine the amount of tension on the anchor cable; and eventually that cable tension can be translated into anchor size.

The stronger the wind, the greater the cable tension and the bigger the anchor needed. But how big is big enough?

Our study of anchors that have proven satisfactory for ordinary use on actual cruising boats in normal conditions (a sand bottom with a scope of five to one) indicates that many of these boats would drag their largest anchor in winds of 25 to 30 knots. While the selection table deals with wind velocities to 63 knots, an anchor that will hold the boat in conditions up to 30 knots would be satisfactory for ordinary use.

Calculating Anchor Size

First, determine from **Table 5-1** the tension your boat will place on the anchor cable, using the column for wind velocity of thirty knots. In the table, cable tension is shown for each three feet of boat length. For intermediate lengths, the tension may be estimated, interpolated, or calculated using the formula: tension = length squared x factor (the bottom row of the table). Length is the length overall of the hull, exclusive of bowsprit or boomkin.

The cable tensions tabulated are for single-masted vessels. For yawls, they should be increased 15 percent; for schooners and ketches, 25 percent. A power cruiser without a flying bridge should be taken as a yawl; when fitted with a flying bridge, consider it as a schooner.

With the cable tension from Table 5-1, enter the column of **Table 5-2** for the type of anchor being considered, and find the weight that would be dragged by that cable tension. Tension values are shown for each five pounds of anchor weight. Interpolate or estimate values for intermediate weights.

From your source of supply, find the weights of the chosen type of anchor that are available. If one is close below the desired weight, have it weighed. (The weights of almost all anchors exceed the catalog weights—some as much as 18 percent. The

Table 5-1. Anchor Cable Tension in Wind and Waves

Boat Length in Feet	\multicolumn{15}{c}{Wind Velocity in Knots}
	21	24	27	30	33	36	39	42	45	48	51	54	57	60	63
21	46	60	76	94	114	135	158	184	211	240	271	304	339	375	414
24	60	78	100	123	149	176	207	240	275	313	354	397	442	490	540
27	76	99	126	155	188	223	262	304	349	397	448	502	560	620	684
30	94	122	156	192	232	275	323	375	430	490	553	620	691	765	844
33	113	148	188	232	281	333	391	454	521	592	669	750	836	926	1021
36	135	176	224	276	334	397	465	540	619	705	796	893	995	1102	1216
39	158	207	263	324	392	465	546	634	727	827	934	1048	1168	1293	1427
42	183	240	305	376	455	540	633	736	843	960	1083	1215	1355	1499	1655
45	211	275	350	431	522	620	727	844	968	1102	1243	1395	1555	1721	1899
48	240	313	399	491	594	705	827	961	1101	1253	1415	1587	1769	1958	2161
51	271	354	450	554	671	796	934	1085	1243	1415	1597	1792	1998	2211	2440
54	303	397	504	621	752	892	1047	1216	1394	1586	1790	2009	2239	2479	2735
57	338	442	562	692	838	994	1166	1355	1553	1767	1995	2239	2495	2762	3048
60	374	490	623	767	929	1102	1292	1501	1721	1958	2210	2480	2765	3060	3377
63	413	540	687	845	1024	1215	1425	1655	1897	2159	2437	2735	3048	3374	3723
66	453	592	754	928	1124	1333	1564	1816	2082	2370	2675	3001	3345	3703	4086
69	495	647	824	1014	1228	1457	1709	1985	2276	2590	2923	3280	3656	4047	4466
72	539	705	897	1104	1337	1586	1861	2162	2478	2820	3183	3572	3981	4406	4863
Factor	0.104	0.136	0.173	0.213	0.258	0.306	0.359	0.417	0.478	0.544	0.614	0.689	0.768	0.850	0.938

Anchor cable tension = (Length)^2 × Factor, with scope of five and boat veered 30° to wind
Table values are for sloops or cutters; add 15% for yawls, 25% for ketches & schooners

data of Table 5-2 are based on the actual weights of the anchors we tested.) If the actual weight of the anchor is somewhat less— say not more than 10 percent—the anchor may still be acceptable. Otherwise, the next larger size will be needed.

Of anchors not in the table, slip-ring anchors of the lightweight and Benson type are made only in small sizes. The holding powers of the former are about 84 percent of standard lightweight anchors of the same weight. Holding power of the Benson is about 42 percent of a lightweight of the same weight.

The Danforth company claims much higher holding power for their new Deepset anchors, compared to their standard and high-tensile lightweight anchors shown in Table 5-2. Presumably, the advertised holding powers of the Deepset anchors were based on tests, but we have not been able to verify the claims.

Additional Ground Tackle

SECOND ANCHOR. When cruising, a second anchor should be carried to be used in the event of loss or temporary abandonment of the first. Preferably, this should be of another type in order to better accommodate the ground tackle to a greater variety of conditions. Its holding powers as determined from Table 5-2 should equal that of the first anchor.

Such a complement of anchors will allow lying to a single anchor in winds to the upper limit of Force 6 (27 knots). If both anchors are deployed properly, they should hold the boat in winds in excess of Force 8 (40 knots).

STORM ANCHOR. Yachts that cruise to remote areas or that may be expected to be anchored in exposed locations should carry a "storm" anchor which alone can hold the boat in Force 8 winds. The holding power for this anchor can be determined from Table 5-1 (use the column for 45 knots, to provide a margin) and an anchor selected from Table 5-2. In the interest of saving weight, a lightweight-type is often favored for this service.

SECONDARY ANCHORS. Owners of boats longer than about 33 feet often consider use of their primary anchor to be too much work for casual anchoring when their boat will not be left unattended. A smaller anchor (lunch hook) limited to this use, or to be used if becalmed when racing, is often carried. A small CQR anchor is suggested for the latter use since, when being raised with way on the boat, it will not tend to kite under the boat as much as would the flat anchors.

Fouling

When properly set, the Bruce and the pivoted fluke-types of anchors are not easily fouled by their own cables. The kedge and Northill-types are most prone to this kind of fouling, because when properly set, one fluke or fluke arm projects above the bottom so that as the boat moves about with changes of wind or tide, the cable can become wrapped around the projecting fluke arm. When there is any possibility that this has occurred, the anchor should be weighed and reset.

The lightweight type of anchor can be fouled by a stone, clam shell, or piece of waterlogged wood becoming jammed in the space separating the two flukes. This may not inhibit the burying ability of the anchor very much, but will prevent proper pivoting action of the flukes if the anchor is turned over by the boat moving about.

All anchors can become fouled by weeds or kelp. Anchors having a large, flat fluke area relative to their weight may be held

Table 5-2. Cable Tension to Drag Anchor

Weight of Anchor	Hi-Tens	Lwt	CQR	Bruce	Northill	Kedge	Babbit	FOB	Forsword	Herr.	Luke
5	288	188*	99	68	60	60	49	48	45	42	
10	458	438	158	109	97	96	78	77	72	68	
15	602	574	207	144	128	126	103	101	95	89	
20	729	696	252	175	155	154	126	124	116	109	98
25	847	809	293	204	181	179	147	144	136	127	114
30	957	914	332	231	205	203	166	164	154	144	130
35	1062	1013	368	257	228	226	185	182	171	161	145
40	1161	1109	403	282	250	248	203	200	188	176	159
45	1257	1200	437	305	271	269	220	217	204	191	172
50	1349	1288	469	328	291	289	237	233	220	206	186
55	1438	1373	501	350	311	308	253	249		220	198
60	1525	1456	531	372	331	327	269	265		234	211
65	1609	1536	561	393	349	346	285	280	264	248	223
70	1691	1615	590	414	368	364	300	295	278	261	235
75	1771	1691	619	434	386	382	315	309	291	274	247
80	1850	1766	647	454	403	400	329	324		286	259
85	1927	1840	674	473	421	417	343	338		299	270
90	2002	1912	701	492	438	434	357	351	331	311	
95	2077	1983	727	511	454	450	371	365	344		
100	2150		753	529	471	467	385	378	357		303
105	2221		779	547	487	483	398	391			314
110	2292		804	565	503	499	411	404			324
115	2362		829	583	519	514	424	417			335
120	2430		853	600	535	530	437	430			345
125	2498		878	618	550	545	450	443			355
130	2565		902	635	565	560	463	455			
135	2631		925		580	575	475	467			
140	2696		949		595	590	487	479	452		
145	2761		972		610	605	500	491	464		
150	2824		995		625	619	512	503	475		404
155	2887		1017		639	633	524	515	486		414
160	2950		1040		654	648	536	527	497		424
165	3012		1062		668	662	547	538	508		433
Factor	97.9	93.4	33.1	22.7	20.0	19.8	16.0	15.7	14.7	13.7	12.2

Cable tension to drag anchor = Factor × (Weight)$^{1/1}$ + 0.4 × (Weight)
Weights and tensions are in lbs.
Data are for sand bottom and scope of five
* Factor for lwt anchors under 10 lbs. = 63.6

clear of the bottom by a heavy cover of weeds. They are then quickly fouled by the weeds as they are dragged. The kedge and CQR types are better suited for use on heavily weeded bottoms.

While not fouling as such, the tendency of the ring of a slip-ring anchor (as made by Benson, Danforth, Hooker, and others) to slide to the crown end of the shank has much the same effect. This feature is dangerous. A change of wind or tide causing a reversal of cable direction will slip the ring, causing the anchor to trip, with no prospect of its gaining a new hold.

While attempting to test Benson slip ring anchors in the Columbia River, it was found that, even though making downstream sternway over the bottom, if the boat was making any upstream headway in the current, the anchor would be swept under the boat as it was lowered and would land on the bottom with the shank pointing upstream. As the boat subsequently drifted back with the current, the slip ring was pulled to the crown of the anchor, which was then dragged.

To facilitate our testing, the travel of the slip rings of the Benson anchors was limited by seizings around the hairpin-shaped shanks. It is strongly recommended that owners of slip-ring anchors limit the travel of the rings with a U-bolt or a strong wire seizing—or, better yet, abandon use of the anchor entirely.

SELECTING THE ANCHOR RODE

The most practical choices for anchor cables are wire rope, fiber rope, chain, or a combination of chain and rope. Wire rope is generally limited to commercial vessels. The mechanical complications, space required, and the expense usually discourage its use on yachts.

Rope or Chain

The choice between rope and chain will be determined in part by the weight of the anchors to be handled. On boats over 40 feet, breaking out the largest anchor and bringing it aboard clear of the hull and over the lifelines can be a difficult operation. This fact alone will encourage the use of a windlass and chain, and stowage of the anchor on a bow roller or in a hawsepipe. Therefore, except for racing craft on which saving weight is a primary consideration, chain will usually be used for the anchor cable. Chain should always be used when anchoring on rocky or coral bottoms.

On smaller cruising yachts and on many large racing yachts, in the interest of saving weight and a more favorable weight distribution, rope will be usually be used for the anchor rodes. When more power is needed to raise the anchor than can be applied by hand, the line can be led through snatch blocks, if necessary, to a jib-sheet winch. Because of its elasticity, and the fact that it doesn't rot or mildew when stowed wet, nylon rope is preferred for this service.

When the anchor cable is rope, a length of chain should be used at the end next to the anchor. The weight of this chain will tend

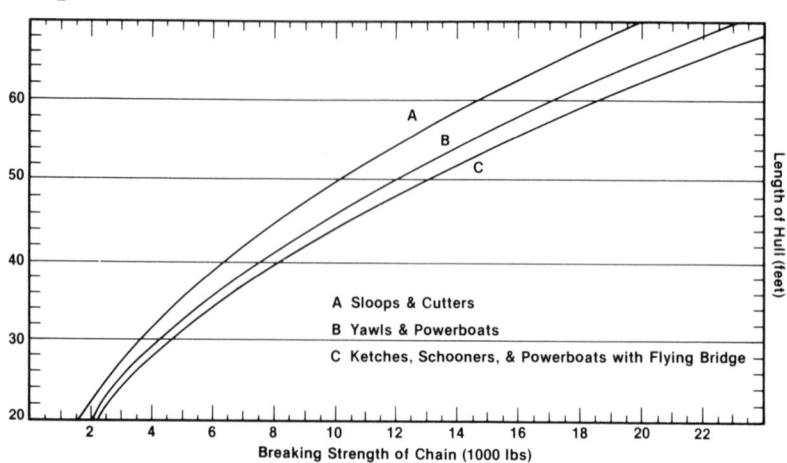

Graph 5-3. Anchor Chain Selection Chart

Graph showing Length of Hull (feet) on vertical axis (20-60) vs. Breaking Strength of Chain (1000 lbs) on horizontal axis (2-22), with three curves:
- A Sloops & Cutters
- B Yawls & Powerboats
- C Ketches, Schooners, & Powerboats with Flying Bridge

to hold the anchor shank down, thereby assisting the initial digging-in action of the anchor, and the chain will withstand being dragged about on the bottom better than will rope.

A suggested minimum length for chain used in this way is the sum of the draft of the boat and the freeboard at the bow. For example, with 5-foot draft and 4-foot freeboard, 9 feet of chain would be minimum. With this length of chain, the anchor will usually be clear of the bottom when the rope-to-chain connection has been brought to the bow chock or roller, so that the boat may be gotten under way while the chain and anchor are being raised and brought aboard.

CHAIN SIZE. Suitable size for chain may be determined from **Graph 5-3.** Begin with the length of boat (exclusive of bowsprit or boomkin). Read across to the curve for the type of rig: A, B, or C. From the point of intersection of boat length with the curve, read vertically to the breaking strength of chain that is suitable for the boat.

Either BBB or proof-coil chain may be used. If it is to be used with a windlass, BBB is usually preferred, though some windlass manufacturers offer wildcats for proof-coil. It is important that the chain and the wildcat are a proper match; otherwise slipping will occur and the wildcat may sustain damage. BBB chain,

Table 5-4. Selected Specifications for Chain and Nylon Rope

Chain Sizes		BBB Chain		Proof-Coil Chain		BBB or PC	Nylon Rope	
Nominal Size (inches)	Actual Diameter (inches)	Weight of 100' (lbs)	Breaking Strength (lbs)	Weight of 100' (lbs)	Breaking Strength (lbs)	Volume of 100' (cubic feet)	Diameter (inches)	Breaking Strength (lbs)
3/16	0.2188	50	3,186	48	2,846	0.26	5/16	2,725
1/4	0.2813	82	5,267	79	4,705	0.43	3/8	3,924
5/16	0.3438	123	7,869	118	7,029	0.64	7/16	5,341
							1/2	6,976
3/8	0.4063	171	10,990	164	9,817	0.89	9/16	8,829
7/16	0.4688	228	14,632	219	13,070	1.19	5/8	10,900
1/2	0.5313	293	18,794	281	16,788	1.53	11/16	13,189
							3/4	15,696
9/16	0.5938	366	23,476	351	20,970	1.91	7/8	21,364
5/8	0.6563	447	28,678	429	25,618	2.33	1	27,904

having shorter links, can pass through a smaller size naval pipe. A shackle of equal size cannot be inserted through an end link of BBB chain, so two shackles back-to-back or a special connecting link (usually weaker than the chain) must be used to join lengths of chain.

Proof-coil chain is better suited for use in conjunction with a rope anchor rode when a length of chain is used next to the anchor. Shackles, a size larger than the chain size, can be put through the end links, for the connections to the anchor or the eyesplice in the rode, and for adding more chain when anchoring on rocks or coral.

ROPE SIZE. To find the size of nylon rope that will have both adequate strength and desirable stretch characteristics, multiply the minimum breaking strength of chain as previously found by a factor of 1.33.

From the table of rope and chain strengths (**Table 5-4**), select the rope size that has a breaking strength equal to or greater than the value thus found. Do not use smaller line; it will be too elastic. For example, a 40-foot sloop will require a minimum chain strength of 6500 pounds. This can be met by 5/16-inch chain, either proof-coil (7029 pounds) or BBB (7869 pounds). For rope, 6500 x 1.33 = 8645 pounds, so 9/16-inch nylon rope having a breaking strength of 8829 pounds is suitable.

These chain and rope sizes will meet the strength requirements for winds in excess of Force 10 (55 knots), provided suitable shackles, thimbles, and splices are used. The strength of the rope exceeds that of the chain to allow for the loss of strength resulting from splices, securing to cleats or bitts, and so forth.

All rodes on board, whether rope or chain, should be made to the same standards, to permit interchangeability or attaching to each other to obtain greater length when necessary.

ANCHOR WINDLASSES

No one seems to be very certain of the distinction (if any) between a windlass and a capstan. Both are mechanical winch-like devices that are used as aids in lifting anchors off the bottom. Both involve wrapping an anchor line or anchor chain around a cylinder or drum, using the friction between the cylinder and the anchor rode, then applying the mechanical advantage of a long handle or powerful motor to do most of the heavy work of retrieving an anchor.

Some people are of the opinion that capstans have vertical drums and windlasses have horizontal drums, but the manufacturers, at least, disagree. They sell machines that they call "vertical windlasses" and "horizontal capstans."

Some are of the opinion that capstans are used only for rope or cable, whereas windlasses are used for chain as well. But again, the manufacturers don't really agree—they sell capstans with or without chain "gypsies" or "wildcats"—those toothed devices that fit the chain links to make the capstan work. So, we'll call them all windlasses. Or capstans.

As soon as you cannot conveniently manhandle the anchors that you carry, you need a windlass. The "conveniently" part is obviously relative, but generally, we're talking about larger boats, over 30 feet, which are carrying anchors that weigh more than 25 pounds, or smaller boats with an all-chain rode.

A more relevant factor is the person handling the ground tackle. For some, hoisting 30 pounds of anchor out of the water and onto the deck is easy; for some it is physically impossible. For the person who anchors out every night for an eight-week cruise during the summer, a windlass may become a necessary convenience, while the occasional sailor can usually struggle with the heavy tackle on a rare overnighter during the year.

We use two common rules of thumb. First, the weakest adult normally on board should be able to lift the primary anchor over the lifelines. If he or she cannot do that, your tackle is heavy enough to start thinking about a windlass.

Second, when the person who normally handles the anchoring—whether it's the husband or wife or teenage daughter—begins to dread the thought of anchoring because of the physical drain (or when hauling anchor often ends in a shouting match), it's time to consider a windlass.

Windlass Selection

In spite of the small market, there are more than twenty-five manufacturers of windlasses worldwide, producing a wide variety of windlass sizes, styles, types, and configurations. So many, in fact, that making a selection can be hopelessly confusing. For example, the largest seller in the U.S., Simpson-Lawrence, lists 25 models, each available with varying configurations and combinations of chain and rope accommodations. Ideal, one of the old-time American companies, has 31 models suitable for pleasure boats on their current price sheet, and Nilsson shows 37 different models in their current catalog. Adding to the confusion is the fact that it's often difficult to be confident about the answers to technical questions received from the equipment manufacturers.

Using a 40-foot sailboat as an example, we ended up with a list of 200 basically similar windlass models and options to choose from—a truly bewildering array. Compounding the problem is the lack of standardization among the sellers regarding what information is published. Consider "current consumption," one of the buyer's major concerns for an electric windlass. The manufacturer's terms and specifications are not at all clear or consistent. Some don't list current draw at all; some list only wattage of the motors (you get a nominal current draw by dividing the wattage number by 12, as in volts); some list ranges (45 to 90 amps, for example) without explaining what the ranges mean; and so on.

Another area of confusion is model names, with meaningless terms like Condor, Cougar, Seawolf, or Ursus competing with number designations that sometimes designate pulling power (Balmar's 600 M, for example) and sometimes designate nothing in particular.

About the most usable figure for the prospective purchaser is the power of the windlass, given in pounds. In manufacturer's brochures, it takes various names: "lift," "load," "capacity," "pull," "power." It generally refers to the maximum poundage the windlass can pull or lift before stallout or breakdown. Power is usually a calculated figure, that is to say that it is not derived from tests. It's usually based on the power of the motor or length of the manual crank, the gearing, and the size of the chain gypsy or rope drum. We found that the figure will always be in the ball park, if not precisely accurate.

On the assumption that you will be able to determine what the various models actually offer relative to one another, what attributes do you want in your capstan, and how much of them do you need? We'll take a look at them one by one.

Capacity

While most of the companies make vague recommendations about capacity ("good for vessels to 35 feet"), it is probably best for the buyer to look at the "lift" or "capacity" figures, usually given in pounds.

What will you be lifting? Suppose you're anchored in deep water, maximum scope, all your anchor rode out, and you break loose and drift into deeper water. As an absolute minimum, you should figure on lifting 100 percent of your ground tackle. For those using mostly nylon rode, the concern is not significant since the tackle itself will be well under the capacity of all windlasses on the market. But those using all chain should calculate actual weights to make sure their windlass can handle it. Figure roughly two pounds per foot of chain, plus the weight of the anchor.

In actual practice, windage and wave action on the boat are more important in figuring how much capacity you need: you expect your windlass to overcome the tension on your anchor cable caused by wind and wave. Here it is best to study the figures in Table 5-1.

Only the buyer can decide which conditions are appropriate to use. Many will want a windlass that is still usable in the most extreme conditions, say 60 knots of wind. Others may figure that they'll rarely encounter anything over 30 knots, and if they do they can "cut and run," returning for the anchor on a calmer day. As an example, the table shows that cable tension in 60 knots of wind is 765 pounds for a 30-foot sloop and 1721 pounds for a 45-foot sloop. These would be minimum figures, then, for windlass capacity. You would probably want to add a safety factor (50 to 100 percent) for common conditions such as the temporary pressure needed to break loose a well-buried or fouled anchor.

Another consideration in determining capacity is the possibility of using the windlass to kedge off a boat that's run aground. Depending on how high aground the boat is, the power needed could approach the actual weight of the boat. More likely, you could be kedging off about 25 percent of the boat's weight. For a 20,000-pound boat, you could need a 5,000-pound capacity in the windlass. Obviously, since such capacity demands an enormously oversized windlass for normal use, most people will want to resort to their sheet winches when they run high and dry.

Again, using a 40-footer as an example, the heaviest anchor might be a 35-pound CQR with 25 feet of chain plus 300 feet of 5/8-inch nylon rode. The total tackle weight would be about 120 pounds. That's enough weight that manhandling is difficult, and a windlass is worth considering.

For coastal cruising, we'll figure anchor cable tension for 36 knots of wind—about the most we would be likely to encounter. The table yields 490 pounds. Since we're conservative, we'll multiply by a safety factor of two, and say we want a windlass with about a 980-pound capacity. (If we were going long-distance cruising, we would use 60 knots of wind and end up with a conservative figure of a 2500-pound capacity windlass.)

The 980-pound capacity would be our primary figure in choosing a windlass. Anything less would mean we would have a machine of marginal value in tough conditions. As we get to more than 980, we would start paying for capacity we would never be likely to use.

Manual Windlasses

The choice is among manual, electric, and hydraulic power. The advantage of the manual windlass is its simplicity. It's a tried-and-true device, with relatively simple mechanical workings,

On larger sailboats, a foredeck hatch permits getting the windlass totally out of the way. Note the large "clutch wheel" next to the chain gypsy.

and is relatively easy for most people to use, service, and repair. About the only significant choices for a potential purchaser are whether to go for the increasingly rare single-action (the pull stroke brings in rope/chain, the push stroke ratchets) or double-action (both pull and push bring in rope/chain), and whether to go for a simple one-speed or a more complex two-speed windlass with a higher power low gear.

The primary disadvantage of the manuals is the slow speed and the physical work involved. Smaller capacity winches will haul in the anchor line fairly rapidly (in the neighborhood of six inches per stroke). But larger capacity in manual windlasses is acquired through gearing down, meaning more strokes to retrieve a given length of chain. Since the low speed (high power) is primarily used for breaking the anchor free, this is a significant consideration mostly for the person with an all-chain rode and heavy anchors. If you have to use the low speed for hauling, that is for anything other than breaking the anchor free, you've got a lot of cranking ahead of you.

Electric Windlasses

Electric windlasses substitute an electric motor for your arm muscles. Capacity depends on the size of the motor and the gearing. The trade-off is in speed of retrieval. A smaller (cheaper) electric motor geared down will yield high power but slow retrieval speed. If you want fast retrieval and high power, you need a bigger motor.

The other major consideration (and the biggest reason for price difference) is the type of motor. The cheaper electric windlasses use motors that are essentially similar to automotive or truck starters, designed for intermittent use. The more expensive windlasses use "continuous duty" motors. The "continuous duty" advocates point to the superiority of their machines; those with cheaper motors point to their record of longevity, and claim that a continuous duty rating is unnecessary in an electric motor which is used only minutes at a time.

For normal coastal cruising, we suspect that the "starter type" motors are entirely adequate. For the full-time or long-distance cruiser, the continuous-duty versions may be worth the extra expense. You can expect a shorter life and earlier replacement if you use a "starter type" continuously.

Incidentally, it is difficult to find out what kind of motor is used (some of the importers don't even know). It's probably safe to assume that a motor is a "starter type" unless the manufacturer specifically says otherwise.

The other consideration in electric windlasses is whether to buy a "reversing" motor. With the reversing motor, you can use the motor to pay out rope or chain as well to take it in. With non-reversing motors, to pay out rode you use the friction of the drum (just like a sheet winch) for rope, or a friction clutch for chain. Although the clutches are notorious troublemakers, we still regard the reversing motor as a luxury—nice but not essential.

The amperage draw of an electric winch can be astoundingly high—400 to 500 amps when the big motors are nearing stall. The wiring for electric windlasses must be heavy duty—at least as large as the cables to a diesel engine's starter motor, and usually bigger because of the inherent loss in long runs of wire to the bow of the boat. Buyers should also examine their alternator and battery capacity, recognizing that for all practical purposes, the engine must be running when the windlass is operating. An alternate possibility with many windlasses is to wire two 12-volt batteries into series so that they produce 24-volts, thus cutting the amperage in half.

Hydraulic Windlasses

Almost every model of electric windlass is also available with a hydraulic motor in place of the electric. If a boat has engine-driven hydraulics for other purposes, such as a hydraulic-driven shaft and propeller, a hydraulic windlass is naturally to be preferred to electric. Otherwise, the hydraulic versions will generally cost considerably more, simply because a hydraulic pump is needed on the engine as well as at the windlass, adding another "system" to a boat that may already be complicated and expensive enough. The piping for the hydraulic fluid can be a bit of a nuisance, but for high-powered windlasses, it's not much more trouble than the electrical wiring.

On the plus side, hydraulic pumps are amazingly powerful and compact. When you start looking at power needs in excess of 1500 pounds, the efficiency of hydraulics makes them an attractive alternative. They will also provide a combination of power and high-speed retrieval better than almost all electrics. The major question with hydraulics, then, is whether or not it's worth the trouble and expense of an extra system.

Construction

The major problem with windlasses is the use of dissimilar metals. Almost all windlasses use some combination of stainless steel, coated or painted plain steel, bronze alloys, and aluminum. (Only one company that we know of uses all stainless steel. Another uses only stainless in the above-deck part of their hydraulic windlass.) One of the recurring complaints is corrosion—usually cosmetic but occasionally structural—resulting from saltwater dousing or spray on the foredeck, and occasionally from stray 12-volt electrical current. The solution to the problem is simple maintenance—cleaning and protecting.

One other noticeable difference in windlass construction is in the lubrication system for the gearing. Most use simple grease fittings or grease-filled gearboxes, while others use oil-bath gearboxes. There appears to be no clear advantage to either lubrication method.

Except for some of the models aimed at the small powerboat market, all the electric/hydraulic winches have some sort of manual backup. The handiest on a sailboat is the socket which takes a standard winch handle, fairly common on the vertical windlasses. Other manual backups are relatively inconvenient, but usable.

Configuration

Vertical or horizontal, above deck or partially below deck, fat and squat or high and skinny; these are all considerations of appearance and installation space. The vertical versions are desirable when differing angles of lead are necessary, such as when the windlass must be close to the bow and the angle from the portside roller is considerably different than the angle from the starboard roller. Otherwise, such specific considerations as under-deck support, stowage space for the anchor rode, routing of wiring, and just plain attractiveness will be more important.

The chain gypsy must be chosen to match the chain size, and some models make the chain strippers (which knock the chain out of the gypsy after one revolution) and chain pipes optional. The electrical fuses and overload protectors are frequently an option, but they are necessary for safety's sake. Otherwise, the chain stoppers, foot switches, chain-run indicators, weather covers, fancy bases, and so on, are convenience items, up to your discretion and pocketbook.

ANCHOR WELLS AND BOW ROLLERS

Ever since some ancient mariner broke a toe tripping over the killick stowed in the bow of his curragh, sailors have sought to solve the mysteries of ground tackle stowage. The solutions have been endless, and as a rule compromises. A significant portion of the interior volume of a 19th century warship was given over to the storage of anchor rode.

Even aboard modern boats, the search for the proper stowage of several anchors, plus hundreds of feet of chain and nylon line, is one that occupies both designers and boatowners.

Two "modern inventions," the anchor well and the bow roller, have greatly eased many of the problems of ground tackle stowage. But even these developments vary greatly in quality and design, some creating more problems than they solve. Of course, neither the anchor well nor the self-stowing bow roller are new. In some form or another, they have existed since time immemorial, but it is only in the last decade that they have become standard features on many production cruising boats.

We don't know who gets credit for the modern anchor well. Like the development of the wheel and the discovery of fire, the anchor well lacks a specific point of origin. Whatever its source, most of us condemned to handling anchors on the pointy end of the boat are grateful for even a minor improvement in ground-tackle handling.

Anchor Wells

Making an anchor well is easy. Making a good one is less so. Most early anchor wells were created by installing a bulkhead in the bow of the boat about three feet behind the stem. A large hatch cut in the deck and hinged on one side provided access. Usually, a small hole was drilled in the stem to provide a drain for water finding its way into the well through the deck hatch.

While this may be the simplest form of enclosed anchor well, it has a number of shortcomings. With a deep anchor well, all the gear ends up in a tight little pile at the bottom, wedged into the "V" formed by the stem and the topsides at the bow.

A deep anchor well invites back problems, as it is almost impossible to avoid bending over into the well to retrieve the anchor and chain. In heavy weather, the anchor and chain can pound hard against the hull of the boat, and could conceivably cause structural damage in some conditions. To top it off, many boats carry a significant amount of water in the well in heavy weather, water located in the worst possible part of the boat when handling is the hardest. Surprisingly, many production boats still have this type of anchor well. Fortunately, it may not be too difficult to improve upon it.

The ideal anchor well is no deeper than is necessary to hold a single anchor and its rode. Unless the well is compartmented in some way, storing more than one anchor in the well is likely

Ground Tackle and Anchor-Handling Equipment

to result in a rat's nest of tangled line, complicating—perhaps dangerously—both the setting and retrieving of the anchor.

If you have a deep anchor well, it may be possible to improve it by glassing in a triangular piece of heavy plywood to serve as a false floor. Unless the access hatch is very large, it may be necessary to cut this plywood floor into two pieces to wrestle it into place. The two pieces can be rejoined with a simple strip of wood on the underside, screwed into one half of the plywood before it is inserted, into the other once both pieces are in place.

It will then be necessary to drill a new drain hole in the stem, just at the height of the new floor. Draining will be made easier if the plywood floor is angled downward slightly at its forward end. If two anchor rodes are carried in the well, a removable plywood partition can be installed to keep them separated.

A cleat much larger than you would be willing to mount on deck can be mounted to the new plywood floor, but only if the floor is heavy, rigid, and very strongly fiberglassed to the hull. Otherwise, cleat, anchor, and rode may take leave of the boat when she is anchored in heavy conditions.

The well should also include one or two large padeyes, through-bolted to either the floor or the adjoining bulkhead, to which the bitter end of the anchor rode can be secured. If you are clever enough to have spliced a thimble into both ends of the anchor rode so that it can be swapped end-for-end yearly, the bitter end is simply shackled to the padeye in the well.

It's also a good idea to mount several smaller eyes that can be used for lashing down anchors. Otherwise, it would be possible in a severe knockdown to lose the anchor and rode.

Boats carrying large quantities of chain would do well to stow the chain farther aft than in an anchor well in the foredeck. If there is a chain locker under the forward berths, a PVC pipe can be run from the inside of the anchor well to the locker. This pipe must be substantially larger in diameter than the chain links, and should be run without sharp turns. It is possible to form PVC pipe to curves if it is heated. The pipe should project far enough above the floor of the anchor well to minimize the chance of water in the bottom of the well working its way down into the chain locker.

Realistically, the lid of the anchor well is usually a problem.

The anchor well of the Nicholson 31 is nearly ideal; shallow, with a large cleat, pad-eyes for tiedowns, a large drain hole, and plenty of room for the anchor, chain and rode.

Lids are often heavy, hard to secure positively, and always seem to be in the way. Strong hinges are required, as are heavy sliding bolts or some other means of latching. In areas where theft is a problem, a hasp for locking it may be in order.

Another type of specialized anchor well is the molded fiberglass vertical well fitted for a particular size and type of anchor. We first saw this on the J/30, which has a well on the sidedeck designed to carry the Danforth anchor that is the class standard. The well has a molded recess for the stock of the anchor, so that it is held securely in place. The advantage of this arrangement is that the vertical well takes up less deck space, so that its location is more flexible. The disadvantage is that there is little flexibility in the ground tackle you can carry. You're stuck with whatever anchor the locker is molded to fit.

Bow Rollers

Bow rollers began to proliferate about the same time as the anchor well, and many suffer from the same shortcomings as anchor wells: lack of proper forethought. Like many anchor wells, the design of bow rollers often appears to be an afterthought, rather than part of a well designed ground tackle-handling system.

For a boat doing a fair amount of coastal cruising, where anchoring daily is a part of the routine, some kind of self-stowing anchor holder on the bow is a real blessing. In the stranger-than-fiction world of family cruising, the person handling the heavy ground tackle on the bow of the boat is often a woman, while the male assumes his dominant position at the controls of the boat. Handling heavy ground tackle without a windlass is a backbreaking chore that rightfully should be left to the strongest member of the crew, whether male or female.

Bow rollers fall into two categories: those designed to stow anchors, and those whose only function is to provide a low-friction pivot-point for retrieval of the anchor.

If the bow roller is not used to stow the anchor, its design requirements are fairly simple. The roller itself should be large enough in cross section to handle both the anchor line and the chain. It should roll freely on its axle. Dense urethane is a good roller material, since it will not chafe the anchor line. Harder materials, such as bronze and stainless steel, can quickly wear the galvanizing off the chain. Even a hard plastic such as nylon, can wear soft zinc galvanizing. Metal rollers also tend to be noisy at anchor, particularly if an all-chain rode is used.

The cheeks of the roller housing are quite important. Forward of the rollers, they should be flared outward, with the edges well polished, to prevent wear on the anchor rode as the boat sails around on the anchor. Most modern cruisers have too much windage forward and not enough displacement to lie quietly at anchor. (A few, in fact, are far smarter sailers on the anchor than they are with the sails up.)

In addition, the roller cheeks should project far enough above the roller to hold the line in position as the boat swings and pitches. There should be a removable pin through the cheeks above the rode to serve as a keeper, in case the rode has a

A custom-built wooden platform with rollers (above) to hold a plow anchor, and a stock stainless steel fitting (below) designed for a Danforth.

tendency to pop out. It is also important that there be little or no space between the cheeks and the roller, to prevent the line from wedging itself in that space.

A fair lead from the aft end of the roller to the windlass or bow cleat is critical. Obviously, the lead should not foul the headstay, the roller-furling pennant, or the lid to the anchor well.

The same requirements hold when the bow roller is incorporated into some type of bow fitting which actually serves to hold the anchor. There are, in addition, even more caveats.

First, the fitting must project far enough forward to keep the anchor from banging into the topsides. This problem is most common with plow-type anchors, whose flukes pivot when the anchor shank is in the horizontal position. If a plow anchor is snugged up against the stem, the stem must be fitted with a metal protecting plate.

There are several ways of mounting Danforth-type anchors at the bow. The problem with stowing a Danforth at the bow is that it makes a formidable obstacle, guaranteed to snag errant sheets and docklines, poke holes in sails, and splinter the teak rubrail of the boat in the neighboring slip. Stowing the anchor vertically in the bow pulpit still requires handling the anchor and chain, something we're trying to avoid, Instead, if at all possible, use an anchor roller specifically designed for the Danforth anchor, making sure that it mounts far enough forward to keep those sharp flukes away from the topsides.

If the fitting is used to house a plow anchor (CQR), it should incorporate a cross pin through the cheeks that passes through the trip line eye just above the flukes of the anchor. This serves the dual purpose of holding the anchor firmly in the fitting, and preventing the flukes from beating against the topsides.

A considerable amount of leverage is exerted on the projecting anchor roller when the boat pitches at anchor. We've seen these fittings twisted like pretzels on several occasions. Be sure that the material is heavy enough for the job it must perform. Don't skimp either on the size of the bolts or the backing plates used to secure the fitting.

* * *

The primary disadvantage to stowing anchors in stemhead rollers is their effect on the boat's pitching moment. The longitudinal center of buoyancy of most modern boats (the point about which they pivot when pitching) is usually slightly aft of the middle of the boat. The further forward the weight of ground tackle is, the greater the tendency of the boat to pitch.

For long passages, therefore, it's better to remove anchors

from stemhead fittings, stowing them further aft, preferably down below. Whenever possible, keep the ends of the boat light to reduce pitching.

This is, of course, contradictory to the idea of handy stowage of ground tackle for in-use convenience. That's not too surprising, for like almost everything else associated with boats, anchor selection and stowage is just one of a seemingly endless stream of compromises.

6

Navigation Equipment and Electronics

PEDESTAL COMPASSES

At once a primitive instrument and one which is likely to survive for ages in similar form, the magnetic compass seems almost an anachronism among modern electronics. A crystal ball which senses the message of direction, it is undoubtedly relied upon less, as Loran-C and SatNav have come into wide use. And yet, the compass continues to occupy the front and center position because when the antennas became deaf and the LEDs fade, it is this crystal ball which will bring us home.

While it is easy, then, to admit that the compass is required equipment, it is not so easy to choose one. The variety available is bewildering, with at least ten manufacturers marketing several sizes, each size having several mounting types and often a choice of card or dial. The discount mailorder outlets reflect this profusion of choices to some extent, but as most merely echo the manufacturer's hype, they fail to clarify the distinctions among models. At many marine stores, especially the larger ones, it is likely that the person assisting you (if you can find one) is young and inexperienced. In short, it's getting easier than ever to make the wrong choice.

With this basic fact in mind, we'll look a wide range of compasses, first pedestal-mounted compasses and then the even wider assortment of bulkhead compasses. Later in this chapter, we'll examine fluxgate compasses, the space-age alternative to the magnetic compass.

Pedestal Compasses: Basic Considerations

In days of old, with either tiller or wheel steering, the compass was traditionally mounted on a binnacle or pedestal forward of the helmsman's position. With the advent of pedestal steering systems, the logical adaptation of the binnacle became the top of the pedestal on which the wheel is mounted. Now most compass manufacturers make at least one model of pedestal-mount compass, and wheel steering manufacturers design their pedestals with "universal" dimensions to accept those compasses.

The first consideration is dictated by the cockpit layout and the skipper's preferred steering position. There is no requirement that a steering pedestal be fitted with a compass, and the fact that most are fitted is no reason, if alternative mountings are acceptable or better, why the steering compass should sit above the wheel. Most boatowners, however, seem to prefer the convenience of a pedestal mounted compass.

The second consideration is the size of the compass for pedestal mounting. It is common practice unfortunately to put small compasses on large boats. The problem with this practice is that smaller boats have a noticeably livelier motion and need greater steadiness than small compasses usually afford. A compass with a 5-inch dome diameter has about twice the volume of oil as a 4-inch compass. The increased steadiness is only one advantage. The greater legibility of a larger compass can be dramatic, a significant factor on voyages with long tricks at the wheel. Greater steadiness and legibility combine to help the person at the wheel be more attentive longer, and perhaps more confident, too. It is an inescapable conclusion that you should buy the largest compass that fits and is affordable, especially if you have a smaller boat.

Selection Criteria

If you steer from a sitting position behind and to either side of the pedestal, then look for 45-degree lubberlines. As beam bearings can be useful, 90-degree lubberlines are desirable as well. Steering from a standing position, looking down on the compass, requires that the forward lubberline be bent over, pointing aft, so that the helmsman does not have to lean back to know his course. Ideally the bent-over section is either a different color, length, or thickness from the graduations below it; otherwise it can be difficult to distinguish. The bent-over part should be far enough above the card to allow the card to rock somewhat without hitting it, but not so far as to create significant parallax error as the helmsman, standing vertical while the boat heels, reads the segment of the compass card directly below the lubberline.

Typically, the compass card is graduated every 5 degrees, has numerals every 30 degrees, and is the traditional forward-reading configuration with slight to moderate dishing of the disc to permit easier reading. The aft-reading card available on some models has no place on a pedestal compass. Cards differ in several other respects, however, especially in how plain or "busy" they are. It is important to like the card you have to look at and to choose one that will not be liable to produce eyestrain.

Covers are standard with some models, while optional with others. With a glass dome, a pedestal compass needs no such protection. But without a cover, a plastic dome will eventually become brittle from exposure to the sun's ultraviolet rays and crack or craze, allowing the compass oil to leak out. Inexpensive canvas and synthetic boots are available at larger marine stores, and we think by prolonging the life of the dome they are a worthwhile purchase.

Although optional on some models, most pedestal compasses come with a built-in corrector system in the cylinder base. A pedestal location generally removes the compass from most sources of deviation, it is true, but it makes good sense to be able to correct any error that may yet exist (as from an instrument, located beside the compass, which has a meter movement and is thus magnetic).

Internal gimballing and night lighting is offered on all models; some have two bulbs and others have one. We don't think the difference is significant, provided the light is red and it works. Construction varies little from compass to compass. With few exceptions, most manufacturers use plastic domes and mostly plastic pieces for the compass body and inner parts. Cards are typically aluminum, supported by a pivot of very hard steel with a polished point bearing on a cupped synthetic jewel. A rubber diaphragm or expansion gasket allows the compass oil, a specially formulated liquid, somewhat similar to kerosene, to expand and contract with variations in temperature. Ritchie uses a metal bellows rather than the typical rubber expansion gasket.

The outer cylinder protects and supports the compass. Some manufacturers have combined function with aesthetics by using polished stainless steel cylinders. The look is eye-catching and the upkeep negligible. Others use aluminum with a polished appearance, or black bakelite plastic. Long-term exposure to the sun slowly makes bakelite turn dull and a dirty gray-brown, which vigorous buffing can partly restore.

The exteriors of all modern compasses are better than the former standard of chrome over brass. The problem was that an intermediate layer of nickel is necessary to produce a good bonding base for the chrome, but nickel is magnetic unless used in very small quantities. The result was thin nickel, a poor bond, and frequent, expensive rechroming. Conversely, those who have had their old binnacles rechromed by people who specialize in auto bumpers may find they need bumpers on their boats as their compasses lead them astray.

Be sure to check serviceability and warranty when considering a compass. Some manufacturers thoughtfully include a list of authorized repair centers, complete with addresses and phone numbers. Other manufacturers either suggest returning the compass to the factory, or they say nothing at all. Since location, mounting, care and compensation can be technical, we favor those manufacturers who have taken the trouble to cover these topics thoroughly in their instructions.

Finally, on the matter of cost, choose your compass first, because you're going to trust it with your life, and then go shopping for the best price.

BULKHEAD COMPASSES

For sailboats without pedestal steering and a binnacle compass, the choice of a compass comes down to three basic types: the compass designed for flush mounting in the deck, one for flush mounting in a bulkhead, and one designed to hang from a deck- or bulkhead-mounted bracket. Even for boats equipped with a binnacle compass, there may be use for a steering compass that is more convenient for the helmsman than the binnacle compass, which may require him to stay behind the wheel to keep the binnacle compass in sight.

Choosing a bulkhead compass is more difficult than choosing a binnacle compass, simply because there are many more on the market and their quality varies more widely. The first step is to decide on the type of mounting configuration.

The Three Basic Types

The bracket-mount compass has the significant advantage of being adaptable to any angle of mounting surface and of being easily removable. The latter feature is unfortunately appreciated as much by the light-fingered as by the boatowner. It also suffers from being a hazardous protrusion, at once vulnerable and a threat to both the crew and thrashing sheets. This drawback strikes us as such a crucial one that we do not recommend their use on sailboats.

The second type is the horizontal deck-mount compass, usually seen in pairs—one on either side of the cockpit—in a wide section of the coaming or on the sidedecks. Wherever it is located, it is prone to damage from being stepped on and from sheets and winch handles. It should be protected by a guard over the dome. For boats such as racing boats where the helmsman sits well outboard and aft, this may be the only type that he can see. However, the typical installation requires looking downward at a considerable angle, which is neither easy nor conducive to frequent checking.

The third choice, and the subject of our scrutiny, is the bulkhead-mount compass, which in many ways is the most attractive choice of all. Many would say that the primary advantage of the bulkhead location is that it is out of the way of people, falling objects, and the snake-basket of lines. True, but there is a more important reason often overlooked or underrated; the compass mounted on a bulkhead allows the helmsman to take his attention only slightly away from his normal view forward as he quickly checks his course. Also, the greatest magnification of the card occurs when looking through the full diameter of the compass sphere, and the bulkhead location almost guarantees taking advantage of this phenomenon—provided the compass card has markings on the top surface. An edge-reading (also called aft-reading or direct-reading) card does not benefit from anywhere near the magnification afforded by the top-reading type. More about this matter later on. Another reason in favor of bulkhead mounting is the increased distance (in most cases) between the compass and certain sources of deviation, especially an inboard engine and its alternator.

There are worms in the apple, naturally. First, almost all boats in the 20- to 30-foot size range have a center companionway, requiring that the compass be positioned on one side or the other or both. If a single compass is mounted on one side, then the helmsman has to read the compass from an angle when he switches sides. Steering by using a 45-degree lubberline as a reference is not bad, but it's not ideal. Having two compasses, one on each bulkhead, is easier and safer, but twice as expensive. Mounting a single compass on either the vertical face of the bridgedeck, if there is one, or in the lowest companionway hatch board may solve the problem, but both locations are vulnerable to people, equipment, and sources of deviation.

Second, most bulkheads are slanted as much as 15 degrees off the vertical. What few know or appreciate is that a compass designed for vertical mounting will, on a slanted bulkhead, incur an error as soon as the boat heels. The error is equal to the sine of the angle of heel multiplied by the number of degrees from vertical. Thus, a boat with a 5-degree bulkhead, heeling at 30 degrees, will experience a compass error of 2-1/2 degrees (the sine of 30 is 0.5, times 5 equals 2.5). In a 12-mile run, the boat will be half a mile off course—an acceptable error in clear weather, perhaps, but not in obscured visibility. A prudent sailor, being told his compass was 2-1/2 degrees off, might want to adjust his compass. The solution to the problem is to shim the compass with a "doughnut" of wood which, on edge, has a wedge shape equal to the angle that the bulkhead is out of vertical. A few compasses are available in models designed to accommodate slanted mounting. Unless your choice is one of these, either shim the compass to true vertical, or else brace yourself for unexpected landfalls.

A third disadvantage of bulkhead mounting is that while the compass may be farther from the powerplant and the strong field created by an operating alternator, it may be closer to other dangers that are less obvious. On the same side of the bulkhead there may be cockpit instruments with meter movements (i.e., analog displays) that are magnetic; and on the inside of the bulkhead, there may be radiotelephones, fire extinguishers, switch panels, stereo speakers, and so forth. Since magnetism passes through almost all materials, the best advice is to put the compass where is belongs, and then find places for the other items at a safe distance.

Selection Criteria

Several factors should control the selection of a bulkhead-mount compass. The most important, perhaps, is legibility. Determine the distance between the compass and the helmsman at his normal station, then go to your marine store and test possible choices for readability from that distance. Are the graduations distinct? The marks at every even 10 degrees should be clearly longer and thicker than those between them. Are the numerals unmistakable? Most compass cards have numbers every 30 degrees, but a few have them every 20 degrees, with the final zero left off to preserve separation.

Another factor, related closely to legibility, is the type of card you prefer. The traditional top-reading card has two distinct advantages and one slight disadvantage. The top-reading card is read at the forward edge, farthest from your eyes, and at the point where a spherical compass dome gives it the greatest magnification. Not only are the numbers and graduations bigger, but the graduations appear to be farther apart than those at the near, or after edge. The result is dramatic relief for the person steering, and probably straighter wakes. A second advantage is that the card as marked is oriented correctly ("N" points north). Neophytes appreciate the stunning simplicity of this scheme, and old-timers would have it no other way.

A disadvantage of a top-reading card is that daylight doesn't penetrate so easily into the recesses of the compass sphere, and a brightly lit outer edge can make the darker inside edge, somewhat less distinct by comparison. The edge-reading card may seem very legible because daylight hits it directly, especially the bevel-edge models, but check the distance between the graduations. They probably look very close together compared to the markings on the magnified portion of a top-reading card. Whichever you select, it is important that you give legibility a high priority.

Another criterion is steadiness. How does the compass respond to boat motions? All good compasses accommodate heel and pitch through the extreme limits, but they differ in their responses to surge, or lateral acceleration and deceleration. Pick up a compass and put it on a smooth, flat surface. Slide it away back and forth, and from side to side. This motion roughly simulates some of the actions of a vessel outside of simple heel, pitch, and yaw. Some compasses remain fairly steady, with little motion of the card and lubberlines. Others have steady cards but lubberlines that sway considerably. Some score poorly both ways. This simple test is effective in separating the good from the not-so-good, and it duplicates to a surprising degree how a compass will behave at sea.

Important, but less so, is the matter of mounting. Given the desirability (or need) for having to shim a compass on a slanted bulkhead and the time and expense to do so, considerable weight should be given to those models which obviate that need. Beyond that, all models require that a hole be cut in the bulkhead, and to many this prospect, like facing surgery and having the choice of where to have the scar, forces one to wonder, if not to wince. It's a decision with permanent consequences.

Top-reading compasses should be mounted somewhat below the helmsman's eye level, and edge-reading models can be mounted somewhat higher. Check to see if you have a choice here; the installation of other instruments or equipment may compel you to choose one type or the other. Nearly all compasses come with a template to help in cutting the proper size hole and locating holes to be drilled. Some come with a back cover, or offer it as an option, to tidy up the view from inside the cabin. A few are fastened from within the cabin (making theft a messy chore), but most screw or bolt from the outside.

Other considerations in choosing a compass are night lighting, extra lubberlines (most have 45-degree lubberlines in addition to the center one), good instructions, and the availability of a back cover. Serviceability and warranty are very important, for few people buy a boat intending to keep it only a year or two. The typical compass can be disassembled, have parts (like a pivot, jewel, gasket, and dome) replaced, and be reassembled at a cost much less than half of replacement. A few are not repairable, but the manufacturer either replaces the capsule outright, charging a nominal fee, or dangles a long warranty in front of the buyer to dispel his doubts. Ask your dealer what happens when the compass needs repair. The chances are it will need some kind of attention in five years or so.

When choosing a bulkhead compass, we recommend an established model that is widely available through catalogs and marine stores, and of about 4-inch diameter as measured across the outside diameter of the dome. When given a choice between a top-reading and edge-reading model, we would choose the former because we feel it has more advantages. Black cards are our preference over colored, "tactical" cards because we think the latter is a gimmick.

The practical matter of cost reveals a vast gulf between the choices in the 4-inch diameter range. Somewhere between these extremes, we think, lies the best buy. As with the 5-inch pedestal-mount compasses, we feel that a good compass is of such importance that it would be wise, in most cases, to choose your compass first and then shop for price.

DIGITAL MAGNETIC COMPASSES

In this age when navigation is so dependent on electronic wizardry, most of us find comfort in the good old-fashioned magnetic compass. You don't have to feed it electricity or push buttons to turn it on. It's just there, turning freely, faithfully pointing the way, requesting only a modicum of annual attention to keep it so.

We may rely on gadgets like Loran to tell us where we are, but the magnetic compass is still the tool used to tell which way we are going. As the 21st century approaches, the traditional compass is so highly refined that there is very little room for improvement in its design. You could say that the modern magnetic compass has been just about perfected. But it is not perfect. When asked for flawless performance, the results are sometimes disappointing.

Take deviation correction, for example. Consumers demand that the compass and its compensation magnets be contained in a compact, neat package, which makes for a simpler installation. But large magnets placed a distance from the compass work much better than the small internal magnets found on most yacht compasses. Internal magnets can induce a healthy error when the boat heels.

Motion in a heavy sea is another problem area. The large spherical bowls of the best magnetic compasses can handle an occasional sharp turn without losing accuracy. But the constant pounding when sailing upwind in a seaway will eventually excite all of the fluid in a bowl and make the best compass card sway, swirl and drift. When it's really rough, you have to mentally average the movement of the card, so the course you think you're steering is, at best, only a guess.

Modern electronics has made it possible to average the motion of a skittish compass card, and display it in a format that is easier to read than an active compass card. Called the *digital magnetic compass*, this system allows the compass to be mounted belowdecks where motion is minimized and more accurate compensation can be achieved. The card is read by an optical sensor and the result is displayed in digital form on one or more remote readouts.

The digital magnetic compass represents an improvement over a traditional compass, and has been pretty well refined by companies like Digicourse. This type of compass has been the safe choice of most autopilot and integrated instrument manufacturers until a few years ago. Yet, it depends on a traditional compass: no matter how many microchips digest the information, they're still reading a swirling compass card, so the course displayed isn't always the course you're steering.

FLUXGATE COMPASSES

One by one, electronics manufacturers are eliminating the digital magnetic compass from products like autopilots and integrated equipment systems. They are replacing it with the fluxgate compass.

The fluxgate compass isn't anything like a traditional compass. It operates on an entirely different principle and holds the promise of much better performance. Briefly, the fluxgate in the compass electronically senses the direction of the earth's magnetic field. When it is perfectly level, it produces very accurate readings that correspond to those on a traditional compass. When it is not level, it produces accurate readings that look like gobbledygook to most of us.

While the electronics and the theory are quite refined, the mechanics of keeping the sensor level still have a way to go. Fluxgate designs differ significantly among themselves, and we have yet to see one that we would call perfected. While some fluxgates only work when interfaced with other instruments, others are available as "stand-alone" instruments.

Displays

The fluxgate compass designs available in the early 1980s were equipped only with analog displays—typically a needle on a three-inch dial that was mounted either on the cabin house or the steering pedestal. Originally, analog displays were thought to be better because they eased the transition from a traditional magnetic compass. Most sailors learn to steer by following the trend of their course on a swinging card. Using an analog dial is similar, and with a fluxgate driving it, it's less affected by the boat's motion.

There are two problems with analog displays, however. First, the small size makes it difficult to read the gradations. The usual interval between markings is 5 degrees, and the numbers aren't magnified like they are in the bowl of a magnetic compass.

Second, analog displays rarely offer adjustable damping, so they are difficult to read in rough weather. Damping allows a compass to average the boat's course in heavy seas so that the number you see is consistent enough to steer to.

Most digital displays have adjustable electronic damping. In calm sea conditions, with the damping to a minimum, the display will react more quickly to course changes. In rough water, maximum damping gives you a steadier number, but you also get a significant lag between the course displayed and the course you're steering.

The lag resulting from electronic damping of a digital display can be a significant drawback. An advantage of a large, spherical magnetic compass is that there is virtually no lag unless the pivot is worn out or sticky. When you turn the boat you see it reflected immediately in the compass card. With electronic damping, you can get pretty far off course before you realize it. Therefore it's important with a fluxgate that you be able to set damping to the minimum level that you can follow for a given sea condition.

Some fluxgates offer only three settings for the damping function: maximum, minimum, and in between. That's probably not enough. Four or five settings seems more reasonable. One fluxgate compass offers 100 settings, from a minimum of 8 seconds delay to a maximum of 300 seconds. Such fine tuning is unnecessary. The range of adjustment is as important as the number of settings. For most fluxgates, minimum damping is still, in our opinion, overdamped.

Digital displays are better than analog, but are they for everybody? Not always. We already noted that most sailors would rather steer to a dial than to a bunch of numbers. Those with "digital phobia" will have to make do with the "trend indicators" found on most digital displays. These are arrows that light up to show that you are deviating from a preset course. The number and direction of the arrows show which direction and how much to correct.

Are fluxgates a replacement for the magnetic compass? For most people, no. They're still going to find it easier to steer by a magnetic compass. They might also worry, with some justification, about a power failure rendering the fluxgate useless. This means the fluxgate is probably a luxury for the daysailor and casual cruiser.

For the bluewater cruiser, the fluxgate has the advantage of being accurate at any latitude (more on that later). For the racer, the fluxgate allows you to spot windshifts better, by virtue of it's fine digital graduations. It also has the ability to plug into an integrated instrument system to figure true wind direction.

Most people who purchase a fluxgate compass will want a magnetic compass as a backup. The only instance where this might not be necessary is the boat that never sails at night. Sailing at night by a digital display can be most difficult.

How The Fluxgate Compass Works

The big difference between the fluxgate and the magnetic compass is that the fluxgate compass has no moving parts. At least, that's what the fluxgate brochures would have you believe. If fluxgates had no moving parts, however, they would not work at all. It's how well these parts move that determines how accurate the compass will be.

A conventional magnetic compass card must "float" level for it to rotate smoothly and read properly. But the earth's magnetic field doesn't flow only horizontal to the earth's surface. There is a downward component in the total magnetic vector, a "dip angle", that varies with latitude. A conventional compass card has weights as well as magnets affixed to it. The weights counteract the tendency of the magnets to tilt the card toward the dip angle. If you decide to take off on a round-the-world cruise, you'll have to provide for the changing dip angle. You can take several compasses, each one weighted for a particular region of latitudes; or you may prefer to have the compass rebuilt as you change latitude. A third option is to have a compass built to be insensitive to latitude, but at the expense of sticky behavior.

A fluxgate sensor determines its position relative to the earth's magnetic field electronically, without the use of magnets. However, like all compasses, a fluxgate is more sensitive to error at higher latitudes because the dip angle is so much greater.

What causes error in a fluxgate? Nearly all fluxgate errors can be traced to one cause—the sensor must be perfectly level. The fluxgate sensor doesn't home toward magnetic north, like a magnetic compass card. It rotates with the boat, sensing its own position relative to the earth's magnetic field. But it must be level. Since boats do not maintain a perfectly level platform, the sensor must be gimballed to swing in both the fore-and-aft and athwartships planes.

Sensor gimballing has a significant effect on the performance of fluxgate compasses. There are two things a fluxgate gimbal must do: find "down" to keep the sensor level, and mechanically damp unnecessary movement. Gimballing can be pretty successful in keeping the sensor level when the boat is heeling. When the boat hits a wave, though, the sensor swings on its gimbals, and during every fraction of a second that the sensor is out of level, the fluxgate is getting readings which in no way resemble the boat's course. Through electronic damping, these wild readings are averaged by a computer to give you an answer which should closely approximate the actual course of your boat. How close will depend on the design of the sensor's gimballing system.

All compasses, fluxgates included, are subject to heeling error. They are affected by magnetic influences like the ship's engine, which bend the straight lines of the earth's magnetic field. These are usually compensated for in only one plane—the plane of the deck of the boat on which the horizontal correcting magnets are located. When the boat heels, these magnetic influences bend the earth's field in a different manner, so the compensation is no longer correct. The resultant error can be significant.

Fortunately, one of the advantages of the fluxgate compass is that the sensor is detached from the readout. This allows you to mount the sensor in a position where there is the least motion and magnetic interference.

Fluxgate compasses are best suited for the racer or the world cruiser. For the racer they provide the precise information needed for tactical sailing. The world cruiser will appreciate the lack of need for dip-angle correction, and features which allow programming local deviation into the readout. The racer will appreciate their ability to interface with just about any integrated instrument system, while the cruiser will appreciate this ability for use with most autopilots.

GLOBAL POSITIONING SYSTEM

The Department of Defense, the government agency that can buy anything more expensively than you can, is hard at work on a radio navigation system which promises to be of practical benefit to the sailor. This system, called the Global Positioning System (GPS), uses radio signals from orbiting satellites to determine the location of the receiver. It promises several significant advantages over currently used navigational aid systems.

As GPS signals will come direct from the sky, they will not be subject to anomalies caused by such factors as passage over land

Navigation Equipment and Electronics

masses that plague Loran signals, which originate from ground based stations. Unlike SatNav, GPS will be a worldwide system with constant fixes available. One of the major drawbacks of the present satellite system is that even under the best conditions, fixes are only available every ninety minutes. GPS's worldwide coverage contrasts sharply with other constant position radio systems, like Loran-C or Decca, that only operate in certain parts of the world and then only relatively close the the coast.

In conversations with the Radio Aids to Navigation office of the Coast Guard, we got the official lowdown on the present status of the GPS system. Originally, the system was supposed to be operational in two dimensions by the beginning of 1988 (three-dimensional capability for aircraft would come sometime later). The system will eventually consist of 21 orbiting satellites, 18 of which will be operational, the other three serving as backups. The disastrous explosion in 1986 of the space shuttle *Challenger* has upset the timetable, but presumably, DOD satellites will be high on the priority list when shuttle flights resume.

Transmitting on two frequencies, GPS satellites will be able to provide two grades of positioning accuracy. The Standard Positioning Service (SPS) uses only one of the signals transmitted. The Precise Positioning Service (PPS) will utilize both frequencies to produce a more accurate fix. The second signal will correct for distortion caused when the signals pass through the Earth's ionosphere. The PPS will be used by the military and others who can demonstrate that their use of the more accurate signal is for the "good of the country."

Although the Department of Defense is aiming for a degraded (civilian) GPS signal accurate to 100 meters, the GPS/SPS (civilian) signal is proving to be more precise than anticipated with an accuracy on the order of 10 meters. The Department of Defense is concerned enough about the civilian signal accuracy that the satellites to be launched from now on will have hardware in them to make the signal less accurate if the DOD believes that this unexpected accuracy is a threat to national security, and if it can weather the political consequences of making the civilian signal intentionally less precise.

Texas Instruments makes a GPS set that operates off the PPS (military) signals for which they have established an accuracy of

14 meters at a speed of 30 knots, with greater accuracy as speed decreases. At present, TI can sell you this receiver for a mere $140,000. It will operate for about 6 hours per day with the present number of orbiting GPS satellites. However, when the system becomes fully operational, the PPS signal will be encrypted and only users approved by the DOD will have the decoding information.

Trimble Navigation is producing a GPS system that operates on the less accurate SPS (civilian) signal. Trimble has found that that their system works with an accuracy of about 10 meters when the set is stationary. Their receiver is "only" $24,000 and is a surveying instrument not designed for marine use. They intend to have a consumer marine system on the market by the time the GPS becomes fully operational.

The Coast Guard is planning a 15-year transition period for the conversion from Loran-C to GPS, meaning that Loran-C will not be disabled before the year 2003. Moreover, if GPS units are thought to put a significant economic burden on users as a replacement item, Loran-C may well be continued beyond 2003. Prognostications point toward a civilian GPS set costing between $500 and $1000 once the economies of scale begin to do their benign magic, perhaps as early as the mid 1990s. If these estimates are accurate, GPS will mean more accurate, worldwide navigation at about the same cost as present Loran-C. Even if GPS sets prove to be more expensive than estimated, their presence will surely drive down the cost of Loran-C, a system that will be operational into the next century.

So, don't hold your breath, but be assured that the GPS/SPS will prove to be better than either of the present systems, Loran-C or SatNav. At the same time, you can feel confident that the Loran you buy today will have an electronic operating system to work from for many more years.

SATNAV

With the promise of GPS satellite navigation on the horizon, one wonders just where the current SatNav (officially known as TRANSIT) system fits in. Like GPS, SatNav electronic navigation devices operate off signals from orbiting satellites, and did, at one point, offer much the same promise as GPS.

The price of SatNav sets has been coming down recently. This can be attributed to the decreasing expense of microprocessor technology and the vicissitudes of the marketplace. As things now stand, however, many sailors are wondering if SatNav is a prudent purchase. Does a bargain price in SatNav hardware offer good value and performance over time?

Consider the present state of the system. The advantage of SatNav is that it provides very accurate fixes anywhere, including the open ocean, where other currently available electronic navigation systems are not useful. The bad news is that, even in the best of situations, one can get a SatNav fix only once every 90 minutes. In some locations, fixes may be as much as six hours apart. Between these fixes, navigation is by dead reckoning, either electronic dead reckoning or the traditional kind. This system offers few enticements for a sailor trying to find his way back to port on a foggy afternoon. For coastwise navigation, Loran is more desirable than SatNav, both for its cost and its reliability. For offshore voyaging, however, SatNav does offer a simple and accurate supplement to (but not a replacement for) celestial navigation.

The SatNav system not only has its full complement of six satellites and one spare in orbit, there's also a whole spare set of satellites built and ready to launch. While the DOD isn't crazy about the "imprecision" of SatNav navigation, a bird in the sky is worth a dozen on the shuttle's launch pad. It now looks as though SatNav may be around till the turn of the century.

Sometime during the coming years, GPS is scheduled to become available, and subsequently the price is expected to fall to affordable levels. Because Loran-C stations have the commitment of the government to be maintained for at least 15 years after GPS becomes operational, there is a convincing incentive to buy into the Loran system. However, unless you are planning a transoceanic voyage during the next few years, SatNav may not be a justifiable investment. If such adventures are not part of your immediate plans, it may make sense to wait until GPS settles into its niche.

LORAN-C

Through at least the turn of the century, the electronic aid of choice for sailors will be Loran-C. While other systems exist or are coming into existence, like GPS and SatNav, price alone will make Loran-C the preferred system for the coastal cruiser.

Loran is an electronic aid to navigation which provides sailors with lines-of-position through the precise measurement of transmitted radio signals. Loran is an acronym for *LOng RAnge Navigation*.

The "C" part of Loran-C simply refers to one version of Loran which operates at a low frequency (90 to 110 KHz—below the AM broadcast band). The original version, Loran-A, developed during World War II, is higher frequency (1850 to 1950 KHz), but is no longer being used except in a few areas near Japan. Loran-D is a short range version, generally limited to military use. (There is no Loran-B.)

Loran systems are based on the fact that radio waves travel in a fairly straight line at a fairly constant speed (161,875 knots) that is, they cover one nautical mile in 6.18 microseconds. (A microsecond is one one-millionth of a second.) So if you are one mile away from a transmitter, a pulse of radio energy will travel from the transmitter to you in 6.18 millionths of a second.

What a Loran receiver receives are pulses from a "master" transmitter and from up to four "secondary" transmitters placed hundreds of miles apart. (The secondaries were called "slaves," until the Reagan administration.)

These transmitters are geographically grouped, with each master and its secondaries called a "chain." Seventeen chains cover a good portion of the northern hemisphere, but there are voids in many spots and geographical overlapping in others. In some areas you will have to choose one chain over another; in other areas, your receiver won't hear the signals well enough to work at all.

Each chain is identified by a name and a number. Since all Loran chains use the same frequency, your receiver identifies which chain it is listening to by measuring how long (in microseconds) it takes a chain to transmit its group of pulses. The identifier is called a GRI (or *group repetition interval*) number. For

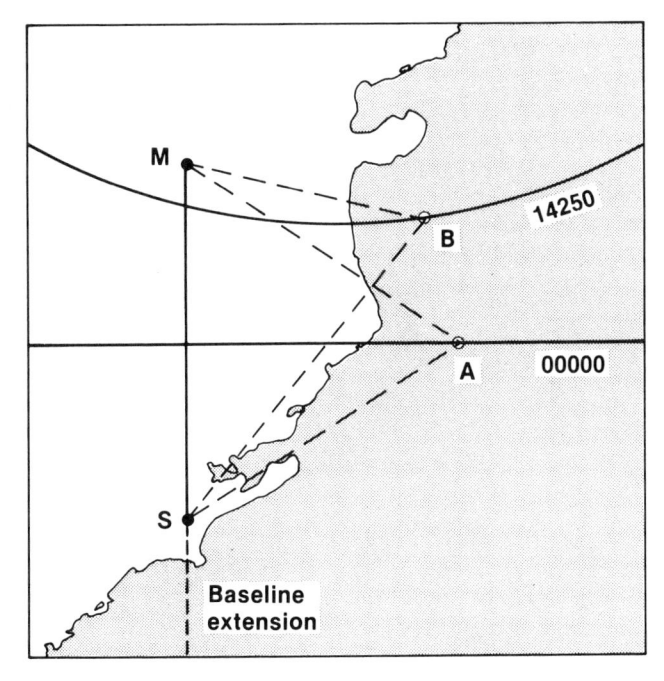

Figure 6-1. Anywhere along line 14250, a Loran-C receiver shows the same time difference between reception of the signal from the master transmitter (M) and the secondary (S). To get a fix, you need a second line crossing the 14250 line. Baseline extension is the area of greatest inaccuracy.

example, GRI 8970 is the Great Lakes chain. (The number is simply the number of microseconds it takes the chain to broadcast all of its pulses, divided by 10).

The transmitters in each chain are further identified by letters: M being used for the master and W, X, Y, Z for the secondaries. Thus the number that appears on the chart identifies the transmitter—for example, 8970-X refers to one of the secondary transmitters in the Great Lakes chain.

Because the pulses are transmitted in precisely timed sequences (cesium atomic clocks are used, and monitors constantly check the system), your Loran receiver can measure the time that passes from the moment it hears the master pulse group to the moment it hears a secondary pulse group.

To take a simplified example, let's say your boat is midway between a master (M) and secondary (X) transmitter, at point A in **Figure 6-1**. If the master and secondary both broadcast a pulse at exactly the same time, your receiver would hear both pulses simultaneously; there would be zero time difference. If your boat moves closer to the master (to point B on the diagram), your Loran set will hear the master pulse before the secondary pulse and it will be able to display how many microseconds later the secondary pulse was heard. You will get a figure like "14250" which stands for 14,250 microseconds later.

Because the speed of the radio waves is known, the time difference (commonly abbreviated *TD* in Loran talk) between receiving the two pulses can be converted into distance and printed as lines on a chart. The lines are identified by their TD numbers—like 14250. If your boat is anywhere along that line, the time difference between hearing the master pulse and the secondary pulse will be 14250 microseconds.

From the master and one secondary transmitter, you get only one line of position. To get a geographical location, you need two lines of position which cross, that is, you need TDs from a master and two separate secondary transmitters.

The Loran transmitters are arranged so the differing lines of position generally cross at suitable angles, the only serious problem being in an area near the "baseline extension," because the lines become very curved and close together. Baseline extensions are always well identified on Loran charts.

In addition to measuring the time difference between two signals, your receiver must also examine the shape of the pulse (the "envelope"), from the weak beginning to peak power and back down to nothing, and the "cycles" within the pulse. The receiver uses this information to determine if it is hearing a master or secondary and if it is receiving "ground waves" which travel along the ground or "sky waves" which arrive a bit later because they bounce off the ionosphere and back to earth. The receiver also has to be sure it is tracking the signal using the right sampling point (or "cycle") in the pulse.

The radio signal can warn your receiver when the system is not working. One of the pulses in the normal sequence can be altered to "blink," and when that happens your receiver will trigger an alarm to warn you that the whole system is not working properly.

How Loran-C Works

When you turn on your Loran-C receiver, it has to choose one of the chains. For most modern sets, you will specify the chain the first time you use it—for example, in Newport, Rhode Island, you would punch in GRI 9960 which is the identifying number for the Northeast U.S. Loran system. Thereafter, the Loran receiver will store that number in memory and automatically listen for the Northeast chain whenever you turn on the set—until you tell it otherwise.

It takes a while for the receiver to get organized and lock on to the signals (to *track* in Loran-talk), up to three or four minutes depending on the location, the capabilities of the receiver, atmospheric conditions, and other radio or electrical interference. The receiver has to identify the pulse from the master station and use it to start up its own internal clock; then it has to sort out the secondary stations (receivers now automatically track all the secondaries they can hear) and choose the best signal.

Once it has acquired the signals, it is operating—measuring and displaying the time difference between the master and the secondary pulse. With the time difference displayed, you can go to a chart with TD lines on it and plot your position.

That is the basic Loran-C receiver. Everything else on the modern Loran-C receiver is an add-on, related to those basic TDs in one of two ways; either providing a better signal (some features can help you receive a purer or cleaner or more accurate signal, and thus more accurate TDs); or additional information (some features calculate all sorts of navigational information from the basic TDs, such as the course to steer to get to a particular location or the time it should take you to get there).

Better Signals

Loran-C is subject to all the problems that affect all radio signals. The major problems are these:

RECEIVER ACCURACY. Some receivers are better—more accurate—than others. You would not expect a $10 pocket transistor radio to receive signals the same way a $1000 transoceanic receiver would. Similarly, a large part of the price spread in Lorans is because of the ability of the receiver to pick a Loran signal out of background noise.

RADIO WAVE INACCURACIES. Radio signals are not uniform. They generally travel in a straight line at a fairly constant speed, but they do bend and twist, especially when they encounter minor obstructions like mountains or thunderstorms. Also, they can change speeds, traveling slower and more irregularly over land than when they pass over bodies of water which are electrically more uniform (technically more uniformly conductive). These irregularity problems are collectively called "Additional Secondary Factors," *ASF* for short.

Radio signals also "degrade." This means that they become weaker and harder to pick up the farther away you are from the transmitter. And with a Loran receiver, you can also be too close to a transmitter (like listening to a symphony from inside the bass drum). As a result, what should theoretically be the time difference between signals is often not the actual time difference; there are inevitable inaccuracies in the system because of the nature of radio waves.

The principal add-ons to deal with these radio-wave inaccuracies are, first, alarms to let you know that the signal is too poor to be accurately interpreted, and second, ASF correctors.

The alarms take a variety of forms and names (signal-to-noise ratio, signal loss, distortion alarm, cycle mismatch, and so forth). You must consult your operator's manual to understand what they mean for your set, especially since sometimes you can get accurate enough information even when alarms are operating. Many of the signals only mean "I'm not sure of this information" so that much of the "art" of using a Loran involves interpreting the machine when something is functioning marginally.

INTERFERENCE. Interference, like static or other electrical signals, affects the quality of the Loran signals. Some onboard things—like alternators, distributor coils for gasoline engines, fluorescent lights, and TV sets—can mess up a Loran signal so the receiver cannot decode the pulses. And nearby things—like the mercury-vapor lamps so common at marinas, or a forest of aluminum masts surrounding the antenna—can thoroughly confuse the signals as well. In addition, there are other radio transmissions in or near the Loran frequencies which may occasionally or regularly interfere with the Loran signals. The Coast Guard has a three-page list of "known sources of interference," mostly broadcasts of military radio signals by the Department of Defense. And from time to time, there may be other transmissions that temporarily "slop over" into the Loran band.

What you do about interference is filter it out. For onboard things, you may have to add "noise suppression filters" to your engine, or make sure the fluorescent lights are turned off. For other radio transmissions, you use filters in the Loran receiver. These are usually called "notch" filters, and what they do is "notch out" or block specific frequencies near the Loran band.

The notch filters may be "fixed" in which case they are preset by the manufacturer to block out the known interfering frequencies. Or they may be internal but "adjustable," in which case you or a technician will have to get inside the receiver and "tune" the filter to block out certain frequencies. Or they may be "external" and adjustable, in which case there will be a meter and a knob that you can turn to minimize interference. Or they may be internal and "automatic" in which case they identify non-Loran signals and adjust themselves to block those signals.

Addition Features

The big sales push from Loran manufacturers has been for the extra information add-ons. It's a good idea to remind ourselves occasionally that these are only extras. As one *Practical Sailor*-reader aptly put it: "I have an antique set—all it does is tell me exactly where I am." Not bad for an aid to navigation.

The most common add-ons are: converting TDs to latitude and longitude (L/L), storing certain locations in memory (waypoints), and calculations of course, speed, distance, and time—both past and proposed. This last add-on takes an incredible variety of forms: conversion from true to magnetic course or bearing; course, distance, and time to, from, and among waypoints; speed over the bottom; velocity made good (VMG) to a waypoint; deviations from intended course; visual indicators to steer right or left, and so forth.

All of these calculations are performed by a microprocessor

in the Loran receiver and most have some inherent inaccuracies. Computing course and distance from one latitude/longitude coordinate to another is mathematically fairly straightforward, but figuring out the same course and distance between TD positions is extremely complex.

So, before the Loran does any calculations, it first converts the TDs to latitude/longitude numbers. Errors creep in, partly because of the inherent inaccuracies related to radio transmission; partly because the conversion and calculation formulas may use "idealized" figures, assuming for example that radio waves always travel at an identical speed; and partly because they may use figures which have varying degrees of correction applied to the idealized information.

The programming of these conversion formulas is very complex, and the attempts to correct the errors that creep in are expensive. In determining the price of a Loran-C unit, this programming is next in importance only to the receiver's ability to pick a signal out of background noise.

Who Should Not Buy Loran

The price of Loran-C receivers is low enough now that they are worth consideration by almost anyone with a cruising boat—the lowest priced units are an accessory costing five percent of a typical used trailerable boat and one percent of a new 30-footer.

Who, then, should *not* consider the purchase of Loran? First, the sailor whose budget is so limited that the Loran will substitute for other basic safety items should not buy Loran. While Loran could be considered part of your safety gear, buying one should not force you to compromise on the quality of your compass, for example, or keep you from buying adequate charts or man-overboard gear, or cause you to put off the purchase of such basic equipment as a VHF radio.

Second, the sailor who will be cruising away from the continental shores of the U.S. doesn't need Loran. There are a few chains elsewhere, but the Loran system is essentially a United States system. Even in the nearby Bahamas you will have trouble getting fixes, simply because the transmitters on the mainland are set up to get crossing lines of position near shore. And don't expect an expansion of the Loran system—in these days of tight budgets, the government is spending its money elsewhere (navigationally, on GPS).

If you plan to cross the Atlantic, don't buy a Loran. If you plan to spend most of your sailing time in the Caribbean, don't buy a Loran. If you're taking off for Tahiti, Tierra del Fuego, Teneriffe or anywhere else south of the Tropic of Cancer, don't buy a Loran.

The current electronic alternative for these travelers is Sat-Nav. The ultimate alternative for the 1990s is GPS.

RADIO DIRECTION FINDERS

The radio direction finder is about the simplest—and cheapest—form of electronic navigation equipment available. For many years, the standard direction finder has been the box-like, multi-band receiver with a built-in, rotating ferrite bar antenna.

There are several disadvantages to this type of radio direction finder, however. They are bulky and require a fair amount of storage space—a scarce commodity on a small boat. They must have a fixed mounting location, so that their orientation in use is always the same. They yield a relative bearing, which must be converted to an actual bearing by making reference to the vessel's heading. Their use belowdecks also makes them subject to bearing errors caused by reflection of the incoming signal from the boat's spars and rigging.

In theory, most of these problems are solved by a hand-held radio direction finder. These have several advantages:
- They are compact.
- They can be mounted out of the way in a locker.
- They incorporate compasses, so that absolute magnetic bearings can be read directly.
- They are portable, so that they may be used away from potentially distorting sections of the boat, notably aluminum masts and their rigging.

We further like the hand-held RDF because it operates on its own power source (flashlight batteries). For this reason, the RDF will still be usable in the event of a failure in the ship's power system that would render the Loran or SatNav set useless.

RDF vs. Loran
Within the last few years the average price of Loran-C has plummeted from almost $3,000 to about a third of that, and discounted prices at the low end of the spectrum are beginning to dip below $500. Given the accuracy and ease of use of Loran, is it reasonable to spend the extra amount for a radio direction finder, which may be harder to use and lack the inherent accuracy of Loran?

Probably. Loran is a remarkable system, and the constantly falling prices make it highly desirable even for a small cruising sailboat. At the same time, Loran can make the navigator lazy, and forget the dangers of relying on a single navigational instrument or technique.

The coastal navigator who depends exclusively on his Loran, who fails to keep his DR up to date, and who fails to confirm his position with other navigation tools—such as an RDF—is asking for trouble. A Loran set is no substitute for traditional piloting skills in coastal navigation, any more than it is a substitute for celestial navigation skills in offshore sailing.

Loran is useful for high-seas navigation as well as coastal cruising. RDF is basically a coastal navigation tool, although many offshore islands have radio beacons to assist in making a landfall. After a handbearing compass, a good RDF is probably the most important navigation tool for the coastal sailor.

Loran has its place, but don't consider it a panacea. Learn to use all the skills of the navigator. When you're socked in by the fog while trying to make port, you may need all of them.

SEXTANTS

Although the age of electronic navigation is in its adolescence, there has already been an irreversible change in the image, if not the function of the navigator. No longer like a druid trying to conjure secrets from silent stars in the distant sky, he has become a technician who from the comfort of his cabin, speaks to the heavens and reads their reply in the constellation of LEDs twinkling before him. Of course he still carries a sextant to use when the batteries fail. Stars have a good shelf life.

With so many sextants to choose from, such a profusion of

details to understand, and numerous priorities to weigh, the prospective sextant-buyer could benefit from a discussion of their features.

Characteristics of a Good Sextant

It is neither feasible nor necessary to take a protracted bluewater cruise in order to evaluate a sextant. The prospective buyer can learn a great deal by going to the showroom of a knowledgeable dealer, presenting himself as seriously interested, and asking permission to handle the instruments. (Be aware that you undertake some risk in handling the sextants, and forgive the dealer if he watches you closely.) This review is intended to be an armchair excursion into a well-stocked showroom, with explanations and advice as they seem appropriate. Nothing can replace your own "hands on" test, however, and we urge you to take time to do so.

What are the important things to look for in a sextant? Few would argue that three major features are optical quality, comfort, and durability. What about accuracy? It is likely that new metal sextants will have negligible instrument error (uncorrectable), as each instrument's certificate will show. Index error (correctable) can be readily reduced or eliminated by following your dealer's instructions (he should know the procedure) or those in the instruction booklet (ask for one if it is not offered).

OPTICAL QUALITY. Optical quality depends on several factors. First, look carefully at the size of the two mirrors. Large mirrors collect more light and reduce eyestrain when taking star sights. Since most small-craft navigators rely more on sun sights, for which large mirrors are not quite so important, you may want to assure yourself that the shades or filters are large enough to cover the viewing area and numerous enough (the range is four to seven) to permit a good range of density combinations.

A very important consideration is which scope to choose, since most manufacturers offer both a 4-power (magnification), and either a 6-power or 7-power scope. There are good arguments for either choice.

The 3- or 4-power telescope is considered the better choice for stars. It is considerably less expensive than a 6- or 7-power monocular because of its simpler construction and fewer parts. The field (diameter) of view with the lower-power scopes is certainly adequate for finding stars and keeping them in view. Furthermore, the objective (larger) lens is large (usually 40mm) for excellent light-gathering in dim or dark conditions. The combined motion of the vessel and the navigator become more amplified with each increase in scope magnification, so for star sights—which can be a challenge under the best conditions at sea—it would be self-defeating to use a high-power monocular. Finally, a 3-power or 4-power telescope is perfectly adequate for taking sun sights, horizontal angles, and distance off. As the only scope, it would be the reasonable choice.

A 6- or 7-power monocular is better suited to taking sun sights. With a greatly magnified apparent diameter of the sun, it becomes easier to discern the point of tangency between the sun's limb and the horizon.

Monoculars have lower light-gathering capacity than 4-power telescopes and are thus poor for use in darkness, but excellent for general daylight and early twilight use. They greatly amplify motion and require a steady hand.

After selecting the scope you prefer, be sure you can stow it securely in the box, separate from the sextant. It will last longer that way.

COMFORT. After optical quality, the buyer should consider comfort. Is the sextant heavy enough to afford some steadiness, but light enough so that after holding it for a minute or so your arm doesn't ache? Is the handle comfortable to hold? It should have a shape which feels natural in your grip, and it should be angled to prevent strain or awkwardness in your wrist. The handle should have its center near the sextant's center of gravity to avoid acting as a lever which might cause fatigue. The switch button for the light, if there is one, should be convenient to the thumb or index finger, so that only one hand needs to be on the instrument. A soft rubber eyecup is very desirable for wearers of eyeglasses. A sextant which is comfortable to hold and operate will allow its owner to exercise the patience sometimes necessary to get a good sight.

DURABILITY. The durability of the sextant is very important, though it is sometimes hard to judge. No one wants to own a sextant which will distort appreciably or corrode when water splashes on it. Plastic sextants change dimension very slightly as the temperature changes. The resulting instrument error may be noticeable with extreme changes, but as the accuracy of plastic sextants is acknowledged to be less predictable anyway, this additional error should not be hard to bear, especially when you remember the low original cost. Metal sextants have no appreciable error as a result of temperature change.

Resistance to damage from impact is very difficult to assess. Most sextants' frames are extremely strong, but you should look at the appendages (mirror frames, light fixtures, legs, shade assemblies, and so forth), and check for secure mounting. One weak point we have discovered is in the way some 6x30 monoculars are joined to their rising posts. At the joint of the rising post and the U-shaped yoke, there is only light brazing and a single screw inside which bond the two together. The prudent owner will remove his 6x30 monocular from the sextant before either carrying or shipping it.

Another durability factor is the juxtaposition of dissimilar metals and the use of uncoated metals which are susceptible to corrosion in a salt environment. Brass is slow to react with salt and needs only to be wiped clean and covered with a thin film of Vaseline or light oil to retard tarnishing. Aluminum alloy, the primary material of many sextants, needs more attention than brass, especially if it is painted rather than anodized. The owner of an alloy sextant must remove salt spray from it frequently, preferably after each exposure, by flushing the affected areas with fresh water and then drying with a clean cloth. The neglected alloy sextant will soon begin to show corrosion where dissimilar metals are in contact, such as where a stainless steel machine screw holding a mirror retaining tab or spring enters an alloy mirror frame, or on the teeth of the exposed arc.

Since sextants spend most of their existence in a box, it is a good idea to check the ruggedness of the container, and especially the way the instrument is held inside it. The best method we've seen for protecting a sextant is the use of rigid foam molded or cut to the exact dimensions of the instrument. Even dropping the box will probably not harm the instrument, as long as the index arm has previously been immobilized or the tangent screw released. Whether the box is plywood, hardwood, or plastic makes considerably less difference to durability than the way the sextant is restrained inside. The important thing is that the sextant be nearly or completely immobilized in the box, even if the navigator intends to remove the sextant again soon. A careless shipmate or unexpected sea may dislodge the box. Examine the clamping mechanism inside, try to move the sextant when it is in the clamp, and decide whether a strong impact could release the sextant.

Further down the list of priorities, but still important, is the matter of illumination. There are two schools of thought about a light. One feels that if it is light enough to see the horizon and the stopwatch, it is probably light enough to read the sextant, so why have a light? If a light *is* needed, they reason, carry a small penlight in your pocket and save your money. The other school prefers a light because if you're paying hundred of dollars, you certainly ought to have a small convenience feature which might, after all, keep you from having to go below to take the sextant reading.

Ease of adjustment of the mirrors is often overlooked by buyers. We prefer those instruments having a square-headed adjusting screw because a wrench can get a firmer purchase and will probably not be deterred by an adjusting screw which has become frozen in place. Those sextants which have Allen-head adjusting screws are more liable to incur damage to the screw or the wrench if great force becomes necessary to dislodge a frozen screw. Plastic sextants need no tools to adjust, but they are harder to adjust accurately.

Resale value may be important to the buyer who intends one day to sell his sextant. The more you pay for a sextant, the higher the percentage of that cost you will likely get back at resale.

While there are other yardsticks for comparing sextants, optical quality, comfort, and durability remain the most important for assuring best overall value.

RADAR

*RA*dio *D*etection *A*nd *R*anging has been around for over 40 years, with little fundamental change until recently. Now radar sets are suddenly appearing in forms and at prices that make them worth considering aboard a sailboat.

The Basics

What radar has always done is to shoot out radio pulses. Then it listens for these same radio pulses being bounced off objects around the boat. When the radar hears a radio pulse being returned, it not only knows that something is in the way, it also knows how far away and in what direction that something is.

The basic idea is not complex. The radar is doing approximately what your depthsounder is doing, but it is using super-high-frequency radio waves rather than the sound waves used by depthsounders.

The radio waves travel at a constant speed—186,300 miles, or about 327,888,000 yards, per second. Since the distance per second is so great, the radar measures not in seconds but in millionths of a second (microseconds).

The radar set transmits a pulse of radio energy (small-boat sets operate in the "X" band, at 9445 mHz) from its rotating antenna (usually called a "scanner" in radar talk). If the pulse comes back in one microsecond (a millionth of a second), the radar calculates that the signal traveled 327,888,000 yards divided by 1,000,000 for the microsecond, or 327.888 yards (call it 328 yards). Since the *total* distance the signal traveled was 328 yards, the radar knows the object was half of 328, or 164 yards away. The signal traveled 164 yards *out*, bounced, and traveled 164 yards *back*.

The radar also knows what direction the rotating antenna was pointing when it received the bounce-back signal, so it knows the direction (actually, the relative bearing) of the object, as well as the distance. The signals are presented on a screen with the presumption that your boat is in the center and that the 12 o'clock position on the screen is straight ahead.

Though these basics are straightforward, there is quite a bit of variation among the different radar sets.

Pulse Length Variation

Old or new, the radars do not usually produce pulses that are one microsecond long. If they did, the closest object they could measure would be 164 yards away. (The signal goes out 164 yards in half a microsecond and comes back in the next half microsecond. However, if the transmitter is transmitting during that microsecond, it cannot receive or measure a signal that bounces back in a shorter time.)

So the radars produce signals in shorter bursts, referred to in terms of "pulse length" or "pulse duration" on the radar's specification sheet. The pulse length of each radar is important because it affects minimum range, maximum range, and the ability of the radar to discriminate between two or more objects that are close to each other.

If, for example, the pulse length is half a microsecond, the minimum range of the radar will be half of 164 yards, or 82 yards. If the pulse length is a tenth of a microsecond, the minimum range of the radar will be a tenth of 164 or 16.4 yards. The spec sheets of most radar sets list both pulse length and minimum range, but the minimums often seem to be "rounded off" and not too precise. To be more accurate, you can perform a simple calculation using the specified pulse length.

The maximum range is also affected by pulse length, since short pulses have less energy than longer pulses. To get a good strong reflection from a long distance away, you need strong (long) pulses. Radar sets could also apply more power to get more strength, but it's far cheaper for the manufacturer to lengthen the pulses than to increase the wattage.

For greater range, most radars have different settings (for example a two-mile, eight-mile, and 16-mile range). The pulse length will change in the radar when you switch ranges—a longer pulse for longer ranges. However, it's not just the maximum range that changes, the minimum range changes as well, and as an operator you need to be aware that close objects can literally disappear on the set when the longer ranges are switched on.

Pulse length also affects the radar's "discrimination," or ability to show nearby objects as separate. For example, if two buoys in a narrow channel are only 16.4 yards apart, your radar must have a pulse length of a tenth of a microsecond or less to distinguish between them. If the pulse length is longer, the first part of the signal bounces off the second buoy and returns to the receiver at the same time that the tail end of the pulse comes back from the first buoy, and both buoys will appear to be one on the radar screen.

Antenna Height and Size

The different radars are also affected by the height and size of their antennas. Range is partly a function of antenna height, since radar is normally line-of-sight, like your VHF radio. A 500-foot-tall smoke stack, ten miles away, will show up before a 4-foot buoy which is two miles away.

Most radars advertise "maximum" ranges. But, you almost always get less range than the specification sheets on your radar set show. You might see a 10,000-foot thunderhead at your radar's maximum 24-mile range, but you'll never see a boat at sea level. Conversely, it's almost impossible to get more range than your spec sheets publish (except for occasional freak atmospheric conditions which can give a temporary increase).

Practically speaking, radar tends to be most useful in the shorter ranges. At sailboat speeds, you will tend to use the shortest range on a multi-range set. In fact, most of the time the longer ranges are really useful only for seeing and avoiding thunderstorms a long way off or for rough position finding when you're well offshore.

The size (width) of the antenna also varies among sets. In all instances, wider is better. Wider antennas provide more "gain" so the transmitted signals are more intense and the received signal stronger. In addition, the antenna width determines the radar's horizontal "beam width," which in turn determines the radar's ability to distinguish between two targets that are at the same range but separated slightly. If the "beam width" is four degrees, two targets that are less than four degrees apart during the antenna's sweep will appear to be a single object.

However, the "dome-type" antenna, with the antenna rotating inside a fiberglass cowl, is the only practical installation on most sailboats. Halyards and sails can get tangled in an open antenna, and windage on an exposed antenna requires a larger, power-hungry motor to rotate the machinery. For a reasonably compact dome, the boatowner is limited to a smaller antenna, with its reduced power, range, and horizontal discrimination.

One change that has recently made radar more attractive to sailors is this reduction in size of the antenna. There is no new technology involved. Manufacturers could have made smaller antennas and given up power, range, and discrimination at any time. They have just recently decided that those trade-offs are something sailboats (and smaller powerboats) could live with, so they're going after a new market.

Displays

The major recent technical development in radars has not been in antennas, but in the way the bounce-back information is digested and displayed.

In the traditional radar set, the display involves an electron gun in a cathode ray tube (CRT). The gun is aimed to sweep around the front face of the tube, synchronized with the rotation of the radar's antenna. When the antenna receives a bounce-back signal, the gun is activated and fires a burst of electrons at the back side of the screen.

Since the screen is coated with phosphor, a glowing blip appears where the electrons hit it. The phosphorescent coating does not hold the glow, but starts to fade immediately. But then another sweep of the antenna and electron gun causes a repeat of the burst and glow so the blip reappears.

The rotating sweep of this old-fashioned CRT display, of course, is well known—universally depicted in old war movies and television shows. However, in reality, there are some aspects of it that are not "user friendly."

First is viewability. The CRTs literally cannot be viewed in much light at all. They're fine at night, but if you want to see the screen in daylight, you must place the set in a dark corner of the navigation station or use a "hood." Most hoods are flexible, rubber-like tunnels, contoured to fit your eyes like a diving mask. Many people felt (or the marketing folks thought people felt) that sticking your head in the hood was a nuisance—not a pleasant way to go cruising. Furthermore, with the fading blips,

Navigation Equipment and Electronics 153

Even though the new radars are more compact than their predecessors, they are still large units. This Raytheon 1200 occupies almost as much space in the navigation station as the SatNav, Loran, and VHF combined.

the circular sweep had to be watched fairly constantly to be sure you were seeing all the returned signals.

Second, and probably more important, interpreting the blips that appear on the phosphor screen is quite an art. To be a good interpreter of the radar's information requires practice and more practice, along with a bit of intuition, some guessing, and lots of good judgment. In short, the old displays could not simply be stuck on a boat and put to work—you first had to develop the skill of "reading" them.

The major change in the "new" radar is in the mechanism for the display. Generically known as *raster* or *raster-scan* radars, they substitute a tube more like a TV set or a computer monitor, in place of the old-fashioned CRT.

A raster "scans" the screen much like you read a page of print, sweeping horizontally left to right, making 512 passes (maybe more, or less, depending on the set) to cover the screen.

Typically, the raster scans the whole screen 60 times per second (again, the figures vary slightly with the sets), the most noticeable result being an image which does not fade. Actually, the screen does flicker, but it flickers so fast that the human eye cannot detect it.

The screens are brighter than the old-fashioned sets, more like a black-and-white TV. They can be read in daylight, although, of course, the image is not as crisp as it would be in a shaded or darkened place. All the manufacturers make claims about reading the screens from a long distance away (for the old-style sets, your eyes were typically inches from the screen), but in practice the screens are generally too small to be able to distinguish the little dots from further than a few feet.

Rather than viewing from a great distance, it's probably more important that you can do chart work while glancing at the screen and that several people can see the screen at once—things you couldn't do with the old hoods.

There is also a considerable variation in the screens in terms of glare control. Some have a good non-glare finish, but on the low-priced sets, the non-glare doesn't seem quite so good, and reflections on the screen can hamper viewing. The problem of glare makes a turntable-mount desirable for daylight viewing, if you cannot position the radar display in a darkened corner. One or two models come standard with a rotating base; other sets can be adapted.

As with a television set, the ease of viewing is partly dependent on physical dimensions, with larger screens much better at displaying the blips in a reasonable size. Most of the new sets have small screens, and in practice, the usable portion of the screen is often considerably smaller than the advertised size. Most of the low-priced sets advertise 9-inch *diagonal* screens, but the displays themselves are circular, with the edges of the screen used for showing the bearing or azimuth. The actual round display is just slightly over 5 inches.

On all the cheaper sets, the displays are currently black-and-white (actually mostly black-and-green), but color displays are available on the big, expensive sets. It's probably not long before cheap color sets will be available. The colors are generally used to show the intensity or strength of the returning signals—strong images in red, medium in yellow, and so on (you've seen the same thing when your TV weatherman displays a line of thunderstorms on your color TV). However, colors may be used for other purposes, where red shows targets and the other colors are used to show bearing and distance information.

In addition to raster-scan sets, there is at least one set which uses a liquid crystal display (LCD). It breaks the screen up into small LCD dots in a grid 128 wide by 128 high. The display operation is similar in principle to the raster-scan units, but it is black-and-white, with the objects displayed somewhat coarser than on raster-scan sets.

Digitizing Radar

Sometimes, these new sets are described as "digitized," an indication that the radar set converts the returned echo into an electrical impulse which is temporarily stored in the computer-like memory of the radar, then converted into a little block of light (called a pixel, on the raster-scan sets, or an LCD). The pixels form a grid, typically 512 pixels wide and 512 pixels tall; that is, there are 262,144 dots of the screen to be either lit or unlit.

The digitizing is necessary for the TV-like display screens, but there are other consequences of digitizing the return echoes in the radar's memory. First, with the computer memory and such a large number of potential dots in a 512 by 512 screen, there is a lot of variety in how the radars work once the signal is received. In fact, there generally is not much consistency among the manufacturers on how to present the information.

In a traditional set, for example, the rotating sweep on the screen followed the antenna rotation, with the blips being "repainted" as the rotating line swept by. In a digitized set, there is no reason to have a rotating line on the display. You could present the information in any number of other ways, but most of the new sets electronically imitate the old, artificially creating a circular, sweeping display.

Similarly, on old-fashioned sets, the strength of the return signal determined the size of the blip displayed on the screen. With digitized information, all signal returns could be displayed the same size, but most sets choose to light up more pixels and make a bigger blob for stronger returns, again in imitation of the old. Consequently, a very weak bounce-back will not show at all, while a big ship will appear oversized.

One odd result of this practice is that some targets (mostly low irregular objects like buoys or breakwaters) appear to disintegrate and re-form while you watch them on the screen. The echoes from such objects are not consistent; weak echoes sometimes don't show up at all, while strong echoes are exaggerated.

Particularly noticeable on the new displays, in contrast to the old, is that plain language and numbers can be printed or overprinted right on the screen while the blips continue to appear. On most of the sets, for example, the operator can push a button to expand a range ring from the center of the display to the edge of the screen. If you stop expanding the range ring at some return echo shown on the display, the machine will calculate the range and print it on the screen in plain language.

While the digitizing of the displays is flashy and generally more readable, more important is that the inner workings of the new machines (basically microprocessors) are now able to do more manipulation of the returned signals than the old sets, or at least do it much cheaper. Since the radar stores a whole screenfull of information and can update it continuously, the brains of the machine can also examine the information to see if and how it is changing.

For example, in old sets there was always lots of "noise" and "clutter" coming both from inside the set and from the seas and atmosphere, all of which were interpretable as return echoes. The user typically adjusted the "gain" on the set to just eliminate what was obviously noise. What usually happened, of course, is that weaker signals (like from fiberglass sailboats) often were hidden in the noise and lost when the gain "tuned them out."

The new sets can examine the returned signals and, in effect, determine if the signals are so erratic and irregular that they must be noise, or so regular and consistent that they must be a target. Those that the computer determines to be noise are eliminated, the others presented as blips.

While there is a potential for better detection of objects (which is what radar is all about), many experienced operators of the older sets find that there is quite a bit lost, too. What is happening is that the microprocessor is now making the judgments and interpretations that were formerly required of the operator. For example, an experienced operator could frequently examine the shape or characteristic of a blip on an old-fashioned radar and determine what kind of object he was seeing—a tanker or a sportfisherman for example. The digital radars tend to give a "blocky" appearance to all blips, more uniform but perhaps less accurate.

Also the sizing of digitized blips according to signal strength can be deceiving. What is a big, steady blob on the raster screen can be very threatening looking, something to attend to and watch closely when it's in your vicinity. But a little tiny blob can sink your boat just as easily.

For cost reasons alone, it seems inevitable that the new digitized machines will eventually replace the old. There is a great potential for software programming, and once it's programmed, the digitizing microchip is just plain cheap. For the manufacturers, it becomes a matter of spreading their engineering and programming costs over a number of sets.

User Friendliness

The manuals for the new raster-scan machines tend to be opaque, written in engineer's language, and often impenetrable for a non-technician. Further, many aspects of operation are confusing. The control panel on some units, for example, identifies the push buttons with mysterious symbols. To operate the set, you have to memorize the button designations and the procedures for pushing, pulling, or turning them.

We would say that none of the radars now selling for under $2,000 is particularly user friendly. They are about at the stage where Loran sets were a few years ago, with all sorts of electronic sophistication blossoming, but with little ability to communicate that sophistication to the buyer.

Radar Installation

It is possible for an owner to install a radar set, and most of the low priced units are packaged and wired to make it relatively simple. Formerly, it was standard practice for an installer (an FCC-licensed technician) to sign the required FCC certificate after the radar was operating aboard a boat. Increasingly, the cheaper radars are being "signed off" at the factory, in the same way that VHF radiotelephones are, so that owners may install the radars themselves.

Many owners, however, find it desirable to buy radar locally rather than through a discount house, for the convenience of local follow-up service. Unlike most other electronics, service problems with a radar are most likely to occur in the antenna, since the antenna is both a mechanical and an electronic device. A midseason trip up the mast to remove a 25-pound antenna and ship it back to the factory may make the value of local service obvious. If that kind of activity is not daunting for you, then buying at a discount and installing it yourself makes sense.

Radar Licensing

Many pleasure boaters don't realize that their ship's radio license must be updated when they install radar. In fact, other equipment which transmits radio signals must be listed on the ship's license, including VHF and single sideband radios, EPIRBs, and radar. The only exceptions are citizen's band radios which require no license at all, and ham radio which requires a separate amateur radio license.

When you install a radar, you will need to complete a form (FCC #506) and mail it to the Federal Communications Commission (Box 1040, Gettysburg, PA 17325). Electronics dealers frequently carry copies of the correct form, or you can write the FCC in Gettysburg or call a regional FCC office for a copy.

Radar Safety

Are there safety problems with radar? Radar signals are in the range of the signals produced by microwave ovens, and there are many stories of birds being instantly cooked as they settle onto some of the super-high-power military radar antennas.

While small boat radars are not powerful enough to do such instant damage to a human being, most experts agree that you should never directly expose yourself to the transmitted signals and that you need to be cautious about prolonged exposure. The primary precaution is to mount the antenna high enough that the transmitted signal will not hit anyone on the boat.

The radar's specification sheet will list the "vertical beam width" or angle (typically 25 to 30 degrees) of the signal coming out of the antenna. If your antenna specs say the angle is 28 degrees, for example, that means the signal spreads out from the antenna at an angle of 14 degrees above the horizontal and 14 degrees below the horizontal. Knowing the vertical beam width, you can use a protractor or compass rose and a diagram of your boat to calculate a safe mounting height.

With the typical mounting on the main or mizzen mast of a sailboat, there is almost never an exposure problem. Mounting on a pedestal (or "stalk") on the transom, however, can create problems, and you should figure the beam width angles carefully to ensure safety.

One other safety precaution—very high voltages are present in radar equipment. It's best to leave internal investigation and repair for someone who's been inside a radar set before.

* * *

There are several things that are making the new radars attractive for sailboat use. First is the downsizing, both of the antennas and the radar sets themselves. The smaller antennas make mast-mounting more feasible for sailboats as small as 28 to 30 feet, and make mounting on a transom stalk more practical for the larger sailboat. With smaller sets, space can be found for the displays in navigation stations that physically could not handle the larger old-fashioned units.

Prospective buyers, however, need to remember that the downsizing is a mixed blessing. The smaller antennas reduce windage and weight aloft, but also reduce power and discrimination. The smaller radar sets themselves are possible partly because of the microchip electronics—a good feature—but partly because of the smaller displays, which are harder to read.

The digitizing of the sets is also a mixed blessing. The resulting brighter displays are generally easier to use, especially for the recreational sailor who is likely to turn on the set only a couple dozen times a season, and the power consumption is reduced relative to the older sets. But the digital processing of the signal often substitutes an engineer's or programmer's judgment for the judgment of the operator—not necessarily a good feature since the radar is usually being used to avert disaster.

INTEGRATED INSTRUMENTS

To make a boat sail efficiently, you need "sensors" to tell what the wind and boat are doing and some way to interpret what the sensors tell you. Many sailors think that the most efficient sensors are the human skin, eyes, and ears and that the best interpreter is the human brain. However, electronic instruments have become standard equipment on both racers and cruisers in the last 20 years, and the latest fad in sailboat instrumentation is hooking the sensors together and feeding the information into an electronic brain—the "integrated system."

What about these new systems? Will they help the sailor refine his intuitive reaction to wind and wave? Or are they merely crutches for the incompetent? Is the advertising hype close to reality? Or are these just high tech playthings?

What Makes an Integrated System?

The new integrated systems are in contrast to the separate or "discrete" instruments which are now standard-issue on boats over 20 feet. The discrete instruments are those electronic devices which measure and report on only one thing, like boat speed or wind direction. With enough separate instruments, a sailor can get all the same information as from an integrated system. However, it is the sailor who has to do the "integrating."

For example, if you have a speedometer and an apparent wind indicator that are separate or discrete, you can read both instruments and calculate the true wind direction, using either a mechanical method (drawing vectors) or a mathematical method (using a calculator). You have to learn the method and the mathematical formulas, but once you know them, the process of calculating such things is not difficult.

The integrated system, in contrast, has a microprocessor (the computer part) that reads the speedometer and apparent wind, does the calculations, and gives you a readout of true wind direction. The two things gained are ease (there is no thinking or calculating on your part) and speed (the computer can do the calculations almost instantaneously and can repeat the process continuously to show you information that is nearly current).

The microprocessor in the integrated systems can also be programmed to perform other functions, like telling you what the wind speed and wind angle will be once you round the buoy ahead of you and start on a new course. You can also have the information displayed for you in a variety of ways: old fashioned digits, analog dials, or even plots on a computer's TV screen or a plotting board.

You can "integrate" as few instruments as you want. Normally, however, a wind speed indicator, an apparent wind indicator, and a speedometer form the minimal system to provide navigational and tactical information to be used in racing or, perhaps, even in cruising. The complexity of the system depends on your pocketbook. For full integration, an electronic compass is the primary addition to the basic wind/water instruments. Then you could add (or "integrate") Loran, SatNav, GPS, a depthsounder, and an autopilot.

A personal computer (most often an Epson, HP, IBM, or Apple) is the final add-on. Its "integrating software" can do a variety of things, like compare your current progress to what your progress should be ideally, tell you precisely when to tack toward a racing mark, display what the pattern of windshifts has been in the last half-hour, and anything else your onboard programmer can dream up.

Incidentally, the simpler "combination" displays should not be confused with an integrated system. The instruments that combine several displays (the "Combi" unit is the best known brand) have no interaction among the different functions. In the accepted sense, they are not integrated at all—the displays are merely packaged differently than the separate instruments.

Exact prices for a full system are difficult to estimate, due to the many options and variations in remote displays and customized software. A complete system, however, with depthsounder, knotmeter/log, wind instruments, electronic compass, and a computer with Loran and SatNav interfaces, plus the necessary software could easily come to $10,000 (and that doesn't count the Loran or the SatNav).

Besides the greater basic cost of system equipment, almost all brands of traditional instruments are cheaper because they are relatively easy to install and widely available at discount prices, from 20 percent to 40 percent off. Most of the integrated systems, however, cannot be bought at a discount. And even if they were available, most owners would probably need to be cautious about owner installation and would want the services of a reliable retail dealer and his technicians—which means full retail prices.

Considering the costs, are these integrated systems practical? Are they all that they're cracked up to be? Is there any sailor for whom they are a reasonable investment?

First, it should be noted that the basic parts of the integrated systems are standard instruments you might buy from any marine electronics catalog. The wind speed and apparent wind senders which are mounted at the masthead and the speedometer paddlewheels and LED displays, for example, are not special or dedicated only to integrated systems. In many cases, the hardware is identical to that of the discrete units from the same company. This is not to downgrade the integrated hardware. The traditional paddlewheels and anemometers that the discrete and integrated systems have in common are generally proven and reliable devices.

Most of the additional expense of integrated systems comes not from the basic equipment, but from additional equipment you would not normally have on board. The first requirement for a fully integrated system is an electronic compass, a piece of high-tech hardware that few boats would otherwise carry—roughly a $1000 investment. This, of course, is in addition to your regular magnetic compass which you will still need to carry as a steering compass and as a backup to your electronic compass in case of a power failure.

The other major requirement is the computer that runs the whole show and does the integrating. The computer part can be a single central processing unit (CPU), or the computing functions can be divided up among the instruments, with each instrument having its own little microprocessor. Which is better is hotly debated; the central advocates claiming greater processing power, and the split advocates claiming backup redundancy in case one part crashes.

As is the case with much electronics, the "hardware" itself is a relatively small part of a high price tag. What you are paying

Navigation Equipment and Electronics 163

for is the engineering and programming that have gone into the brains of the system—the software.

Integrated systems need lots of attention and careful tuning in order to operate as they should. Almost anyone can install a anemometer and get it to work. Most people can install a speedometer and get it calibrated close enough for general piloting. Some people can install an electronic compass and correct its errors. But to install them all and get them working together is another matter.

For example, a 5-degree discrepancy in apparent wind readings on port and starboard is quite tolerable to a helmsman, but it will make nonsense of a computed VMG. And a baby barnacle attaching itself to your speedometer's paddlewheel, changing your speed readings by 10 percent at the low end and 5 percent at the top end, can render all calculations totally inaccurate.

In fact, the basic sensors are the weak link in the integrated systems. Consider, for example, these critical elements:

SPEEDOMETER. The paddlewheel has to be located properly, on the centerline of the boat, not too close to the keel, not too close to the bow, since water flowing around the keel or wave action could affect its readings. It must read equally on either tack and when beating, reaching, or running. If the paddlewheel is removed to be cleaned, it must be replaced exactly as before (no 2-degree turns) or the speedometer must be recalibrated. A bit of growth on the boat's bottom or on the paddlewheel may affect speed readings enough to throw the whole system off.

APPARENT WIND INDICATOR. In a discrete instrument, your only concern is to get the AWI pointing more or less straight ahead. With the boat tied to a dock, you go to the masthead in a bosun's chair and twist the indicator until the cockpit readout says straight ahead. However, for the AWI to work in an integrated system, the instrument has to be calibrated for a variety of effects: upwash from the sails, amount of leeway by the boat, degree of heel, and turbulence from other masthead instruments, since all those things affect the apparent wind direction enough to affect the advanced calculations.

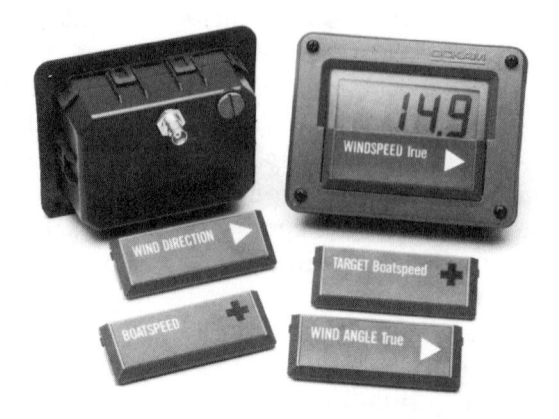

The integrated displays from Ockam (top) and Rochester (bottom) appear to be little different than those of stand-alone instruments.

APPARENT WIND SPEED. In a discrete instrument, it doesn't really matter how far off your wind speed is, as long as the reading is repeatable. For example, based on your experience, you know to put the first reef in the mainsail whenever the wind speed reads 14 knots. It doesn't matter if the actual wind speed is 10 or 18, just as long as the meter always reads the same. With an integrated system, the wind speed has to be not only repeatable, but also close to accurate over a wide range of wind speeds. You may also have to calibrate the wind speed readings to account for peculiarities, such as having the anemometer cups blocked by other masthead instruments when running.

ELECTRONIC COMPASS. Most sailors feel that a compass accurate to plus or minus 3 or 4 degrees is pretty good. In cruising, you can't steer much better than that, and in racing you're primarily looking for relative changes (are you getting a header or a lift?). But if your compass is 3 degrees off on one heading and 4 degrees off the other way on a different heading, you've got enough error to make integrated calculations quite inaccurate. Your electronic compass needs to be fully corrected, for heeling errors as well as normal deviation—an undertaking that will push the limits of competency of almost all amateurs.

For an integrated system to work, the basic sensors of wind speed, boat speed, wind direction, and heading must be much more precise than most sailors are used to. You can't just plug in the instruments and go. And the more sophisticated the computations you want the system to do, the more accurate must be the basic sensors. Small input errors, when used in calculations, are *compounded*; they don't cancel each other out.

The integrated systems are designed to handle the fine tuning needed to make the basic sensors accurate, and if you're willing to make the effort, it's not difficult, just time-consuming. In practice, however, we have rarely seen the fine tuning actually done on the more complex systems. Such tuning takes considerable time on the water with calculations and adjustments. Aside from the 12-Meters, we have seen reasonably calibrated systems only on boats which have an expert navigator who is willing to put in the extra time to do the necessary work.

With an integrated system, you can't expect a dealer to do the fine tuning; it simply takes too much time and effort on the water. If the system goes out of tune during a race, the dealer won't be there to fix it. Furthermore, most dealers have learned that the only way customers will be happy with a system is if they are involved enough with its details to understand it fully.

The programming of the integrated systems is generally not "user friendly." Those who can do a bit of computer programming and have general math competence will have little problem, but for the nontechnical, the advanced stages of integration will be impenetrable.

Who Needs Integration?

If you're sailing a 12-Meter for the America's Cup, you need an integrated system. Even the seat-of-the-pants sailors grudgingly accept the system, provided there is an expert aboard to care for and interpret it, and provided it is used only for "advice."

In grand prix racing, such as the SORC or the Admiral's Cup, an operating integrated system is necessary. In fact, a racing series which includes triangular and long-distance offshore races provides the situations where the complex calculations of an integrated system work best, especially when combined with electronic navigation like Loran.

However, it should be noted that, in practice, most grand prix racers don't make full use of the systems they have onboard. We have never heard that an integrated system placed very high on the list of things contributing to success in a race.

For local racing, a minimal integration—to get true wind speed—is feasible, but we doubt if a fully integrated system is a reasonable investment. The breakpoint, probably, is when you have a crewmember aboard who does nothing but navigate. If your crew work is not that specialized or sophisticated (if your navigator is also a sail trimmer or the helmsman, for example) you're unlikely ever to get the integrated system tuned well enough to be of real use during a race.

In cruising, we cannot see any practical use for an integrated system. The systems do not have the potential to make a major contribution to cruising methods or techniques. They will provide none of the revolutionary changes that seem to be coming from electronic navigation, like GPS for example. The potential of integrated systems is to make relatively small contributions to boat speed and to provide information of tactical value to the racing sailor. For the cruiser, that potential is scarcely practical.

Toying with the complex instrumentation and the software of the integrated system can be a time-consuming, fascinating pastime, a new upward modulation of the classic theme of "messing about in boats." The system will be very "practical" on a rainy day when you've got nothing else to do but sit below-decks and play.

VHF RADIOS

Although inexpensive compared to other pieces of electronic gear, the large number of choices can make the selection of a VHF radio difficult. We count twenty-three manufacturers currently marketing VHF radios in the United States, and another half-dozen retail companies selling radios under their own "house" labels. Almost all of them are made in Japan, Taiwan, or Korea, with just a few made in America or Europe.

The number of models varies from month to month, and even those rare models that stick around for several years will inevitably have changes made to their insides or outsides ("specifications subject to change without notice"). So even if a trusted friend recommends that you buy the model he's had success with, or if you want to replace a good radio that has been damaged, you may find it impossible to match.

After talking with engineers, manufacturers, and marketers, we've reached two conclusions regarding VHF marine radios. First, not surprisingly, the more expensive sets are of better quality than the cheaper sets. And second, for most sailors, the cheaper sets are perfectly adequate.

Are you the one in ten who should buy an expensive set? Or are you the more typical sailor who, we think, will find happiness with a cheap seat. The criteria offered below should help in choosing your set, and hopefully will keep the salesmen from bamboozling you.

Selection Criteria

What makes a better set better? To generalize, we can say that there are three areas to consider:
1) the amount of power that is put out in the form of the transmitted signal;
2) the ability of the radio to isolate and receive a signal; and
3) the auxiliary or "convenience" features.

Generally, better quality radios produce a stronger signal and do it more efficiently. They have more "sensitive" receivers, and they have more gimmicks, or "bells and whistles."

The Transmitter

By law, VHF radios onboard are limited to a maximum of 25 watts, and every full-sized radio on the market is nominally a 25-watt set. Every set must also be switchable to "low power" of one watt. Technicians who check the output of radios tell us that no radio actually produces 25 watts, though the most expensive ones come close.

Instead of 25 watts, high-power output in the range of 17 to 22 watts is more typical. Furthermore, output will vary somewhat. On a sailboat, the two big variables are power input from the 12-volt system and the antenna system.

With the engine and an alternator running, electricity going into the radio can be over 14 volts. But with the engine off and the batteries discharging, the radio can still be operated with the voltage down as low as 11 volts or even 10.5 volts. Although the radio will operate, the output power will drop whenever the voltage is low.

Since powerboats are the biggest market for VHF radios, the radios are generally optimized for operation at 13.8 volts which happens to be the "float" voltage of a fully charged battery, and is the voltage that a radio will actually receive most of the time on a powerboat underway. Although 13.8 is the nominal voltage, all VHF radios will operate adequately between about 10.8 and 16 volts.

Interestingly, none of the companies we talked with had tested their radios at the lower voltages typical of sailboats, and couldn't even tell us for sure which one of their own models would be best for us. But the engineers all believed that the higher-quality, higher-priced sets would operate slightly better at low voltage than the cheaper sets.

In addition, the long antenna cable leading from the navigation station to the masthead antenna on sailboats is another cause of power loss. Although a radio may put out 22 watts on a meter plugged into the back of the set, the same meter at the masthead may show only 18 or 19 watts output. Smaller diameter cables result in a greater loss than larger cables, and in a real-life situation, there is likely to be additional loss because of corrosion in the antenna or connectors and because of poorly soldered joints.

What does this all add up to when it comes to buying a radio? Engineers say that it doesn't add up to much. "As a matter of fact," one said, "with their high antennas, sailboats could operate 99 percent of the time on low power (one watt) and never know the difference."

The reason is that VHF frequencies produce radio waves that are relatively short and do not bend around the horizon, the way that longer (lower frequency) waves will. This means that the radio waves will generally travel only to the horizon, or to use the more common phrase, they are "line-of-sight" waves. (They actually travel about 15 percent further than light, or "sight," waves.) Of course, horizons are relative. If you are three feet above the water, your horizon is much closer than if you are 50 feet above the water.

The distance to the radio horizon is easily calculated: take the square root of the antenna's height and multiply it by 1.22. For example, an antenna at the masthead, 49 feet above the water, would have a range of 7 (the square root of 49) times 1.22, or 8.54 nautical miles. That would be the distance from your antenna to another antenna which was at sea level. If the other antenna is not at sea level—say at the top of another sailboat's mast—you would calculate that antenna's distance to the horizon and add the two distances together to get the maximum range between the two radios.

For shore stations, like the Coast Guard and marine operator, putting the antenna at the top of a 200-foot tower on a 300-foot hill obviously increases the range dramatically.

All of this is theoretical propagation of radio signals. Users commonly report 10-percent to 20-percent greater ranges, and it's hard to know if these reports are mere exaggerations or if the 1.22 multiplier is simply wrong. In any event, relatively little power is required to push the radio signal all the way to the horizon. One watt will do it almost all the time, and the greater range of Coast Guard and commercial land stations is primarily the result of their higher antennas rather than their greater (100 watt) power.

What a more powerful signal will do for you is to keep you from getting "stepped on." On any given frequency, only one signal can be heard at a time. You never get two signals at once, garbled together. In all cases, the stronger signal will be heard and the weaker signal blocked out, so if you are talking to someone and a stronger signal shows up, it will "step on" your signal, and the person you're talking to will hear only the other person's signal.

Overall, the difference between a set that produces 17 watts and one that sends out 24 will almost never be of any value in transmitting a message. In fact, one installer said flatly that sailors would be much better off if they would pay more attention to their antenna system rather than worrying about the power of their radios.

What about power in the handheld VHF radios? They all have a low-power, one-watt switch, but their high power isn't very high—typically between three and six watts. Although the salesman may tell you otherwise, there is really no significant advantage in choosing a six-watt rather than a five-, four-, or three-watt set.

The low antenna on the handheld will diminish the practical range anyway, and the extra watt or two will be of no value in keeping you from being stepped on by regular radios. It doesn't hurt to have the extra power, but it's not a good reason to choose one set over another.

The Receiver

Generally more important than transmitting power, is receiving ability. Every expert we talked to agreed that receiver sensitivity is of primary importance for fringe reception—when you're near the limits of line-of-sight distance. The closer you are to another radio, the less important sensitivity is, even though a more sensitive receiver will always "hear" better.

Another form of hearing quality, the ability to hear signals on one channel while rejecting those from adjacent channels, is also important. This is sometimes called "selectivity" to distinguish it from "sensitivity," although the two are related and represent one of the trade-offs inherent in receiver design.

Sensitivity is the radio's ability to accurately receive the radio signal amidst all the other electronic "noise." There are all sorts of noises around (within the circuitry of the set and in the atmosphere) and the set has to "quiet" that noise in order to hear the radio signal. (If you want to hear some of that noise, just turn down your radio's squelch control.)

Unfortunately, sensitivity is measured in a number of different ways, so comparing sets is not always easy. The most common way is to measure the strength of an incoming signal that is needed to overcome the radio noise in the receiver. What is measured is the ratio of signal to noise, or *SNR*. If a radio signal, measured in microvolts (µV), is twice as strong as the noise, you have a SNR of 2 to 1. For VHF radios, a signal 100 times as strong as the noise will overcome all noise and is often referred to as "full quieting."

The 100 to 1 ratio is not expressed as 100:1, but instead in a mathematical calculation of decibels (dB). The formula is dB = 10 log (signal strength/noise strength). If you use 100/1 in that formula, you end up with 20 dB, which is the level usually stipulated in receiver specifications of full quieting. In looking at the 20 dB quieting specifications, remember that the lower the number for microvolts, the weaker the signal it can hear, and the more sensitive the receiver is.

Increasingly, manufacturers are using a different measure of sensitivity which they've called the "SINAD" ratio. Rather than signal to noise, it is a measure of "voice modulation" to noise; that is, how well the receiver can hear the speech that is carried by the signal. The typical ratio used is 12 dB, which is a ratio of 16 to 1.

What difference does sensitivity make? There will be a significant reduction in range with a less sensitive receiver. Frederick Graves, in his *Big Book of Marine Electronics*, calculated the likely range at which radios could receive a signal from a 25-watt transmitter, given identical antennas. An expensive radio with a sensitivity of 0.25µV at 12 dB SINAD (among the most sensitive on the market), could hear the signal at 22 miles. A cheaper radio with a sensitivity of 0.5 µV at 12 dB SINAD (typical of the lower-priced sets), could only hear the signal to a distance of 16.5 miles.

For the primary purposes of VHF, the minor differences in sensitivity are almost insignificant, particularly in light of the major differences in the cost of the equipment. For safety calls, your transmitter will likely reach to the limits of your line-of-sight range, and the Coast Guard's and shore station's high antennas and good receivers will hear you, even though you might not hear them when you're at the fringes. And for navigation calls, your receiver is likely to hear any ship or other boat that is anywhere within range of being a navigational concern.

For the less essential uses of VHF—calling friends, reserving dock space, harassing the race committee—each individual has to decide whether the greater sensitivity and greater range is worth the cost.

Unfortunately, it is difficult to come up with specifications to compare. Most catalogs don't list these specs, so you have to visit a dealer, write the manufacturer, or pick up a brochure and hope the specs are there. Then, the available specs are often not directly comparable. While knowledgeable electronics people believe that "speech-to-noise" (the SINAD ratio) is a more important measure of quality than "signal to noise," some manufacturers don't report the SINAD ratios at all, while others list it along with the "full quiet" ratio. Fortunately for the consumers, receiver sensitivity generally follows price. If you feel you need that extra sensitivity, you're pretty sure to get it at the high end of the price scale.

There are several other characteristics that will vary in receivers: rejecting adjacent channels, squelch sensitivity, the amount of hum and noise, the ability to reject "images" produced by the receiver and not by an incoming signal, audio output, and so on. While these all are potential problems, none is as important as receiver sensitivity, so sensitivity is the key figure to look at if you're one of those 10 percent who want or need a high-quality radio.

"Bells and Whistles"

To take the least important last, consider the auxiliary or "convenience" features. The most obvious differences between a VHF radio that sells for $150 and one that sells for $500, are nonessential features that are intended to make the radio easier to use in some way (although often they make the set more complicated in some other way):

CHANNEL SCANNING. This features allows the receiver to "scan" through all the channels, listening for someone talking. When the radio hears a signal, it stops on that channel until the transmission stops, at which points it resumes scanning. More sophisticated models let you select which channels you want the radio to scan.

In practice, this feature is relatively useless on weekends during the season, simply because of the intense traffic on the pleasure-boat channels. Channel 16 may be so busy that the radio is never able to scan past it. But by law you are required to monitor channel 16 whenever your radio is turned on; programmable scanning can be helpful if you wish to monitor another channel in addition to channel 16.

CHANNEL 16 REVERT. This can take several forms. At its simplest, it is a button which you push to listen and talk on Channel 16. When the button is off, you use the channel dial normally. This can be convenient if you would otherwise have to turn a knob through 30 channels or press some combination of keys to move from 16 to a working channel.

Other sets will automatically revert to channel 16 when a working channel has been silent for a while, and a few will revert when you hang up the microphone or handset.

U.S./INTERNATIONAL CHANNELS. There are 55 channels (broadcast and receive frequencies) assigned for marine use by the federal government. Of these, 40 are usable internationally. The other 15 are only usable in U.S. waters since the international versions of these channels use different frequencies. In addition, almost all modern sets offer up to ten "receive only" channels, sometimes called "weather channels," even though U.S. weather broadcasts are currently limited to three channels.

Almost all sets on the market today offer the 55 transmit and receive channels and the weather channels. For a slightly higher price, you can usually buy a similar set which offers the extra international channels.

It should be noted that of the 55 channels, 19 are not for pleasure boat use, but instead are restricted to "commercial" or "official government" use. Then, 10 channels are set aside for marine operator use, and 14 are reserved for specific uses, such as talking with the Coast Guard or for "port operations." Channels 16 and 6 are set aside for calling and safety. In short, out of the 55 channels, you can only legally use a handful on your boat, for normal talking. Most of the international channels would be similarly restricted.

Obviously, if you don't intend to leave the U.S., the international channels will be useless. If you are planning to sail in the waters of a foreign country, you can easily get by with only the U.S. channels, since 40 of them—including all the essential ones like 6 and 16—are also international channels. The extra cost of the foreign channels is usually so small, however, that they may be worth buying if you intend to travel through a variety of foreign countries.

There are still a few sets available with fewer than 55 channels, usually with 30 to 40. They are worth considering, since the eliminated channels are ones you would rarely or never use. But, given the economics of volume, the limited channel set has a dim future and it will be increasingly difficult to find.

CONTROLS AND DISPLAYS. The variations in controls and displays basically comes down to knobs, buttons, or keys and LED or LCD displays. One look at the available radios shows there's no clear choice on the controls.

The membrane keypad is generally considered superior in use and reliability to the best knobs and buttons, but a high-quality twist knob is better than a cheap membrane keypad. "Feel" will give you a crude indication of quality, assuming you can get two sets side-by-side, but there is no sure way to tell if you're getting better or worse.

Most engineers believe that the quality of the knobs or keypads generally follows price, but in choosing between two similarly priced radios, you are entirely dependant on the integrity of the company. Fortunately, most pleasure-boat radios are used seldom enough that wear and tear is not a significant factor on the knobs and keys; however, this is the one area where the high-priced sets will generally outlive the low-priced sets.

For the displays, light-emitting diodes (LEDs) are cheaper than liquid crystal displays (LCDs), but both work well. For the sailor, the LCD displays are sometimes preferable just because the light in them can be shut off during the day. Given the efficiency of modern electronics, the lights for the radio dial often use up more power than the radio itself when it is on standby. However, for normal cruising, power consumption is so minimal that it's not a significant concern.

PACKAGE. How the radio is packaged is your choice; there is a great variety in physical size, shape, color, and appearance. Your choice will depend partly on where you're going to install the radio in the boat, and partly on taste.

Most radios are designed for console-mounting on a powerboat, and a buyer should look at some of the potential problems in installing the radio in a sailboat. For example, your choices for installation may be limited by the size and shape of the mounting bracket, the location of the speaker, and the location of the receptacles for the microphone, antenna, and power cord.

The best choice for each of these will depend on where you install the radio. If you have a large navigation station, you'll obviously have more room than if you want to tuck it in a nook above a quarter berth, to keep it out of the weather but still accessible to the cockpit.

While most of these choices are cosmetic, a few can compromise the use of the receiver. For example, if the speaker is muffled by being installed against a bulkhead adjacent to the engine compartment, the radio may be virtually unusable while you're underway, or you may have to add an auxiliary speaker in the cockpit if you want to hear it.

OTHER CONSIDERATIONS. Warranties do vary. Not surprisingly, the more expensive sets have better warranties than the cheaper sets. Even though VHF radios are quite reliable, the warranties are worth comparing if you can't decide between two otherwise nearly equal sets.

Service from the manufacturers also varies. Most noticeably, only the more expensive lines are available through local electronics dealers. Most cheaper sets are available through discount houses or by mailorder, and owner-installation and owner-troubleshooting is assumed. Sailors who "hire out" most of their work may not be able to buy a cheap set from a local electronics dealer. (Service is generally better from a local dealer than from a discount house, but usually the dealer will do little more than box up the radio and ship it to the manufacturer's service center.)

There's a general feeling among electronics experts that the Japanese-made sets are best, with the Taiwan/American/European sets not far behind, and the Korean and other Oriental sets a distant third, but there seems to be no hard evidence to back up that feeling.

Antennas

For a sailboat, masthead installation is generally preferred because of the increased range which comes from height. Some racers prefer to mount the antenna on the stern rail, thinking that they will reduce windage aloft and also have a good antenna installation in case they are dismasted. Most find that the loss of range is not very significant in actual use.

Where ever you mount it, you want it to be a "low-gain" antenna. "Gain" refers to the way the radiating signal can be focused. A no-gain antenna radiates in all directions—straight up toward the heavens and straight down toward the water, as well as horizontally to other boats. When you increase the gain, you focus the radiation increasingly toward the horizontal. The most commonly available antennas are low-gain (3 dB), medium-gain (6 dB), or high-gain (9 dB). The higher-gain (6 and 9 dB) antennas are generally impractical for sailboats. They focus the radiated signal too much—in a narrow horizontal pattern.

Though it is not so readily available, heavier (RG8U) coaxial cable is better than the more common (RG58U) cable for antenna wire, especially in long runs to the masthead. It will cost twice as much, but it is a worthwhile investment on a sailboat. Good soldering of the antenna connections is essential; in fact, the chief causes of poor radio performance and transmission problems are poor connectors.

Every sailboat should carry an emergency antenna in case of dismasting. Compact roll-up coils are available, or you can make one out of a piece of heavy wire, like a coat hanger. Just cut the wire to 18-inches, bend the bottom 3/4-inch at a right angle, and insert it in the antenna outlet at the back of the set. You must be sure that the antenna wire does not "short" across from the center hole of the antenna outlet to the edge. As with antenna wire, the center carries the signal and the outer edge is the shielding. Short across them and you've got a worthless antenna.

* * *

With no two sets alike, there is an astounding combination of features available—so much so that a buyer's response is more likely to be confusion, rather than a considered choice of the desired elements.

For most sailors, we recommend one of the lower-priced 55-channel sets. In terms of quality, the low-price sets are nearly enough equal that there is no clear choice among brands or models. We recommend that you consider the specifications and features, in order to choose one that is good looking, fits the available space, and serves your needs.

When should you consider a more expensive set? If you have specific uses for an additional feature, like channel scanning, or international channels, or compact size, you will have to spend more. If you expect to operate often at maximum range and the limits of reception, you will have to spend more yet to get the highest quality receiver and the higher powered transmitter. If you want a prestige brand with good local service, you'll have to spend even more.

With all the variables, it is difficult to quantify things, but we think of it this way: For $200 or less, you can get everything in a VHF you need. Double that expenditure and you will get a better set—but nothing like twice as good.

HANDHELD VHF RADIOS

What is true of full-size sets generally holds true for the handhelds. We would add just a few considerations.

For the daysailer or weekender, a handheld VHF makes a lot of sense as the primary radio. The addition of a masthead antenna would remove the chief shortcoming of the handheld—its limited range. With an extra battery pack, the radio could provide for fairly extensive use for a weekend of sailing.

For the larger boat, the handheld can serve as a good backup and emergency radio. Many offshore and singlehanded races are now requiring one, to be taken along if you must take to the life raft. For most sailors, however, the primary use is in the cockpit, to reduce the number of times you have to run below to the navigation station to make or answer a call.

Many people use the radio as a personal "ship-to-shore" system. Although sellers never say a word about it, using the handheld off the boat is illegal. And without the required ship's station license and call letters, every call made from the handheld when in the dinghy or ashore is technically a violation and subject to fines and impoundment of equipment, though we have not heard of anyone being prosecuted. Enforcement has been lax during the recent "budget-cutting" years. Nonetheless, if you buy one for such uses, you should be aware of the law. The FCC is under increasing pressure about the crowded marine bands, and enforcement practices could change overnight.

Another consideration for handhelds is the method of recharging. While all come with some sort of shore-power charger, you will have to buy or adapt some means of recharging the handheld's battery when it is aboard the boat and shore power is not available. It's confusing because there is no standard battery voltage for the handhelds. the most expensive sets operate on 12 volts, and can be plugged directly into the ship's system, but most operate on 10.8-volt batteries. A few operate at other voltages, so an adapter is required to charge up the radio using the ship's supply. In addition, the plug-in jacks come in half a dozen different shapes and sizes, so making up adapters is a nuisance. (Radio Shack sells a multivoltage unit with several jacks that should work in most situations.)

Finally, all the handhelds need to be protected from water when outside. There are special heavy-duty plastic bags sold for the purpose, but an ordinary zip-lock bag will also serve.

HAM AND SINGLE SIDEBAND RADIOS

Sailors generally know about short-range radio communication, since the standard VHF radiotelephone is relatively cheap, effective, and found on almost every cruising sailboat. Once beyond the 30- to 40-mile range of VHF, however, a sailor must choose a different kind of radio if he wants to communicate with another yacht or the rest of the world. For longer-range or "worldwide" communication, the sailor has a choice: amateur radio (ham) or marine single sideband (SSB).

Frequency Bands and Range

Ham radio operators and mariners are allocated side-by-side frequency bands in the worldwide spectrum. On these bands, their type of radio transmission is called "single sideband."

This is a type of amplitude modulation (AM, as opposed to the frequency modulation, or FM, of your VHF radio) that is best suited for long-range ionospheric "skip" communications, where the radio signals do not follow the earth's curvature (groundwave), but instead bounce off the ionosphere and return to the earth thousands of miles away (see **Figure 6-2**). Depending on the frequency band you choose, this type of voice radio communication will bounce all over the world, for excellent long-range voice transmissions, day or night.

Figure 6-3 illustrates the relationship between the worldwide marine frequencies and the worldwide ham frequencies. The marine bands of frequencies are located approximately one MegaHertz above each ham radio band of frequencies. The lower bands are best suited for long-range nighttime communications. The higher bands offer worldwide communications during the day.

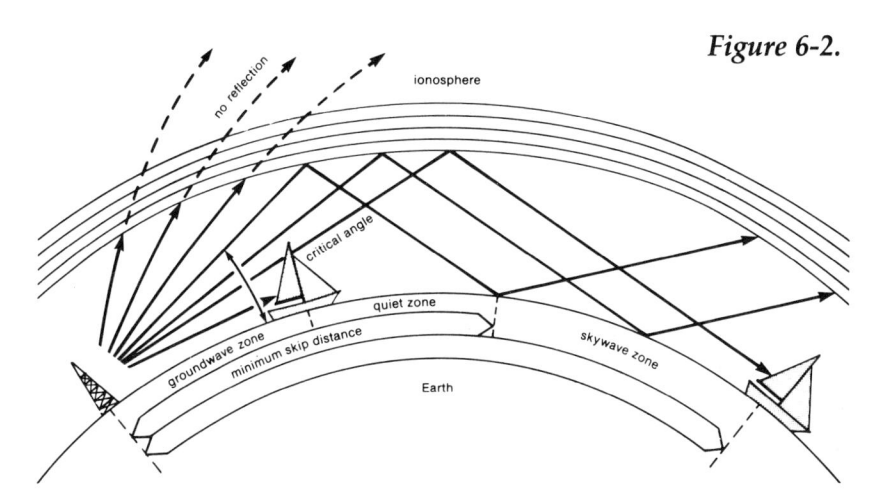

Figure 6-2.

Figure 6-3.

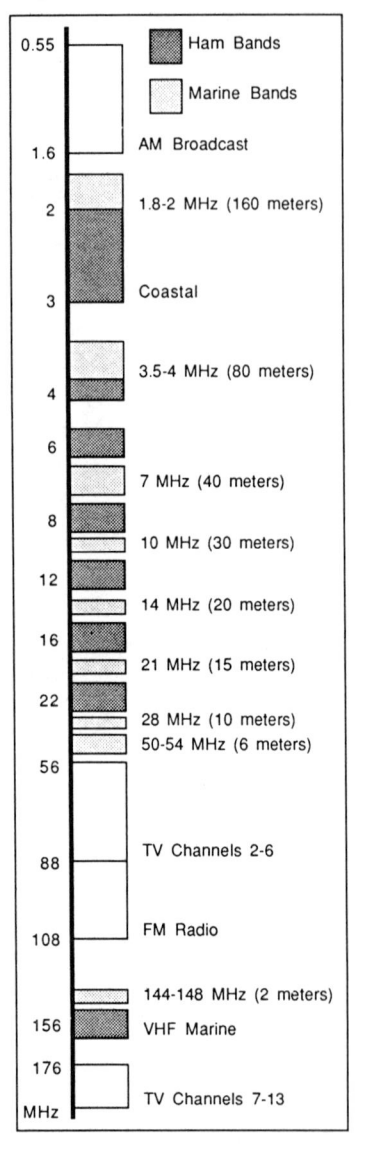

MHz	Band
0.55 – 1.6	AM Broadcast
1.8–2 MHz (160 meters)	Ham / Marine
2 – 3	Coastal (Marine)
3.5–4 MHz (80 meters)	Ham
7 MHz (40 meters)	Ham
10 MHz (30 meters)	Ham
14 MHz (20 meters)	Ham
21 MHz (15 meters)	Ham
28 MHz (10 meters)	Ham
50–54 MHz (6 meters)	Ham
56 – 88	TV Channels 2-6
88 – 108	FM Radio
144–148 MHz (2 meters)	Ham
156 – 176	VHF Marine
176 –	TV Channels 7-13

■ Ham Bands □ Marine Bands

FCC Regulations

To operate a single sideband radio on marine worldwide frequencies, you need only your regular FCC ship's station license, with no test involved. This is the same license assigned to your VHF radio.

When you put a marine single sideband radio on board, you need to modify your existing license if it covers only VHF. You use FCC Form 506 to modify your license, for 2000 KiloHertz to 23,000 KiloHertz marine single sideband privileges. You will use the same call letters on marine single sideband as you do for your marine VHF set. There is no longer a personal operator's permit required. The amateur radio license for ham frequencies requires an entrance examination. The Novice license, now allows for voice communications on one worldwide band and two bands which use "repeaters," devices which re-broadcast shorter range signals. (Previously, the Novice license only permitted the use of Morse code.)

The Novice license is easily obtained with home study courses. The requirements are competence in the International Morse code at a rate of five words per minute, and elementary radio theory and knowledge of radio regulations. You do not need to go to the FCC to take your entry-level ham test. The 30-question, multiple-choice examination, and the Morse code exam, is now given by two fellow hams.

For full worldwide ham radio privileges on every ham band, you will need the "General class" license. For most people, the General class requires about two months of study after they have passed the Novice test. The Morse code requirement is 13 words per minute, and a passing grade on a 25-question, multiple-choice exam is required for the General. The theory could be memorized quite easily in a few weeks, but the code at 13 words per minute takes most people some time to master. The General class examination is also given by a team of three volunteer ham examiners. It can be administered anywhere in the world, providing the three hams are registered with Volunteer Examination Coordination (VEC).

Ham or Marine SSB?

Given that considerably more effort is required to become an amateur radio operator, the main question for most people will be, "Is it worthwhile becoming a ham?"

If you don't plan to do a lot of talking, you may wish to forego studying to become a ham. If you only want your marine long-range radio for safety calls to the Coast Guard and an occasional telephone call to your office on shore, then go with the single sideband set and forget about ham.

But, if you are into gadgets and enjoy twiddling knobs, you might find amateur radio fascinating. More importantly for the sailor, if you wish to use your radio to gab with other sailors and discuss weather conditions and interesting ports of call, then you should plan to become an amateur radio operator. It is on the ham bands that most talk among cruisers will be heard.

If you decide to become a ham operator, first get the Novice license. Even if you go no further than Novice, this gives you call letters and will put you on the air, using voice on some frequencies. Although the Novice class doesn't give you all the worldwide bands here in the U.S., some countries will issue a reciprocal license with worldwide privileges, based on just your Novice permit. For example, if you cruise to Mexico with just the Novice, you may obtain the General-type Mexican license that allows you voice privileges on all worldwide ham bands.

The ideal license is the General class. Though this will take some hard work, it will be worth it for the serious cruiser. The

General class license allows you to talk on all worldwide frequencies and receive full reciprocal operating privileges when you visit other countries. It is necessary to check in with each country's communications office before operating within their jurisdictional waters, but hams can do this ahead of time by writing to the American Radio Relay League, Reciprocal Licensing Division, Newington, CT 06111.

Can You Cheat?

It's quite true that it is no longer possible to determine anyone's grade of license when they operate with their beginning set of call letters. Hams now can keep their original set of call letters, all the way through the highest Extra Class license (formerly, Novices had distinctive call signs). How will anyone know if a Novice is operating on General Class frequencies? Only if someone were to call the FCC and request the license data. Ham radio call books are perpetually a year behind in upgrade information.

An exception is the organized maritime mobile networks where most of the cruisers communicate. Attempting to operate through one of these nets will soon lead to discovery. Most maritime net control operators routinely check with the FCC on all new members, and they are quite clear that they will work only with stations with General class (or higher) privileges, even though they may be in international waters. The FCC rules still apply to any vessel flying a U.S. flag, regardless of where it is.

Aside from the maritime nets, most hams don't bother to check on the license class of others with whom they talk, however, the last thing you want to do is to use someone else's call sign or simply dream one up. If you plan to operate on ham radio, at least get your Novice license, and use your own call sign.

Where to Buy Ham

While marine SSB sets are easily bought through the discount houses that specialize in marine electronics, most sailors have no idea where to go for ham equipment.

There are numerous discount mailorder dealers that sell ham equipment at very low prices. Their ads can be seen in any one of the several ham radio magazines that you can pick up at a ham radio store.

The least likely place to find ham radio equipment is at a marine electronics dealer. They generally don't like ham radio, and they usually refuse to sell it, feeling that ham radio set-ups are cheating them out of their marine single sideband business. It's unfortunate, but many of these marine electronics dealers will also refuse to install a ham set. Ham sets install exactly like a typical marine single sideband set. However, if you're looking for a professional installation, it's worth searching for a marine electronics dealer who will do it.

Purchasing equipment directly from Japan is not advisable. Many Japanese transceivers not intended for export do not contain the same frequency band limits that we have here. What might seem like a good deal there could be only half a radio here.

Ham and SSB: Comparison of Use and Features

Worldwide amateur radio transceivers and worldwide marine single sideband sets are very similar in circuitry; in fact, both sets possess identical operating characteristics: power output of 120 watts, single sideband transmission, frequency capabilities from 1 to 30 MHz, all transistorized, and 10 Hz frequency stability. On the air, both sets sound identical to a listener; it would be literally impossible to detect by listening whether the equipment in use was a ham or a marine single sideband set.

Among mariners thinking about using a ham set for marine radio applications, there has been a concern about frequency stability, but modern ham sets will stay on channel as well as marine single sideband. A modern ham set would also be far superior to older sideband sets using crystal frequency selection.

Set Operation

Although the ham and marine sideband sets sound the same on the air, the likeness does not carry over to how they operate.

Dialing channels and tuning into marine radio calls on a marine single sideband is easy. The marine sideband sets are designed to be almost foolproof. There is nothing to fine tune. Turn the set on, select the marine channel by channel number, adjust the volume, push the mike button, and you are on the air.

When you operate your set on marine telephone and Coast Guard channels, your set automatically switches itself to "duplex" operation, separating the transmit and receive frequencies for these services. The sideband sets also have companion antenna tuners that achieve the best match between your set and your antenna system. Again, this is all done automatically.

Not so with a ham radio. The first problem is tuning to the exact frequencies—not by channel number but in MegaHertz and KiloHertz. If you are a little off, you will soon be detected and probably won't hear the station you are calling. For the marine channels, you must calculate the frequencies. (The better ham sets allow you to store those calculated frequencies into memory channels for repeated use.)

Second, the ham set must be dialed in for the proper sideband. Upper sideband operation is used on the marine frequencies. But on ham bands, lower frequencies use lower sideband, so you must be careful that you have the right sideband selected.

For high seas marine operator and Coast Guard transmissions, you must set your ham radio for split-frequency operation. This does not make for ease of operation. First it requires loading the receive frequency into VFO-A and the transmit frequency into VFO-B. Then you switch back to VFO-A and set the split switch. Then go to VFO-B and tune the antenna tuner. Then back to VFO-A to begin receiving. Then, on most sets there are about five knobs that will improve or smear incoming reception—five knobs that must be adjusted exactly.

In operation, it boils down to this: if you plan to get your ham radio license and you like fooling around with dials and knobs, the ham radio set will probably serve you best. However, if you don't like radios in the first place, and you just want to grab the mike and place a call for help, your best bet is a marine SSB.

"Crossing the Barrier"

Operationally, it's easy to use a ham radio for marine frequencies, and vice versa, although it is illegal. The FCC does not allow a ham set to be operated legally on marine frequencies because it does not carry the necessary type-acceptance for marine operation. When you fill out your blue FCC marine form 506 to get a ship's license, you check a box that states you will use only type-accepted equipment on the marine airwaves.

However, most amateur radio operators go ahead and make

the modification of the ham radio equipment so it has the capability of transmitting on these marine frequencies "in an emergency." It would not be illegal for a ham to modify his equipment for this emergency purpose. It would only be illegal if the operator were to go on the marine airwaves with ham equipment, with no emergency at hand.

The FCC rules also prohibit ham-radio capabilities in a marine single sideband set. This rule is very strange, as marine sideband meets all the FCC's stringent rules, so why not use it for the ham service as well? The regulations state that a ham installation shall be separate from a marine radio installation. (We have never heard of anyone getting a ticket from the FCC for having some ham frequencies programmed into their marine radio.) The FCC refuses to overturn this rule because they state that cluttering a marine set with ham frequencies could cause the marine set to be less effective on marine channels.

Although most marine sideband sets are difficult to modify for ham radio reception, with some (like the ICOM M-700) you don't even need to remove the cover to punch in marine frequencies or to switch to lower sideband.

Installing Ham and SSB

Most sailors install their own VHF radios with few difficulties. Bad soldering of the end fittings on the antenna coaxial cable is about the only serious problem that occurs regularly. However, because of their operating frequencies and their higher power, marine single sideband and ham radios are trickier to install than VHF radios, and their performance depends more heavily on the quality of the installation—particularly the antenna, the antenna tuner, and the grounding.

The non-technical sailor should consider having the radio installed professionally, even though this can be very expensive. (In the busy season, a rush job can cost you one-third of the price of the radio equipment.) For sailors who do most of their own maintenance and other work on board, owner-installation is definitely feasible. However, a serious study of the manual beforehand is recommended.

7

Safety Equipment

PERSONAL FLOTATION DEVICES

Most sailors hate to wear life jackets. We don't like to think of the time when we might need one. We don't see ourselves floundering in the water. We can't imagine the terror of trying to catch a boat that blows downwind faster than we can swim. Neither do we see ourselves sinking face-down with the imprint of the boom on the back of our heads as the rest of the family struggles to pull us onto a five-foot-high deck.

Like poor drivers who refuse to wear safety belts, poor swimmers too often are the last to wear life jackets. Instead of facing the real dangers, most sailors associate life jackets with a humorous image of the stereotypical novice sailor.

The problem is that modern life jackets, although more comfortable than those of a decade ago, are still too cumbersome to suit most people. The United States Coast Guard may insist that life jackets be aboard all recreational boats, but they do not require that they be worn. Because of the current standards for Coast Guard-approval, and the unwillingness of life jacket manufacturers to construct non-approved devices, the few truly comfortable personal flotation devices (PFDs) are imported from Europe.

When deciding whether or not to don a PFD, sailors must think hard about what they would do if they fell over the side. When deciding what type of life jacket to wear, sailors must be honest with themselves about their swimming abilities, and take a close look at their physical condition and the climate in which they will be sailing.

The History of Coast Guard Regulation

The Coast Guard didn't concern itself with life jackets for recreational sailors until fairly recently. It has been regulating commercial vessels since 1852, when a law was passed requiring river steamers to carry floats for each passenger aboard. In 1940, the Motorboat Act was passed which required life jackets on recreational powerboats.

The Coast Guard claims that by 1940, it had realized that the commercial boater and the recreational boater needed different types of life jackets. The commercial vessel tended to meet with disaster farther offshore, so presumably the passengers would be in the water longer before rescue and hence need more buoyancy. The fact that more flotation means more bulk was not a concern because commercial vessels sink slower, so their passengers would only have to wear a vest in an emergency.

The recreational boater has different needs. He usually sails closer to shore, so if he were to find himself in the water he could expect to be rescued sooner. This means he needs a jacket with less flotation (how much less is a matter on which we disagree with the Coast Guard). A jacket with less flotation will be less bulky and hence can be comfortably worn at all times. This is important because a small boat sinks or capsizes quickly and rarely allows time to dig out and put on a PFD.

Even though the Coast Guard claims it came to this revelation nearly 30 years ago, it wasn't until 1955 that it established standards for life preservers for recreational boaters. These standards mandated the buoyant vest shaped like a horsecollar. While this type of PFD may have been marginally more comfortable than the "Mae West" jacket on commercial vessels, it is difficult to understand how the Coast Guard could have reasoned that anyone would wear these horsecollars in anything short of a near gale.

The Coast Guard had critics, most notably Maurice O'Link, founder and Chairman of the Board of Stearns Manufacturing Company (a major manufacturer of PFDs). O'Link says the Coast Guard, federal government, and even much of the industry deliberately dragged their feet when it came to solving the problem of developing more comfortable life jackets for the recreational boater. Through Stearns, O'Link produced non-approved life vests from 1964 to 1971. They became so popular among small boat sailors that the Coast Guard had to admit that the Stearns life vest was more effective in saving lives than the uncomfortable horsecollars that were never worn.

Finally, in 1971, the Federal Boat Safety Act was passed. When it went into effect on October 1, 1973, recreational sailors were legally freed from the confines of the horsecollar life jacket and were allowed to carry the modern lightweight life vest. With the Federal Boat Safety Act in force, the federal government was satisfied that the recreational boater was adequately protected. We disagree.

The Law Today

The 1971 Federal Boat Safety Act requires at least one serviceable, readily accessible, Coast Guard-approved PFD for each person aboard a boat. There are four different types of approved PFDs. A Type I PFD is the most uncomfortable and bulky. It is designed to make an unconscious person float on his back so he can still breathe. Type I vests have been common on commercial vessels and military vessels for many years. They are not well suited for sailboats because they take up too much space and practically immobilize the wearer.

A Type II PFD is what we all know as the traditional horsecollar design. Like a Type I device, the Type II PFD also is designed to turn an unconscious person from a face-down to face-up position. However, the motion is not as pronounced. This is the least expensive type life jacket and hence (unfortunately) the most popular. When worn, it is uncomfortable, and makes working on a sailboat awkward. We would recommend a Type II PFD only for the sailor who wants to wear a non-approved life vest but still needs to carry a cheap approved PFD in order to comply with the law.

In concept, the Type III PFD is a minimum-bulk life vest that doesn't inhibit activity such as fishing, sailing, and waterskiing. The theory is that the best life jacket is the one you wear—logic that may seem hard to fault—but the fact is that these types of life jackets have so little flotation that they are more likely to engender a false sense of security than they are to provide genuine lifesaving capabilities.

The most damning evidence comes from the U.S. Coast Guard itself. In Commandant Notice 10470, issued in 1984, the Coast Guard warned its personnel that their own experiments had shown that float coats and other Type III devices were inadequate to keep test subjects comfortably afloat for periods exceeding half an hour. The Type IIIs have adequate buoyancy, the report notes, to keep one's head above water in calm seas, but they could not provide similar flotation in rougher waters.

A dramatic film provided to the editors of *The Practical Sailor* by Wayne Williams of the National Transportation Safety Association shows similar testing carried out in a recreational wave-generating pool. Despite the fact that the "waves" were really only 3- to 4-foot non-breaking swells, the test subject's head is clearly a foot or more underwater at regular intervals as the swells roll over him. An unconscious or semiconscious person would quickly drown in these conditions.

Ironically, crews aboard boats of the Naval Academy Sailing Squadron which sail offshore do not wear Coast Guard-approved PFDs. Instead, they carry belt-mounted U.S. Navy inflatable flotation devices which provide 32 pounds of buoyancy—twice that of any Coast Guard Type III flotation device. The Annapolis boats are still required to carry Coast Guard-approved PFDs to comply with the law, but you can be sure that no midshipman will rely on one if the Navy device is available.

The U.S. has lagged far behind other countries in the development of lifesaving equipment, and personal flotation devices are no exception. In Europe, one of the most common life jackets is an inflatable device providing roughly 35 pounds of flotation. These are similar to the inflatable life jackets found under the seats of commercial airliners. Until inflated, they do not inhibit activity and are actually lighter than many Type III PFDs. European standards also recognize life jackets similar to our own Type I PFDs.

There has been a great reluctance on the part of the Coast Guard to approve inflatable devices for use here. The argument is that inflatable life preservers require fairly careful handling, and need to be professionally inspected at reasonable intervals to make sure they will function properly. American PFDs, which usually depend on flexible, non-absorbent foam for flotation, are subject to and survive incredible amounts of abuse, such as being sat upon, jammed into cockpit lockers, and punctured. The fact is that you can't treat an inflatable device that way.

But when push comes to shove, it isn't that hard to take care of a PFD, to have a special locker that isn't jammed full of other stuff as a storage space for life preservers, and to take them in the off-season to an inspection station to be examined. It's a reasonable trade-off for the security a "real" life preserver provides.

A Type IV PFD is a device designed to be thrown to a person in the water. Seat cushions and life rings fall into this category. The law says that on a boat smaller than 16 feet in length, any one of the four types for each crew member will suffice. If you sail a boat bigger than 16 feet, you must carry a Type I, II, or III device for every person on board and a single Type IV device as well.

"Adequate" Flotation

How much flotation do you really need? Since the body is mostly water, most people are neutrally buoyant when their lungs are full of air and their heads are immersed. Replace the air in your lungs with water, and you sink. People with a low percentage of body fat, are likely to be slightly negatively buoyant under the best conditions.

Often ignored is the difference in specific gravity of saltwater and fresh water. Pure fresh water has a specific gravity of 1.000, while the nominal specific gravity of saltwater is 1.028. What this means is that you float deeper in fresh water than in saltwater, and therefore need more buoyancy in a PFD that will be used in fresh water.

The problem, of course, is to keep an overboard crewmember's head well above water. Without a life jacket, a healthy person can keep his or her head above water for a long time in warm, calm water by treading water; while an injured person in cold water is likely to succumb in minutes. Adequate flotation is particularly important for an injured person. The more buoyancy a PFD has, the higher it will float the crewmember in the water. The higher he floats, the less likely it is that his face and head will be submerged by waves.

Type III: "Vest" PFDs

The Type III PFD is usually a contoured vest filled with a thin sheet of flexible foam. It is the most comfortable to wear and the least restrictive of movement of all PFDs, but it provides at best marginal protection for someone in the water. Its buoyancy of 15 to 17 pounds is likely to be just barely adequate to keep your head above water. You will find that you probably have to tread water to keep your nose and mouth constantly clear with a Type III PFD, particularly if the surface of the water is rough.

The only advantage of the Type III PFD is that it does not restrict movement. This is important for activities such as dinghy sailing or boardsailing. But the flotation provided by Type III devices is so minimal that they should only be used under carefully controlled conditions, such as a yacht club sailing program where a crash boat is standing by, so that there is a high likelihood of immediate rescue.

It is misleading to equip non-swimming friends aboard your boat with Type III PFDs. People don't usually fall overboard in flat calm conditions. Injury or unconsciousness are not unusual in man-overboard cases, particularly in cold water and rough conditions. The physical activity required to keep your head above water when wearing a Type III device can cause you to lose body-core temperature, accelerating the onset of hypothermia. According to Williams, hypothermia is a major contributing cause in most cases of drowning.

In our opinion, Type III PFDs should not be used as primary life-saving devices aboard any boat larger than a sailing dinghy or boardboat. They should never be used by children, or in unsupervised conditions where immediate rescue may not be possible. Using Type III PFDs to meet Coast Guard requirements for personal flotation devices aboard your boat is irresponsible.

Type II: "Yoke" PFDs

The most common PFD found aboard most pleasure boats is the Type II, the familiar bib or yoke PFD, available at discount department stores, marine chandleries, and anywhere that sells anything remotely related to boating. Type II PFDs have almost the same buoyancy as Type III PFDs (minimum buoyancy is 15-1/2 pounds) but their design is such that, in theory, they will turn an unconscious person face-up in the water. Part of the flotation material is behind your neck, and the rest is on the forward side of your upper body, which means that you should float face upwards without having to work at it.

However, tests by *Consumer Reports* in 1982 showed that most Type II devices will not turn your face upwards without some effort on your part, meaning that an unconscious person could easily drown while wearing a Type II life jacket. In addition, since the buoyancy of a Type II device is the same as that of the Type III device, you are still faced with the problem of having to work to keep your head above water, particularly if there are any waves.

Because Type II devices are bulkier than Type IIIs, they are less likely to be worn by your crew unless you require it. Most people—even non-swimmers—are self-conscious about wearing PFDs. Wearing a PFD implies that sailing is somehow dangerous, rather than purely fun, or that the wearer is somehow not up to the sport. How many boat ads have you seen where the people aboard are wearing life jackets? How many boats have you seen with crews actually wearing life jackets?

Type II PFDs offer a marginal advantage over Type III devices, but not enough to make them useful in conditions any worse than those prescribed for Type III devices. It's a $5 to $10 PFD, and that's about the amount of protection you get.

Type I: "Mae West" PFDs

The Type I PFD provides a minimum of 22 pounds of buoyancy. Type I PFDs will float you face-up, and will hold your head above water with no effort on your part. In rough water, however, wave action is sure to keep you underwater part of the time.

Type I PFDs are bulky, and generally cost about $25 to $30. Most offshore sailors carry them to meet the Coast Guard requirements, but few wear a Type I device as a matter of course: they're simply too bulky. However, Type I PFDs are the only Coast Guard-approved personal flotation devices that give an injured or unconscious person a reasonable chance of survival.

The distinction between an unconscious person and a dead person is a very important one. The time between the onset of hypothermia and the unconsciousness that follows varies with the water temperature, physical condition, and a host of other variables. Once unconscious, however, you're not yet dead. There is a substantial time period between unconsciousness and death due to hypothermia, and you might well be rescued during that time—if you don't drown in the meantime. If you're wearing a Type II or Type III PFD and you lose consciousness, you're probably as good as dead. If you happen to be floating face upwards when you lose consciousness wearing a Type II PFD, you many not drown in flat calm waters. But if seas are washing over you and you are submerged part of the time—which you almost definitely will be in anything other than a flat calm—you're likely to drown sooner wearing a Type II device than if you were wearing the more protective Type I PFD.

There's a certain irony to the fact that the Coast Guard-approved personal flotation devices carried by a significant number of pleasure boats offer minimal protection to anyone except a healthy, uninjured person in calm waters for a fairly short period of time. If the Coast Guard sees fit to warn its own personnel that Type III PFDs are inadequate, they owe the same responsibility to the public. The fact is that the published warnings about the limitations of Type II and Type III PFDs do not adequately convey the risk involved.
Given the current choices of Coast Guard-approved personal flotation devices, there is certain justification for the existence of the Type III PFD. Type I PFDs carefully stored away do nothing for the person who falls overboard. A Type III worn by the same person falling overboard will increase his or her chances for survival in the short run.

One logical question that emerges is whether the whole concept of approved PFDs needs to be reconsidered. The answer is a resounding "yes." If the U.S. Navy feels that inflatable life preservers are superior to existing Coast Guard-approved PFDs for its midshipmen, then it's time to turn serious attention to the question of approving inflatable life vests for the general public.

Type V: Semi-Inflatables—and Beyond
The timid first step in this process has been the approval of hybrid vests—limited permanent flotation, plus an inflatable vest. The hybrid vest (Type V hybrid) is acceptable on vessels 40

feet or smaller not carrying passengers for hire, but is only acceptable if it is actually worn. In other words, a locker full of Type V hybrids won't meet the Coast Guard requirements for personal flotation devices if they aren't being worn by the crew any time the boat is underway.

Without the additional buoyancy of the inflated chamber, the hybrids offer very limited flotation, definitely requiring assistance from the wearer to keep his head above water. The Sterns Performance II Vest, for example, has a permanent buoyancy of only 7-1/2 pounds—half that of a Type III device. Inflated, buoyancy of the Stearns hybrid is 22 pounds, the same as a normal Type I PFD.

There are two other options the Coast Guard should consider for approval: belt packs, such as the Navy model, and full-inflation vests of the European type. At least two belt packs are currently available in the United States: the Stearns unit is actually a vest, like the Navy and European inflatable PFDs. The other is an inflatable horseshoe. In our opinion, the vest configuration is the better option because an unconscious person is less likely to slip out of it.

These belt packs are not flawless, however. You have to be conscious to put the Stearns vest around your neck, even though it inflates automatically. But once inflated, the 28 pounds of buoyancy will hold you higher in the water than any Coast Guard-approved PFD, reducing the chances of waves washing over you. If you lose consciousness once you have put on and inflated the Navy-type flotation device, you probably have a better chance of survival than with even an approved Type I personal flotation device.

An even better PFD than the Navy belt pack is the European-style inflatable vest, approved as a PFD by the authorities in almost every civilized country in the world—except the United States. These are worn uninflated as a yoke around the neck, with a strap around the waist. Uninflated, they are no more bulky than a Type III vest. They are inflated by pulling a handle attached to a CO_2 device, or by an oral inflation tube should the CO_2 system fail. Automatic CO_2 systems which activate on immersion are also available. When inflated, the European vests provide 35 pounds of buoyancy.

In this country, the marine product most similar to European inflatable vests is the Switlik Fastnet Flotation Collar. The Flotation Collar can be mounted on most safety harnesses, and consists of a double-tube inflatable yoke, packed for protection inside a Velcro-sealed, nylon oxford-cloth cover. There are two CO_2 cylinders with firing heads, each with an activating lanyard. Combined with the Fastnet Safety Harness to make up the Fastnet Crew Vest MKII, this is probably the most formidable piece of personal safety equipment available anywhere. However, in addition to being expensive, the Fastnet Crew Vest is fairly heavy at three pounds, and is a little bulkier than the typical Type III life jacket. It does provide 35 pounds of buoyancy, far in excess of anything else on the U.S. market. The redundancy of the two chambers is a comfort for those worried about the possibility of puncture. It's not surprising that Switlik would build in redundancy, since the company is in the parachute business.

Mass-produced inflated PFDs need not be as expensive as the Fastnet Crew Vest. The British Crewfit inflatable life jacket, with 35 pounds of buoyancy and automatic inflation, sells for less than $100 through British mailorder chandleries. This price is typical of European inflatable PFDs, which are also available in hybrid models (part permanent flotation, part inflatable), and as part of a safety harness (similar to the Fastnet Crew Vest).

Inflatable life jackets are not without problems. To avoid corrosion of the inflation systems, the jackets should be kept dry when not in use. To avoid puncture, they should not be stowed in lockers with sharp objects. It takes more responsibility on the part of the owner to inspect, maintain, and repack an inflatable if necessary, but none of these tasks are unreasonable.

The primary argument against inflatables in this country is the degree of maintenance and care required. In our opinion, those problems are vastly overrated. For some reason, the federal government feels that we must have thoroughly idiot-proof PFDs. If sailors are indeed a bunch of idiots, then perhaps we can't deal with inflatable life jackets. Millions of people in the rest of the world seem able to cope with them, however, and millions of Americans fly every year on aircraft with inflatable personal flotation devices.

It would be fairly simple to either adopt or adapt the European standards for inflatable life preservers; we need not start from scratch to formulate a set of requirements. The research required would be minimal; it's been done by Europeans in creating their standards, and it's been done in the U.S. to create the FAA's standards for life preservers for aircraft.

Inflatable life preservers aren't for everyone. If you won't check and change the oil in your boat's engine, you probably won't check and maintain an inflatable PFD. That's about the total amount of time and degree of sophistication required to service and maintain an inflatable.

Perhaps the short-run answer is to follow the Navy's example: keep approved PFDs on board to meet the letter of the law, but provide higher-quality inflatables to protect the crew. At the very least, make your crew aware of the limitations of existing approved PFDs. Don't use Type III or even Type II PFDs as the primary life preservers on your boat, even though they meet Coast Guard requirements.

MAN-OVERBOARD GEAR

Struggling to remove the genoa in a squall, the bowman momentarily forgets the "one hand for yourself, one hand for ship" axiom. You've taken the boat almost head to wind in an effort to make it easier to get the flogging sail inboard. There are only two of you aboard, and one has to steer. An errant wave knocks the boat completely head to wind, and the jib backs. Plunging over the back of the wave, the bow is buried in the trough behind, with green water two feet over the stem.

The man on the foredeck had unwisely clipped his harness to the lifeline; as he is knocked over the side by the backed jib, his weight fetches up on the end of the tether, and the sudden loading parts the lifeline.

What next? Get the man-overboard gear over the side, right? As you struggle with the man-overboard pole, which is attached to the backstay, the flag catches in the upper pole holder, and tears off as you yank on the pole in an effort to free it.

With the pole at last over the side, its tether fetches up on the horseshoe ring in its rack on the stern rail, jamming the ring in its holder. You feverishly tear the ring out, tossing it over the side. Fortunately, you remember to disconnect the strobe from the stern rail, so it gets over before the combined drag of the pole and horseshoe can tear the lanyard out of the light.

A seeming eternity, all this has taken only 30 seconds from the time the man went over the side. With the boat traveling at six knots, the man is only 100 yards astern. But if the gear had hung up at any stage, or if you didn't react instantly to the man overboard (suppose the errant wave also knocked you off balance in the cockpit, disorienting you) he could easily be 200 yards away or more.

While perhaps nothing can reduce the time it takes you to react to such an emergency, there's a lot you can do to improve the deployment of man-overboard gear.

You can start by practicing. It's doubtful if one sailor in ten has ever bothered to toss a life ring over the side, much less test the whole system. For some reason, we don't particularly like to think about disasters like a crewmember lost overboard; it's as if by ignoring it we reduce the possibility of it happening.

Boat manufactures hardly help, either. Despite the fact that most boats that undertake even moderately venturesome coastal cruising are equipped with horseshoe rings, strobes, and man-overboard poles, boat manufacturers rarely make allowance for the stowage and deployment of this simple safety gear, much less such heavy and awkward items as life rafts. Instead, the safety-conscious owner is left to wrestle with the problem, which aboard most boats lies somewhere on the priority list behind the color of the cabin cushions and a little ahead of the tablewear.

Usually, after a bit of soul-searching, the owners of most cruising boats end up with some variation on the same arrangement: horseshoe rings in racks on the stern rail, a man-overboard strobe light hanging on the lifeline nearby, and a man-overboard pole either attached horizontally to the lifelines or vertically to the backstay. This is an acceptable system, provided that the lines are coiled up and secured in some fashion, and that the gear can be deployed quickly in an emergency without becoming hopelessly tangled.

Racing boats typically give safety gear more thought. First,

Figure 7-1.

they are required to carry extensive man-overboard equipment to compete in offshore racing events; second, the equipment must not interfere with the racing efficiency of the boat. For example, boats racing in Category One events (offshore) must carry two horseshoe rings equipped with drogues, dye markers, and man-overboard lights, plus at least one man-overboard pole. (To this list you should consider adding a whistle and a package of three waterproof hand-launched flares such as the S.S.I. "Skyblazer," taped to the horseshoe ring.) The stowage of this formidable array of equipment is done in a number of ways—some good, others not so good. The good systems, however, are rarely seen aboard cruising boats.

Figure 7-1 shows the man-overboard gear stowage aboard Murray Davis' motorsailer *Turtle*. The storage is fairly typical of cruising boats with divided rigs. Horseshoe rings are mounted

Figure 7-2.

in racks attached to a stern-rail upright with stainless steel hose clamps, which are taped over to prevent snagging. Taping is particularly important, as lines can easily foul on the tail ends of hose clamps. The man-overboard pole rests in a piece of PVC pipe which is clamped to a mizzen shroud. The bottom end of the pipe is open to allow water to drain out, but a grid of stainless wire keeps the pole from falling through. Care must be taken with this system because the bottom strap of the ring (the function of which is a mystery) will hang up on the stainless steel rack if it is not led properly when installing the horseshoe. Installed as shown, the ring cannot pull free without unclipping the bottom strap, which no one is likely to do in an emergency.

The chance of accidental deployment of the man-overboard pole is reduced aboard Jim Kilroy's *Kialoa* by a stainless steel pin across the opening of the transom tube for the man-overboard pole shown in **Figure 7-2**. The transom tube is one of the racing boat's great contributions to safety gear stowage, and one almost never seen aboard cruising boats.

Figure 7-3 shows the storage aboard *Scaramouche*, another

Figure 7-3.

ocean racer. To reduce windage, the horseshoe rings are stored flat on deck, with the ends of the rings straddling the stern-rail stanchions. To keep the rings from sliding around, shock cord is fitted from the bottom of the rail to an eyebolt on the deck, keeping some downward tension on the ring. Unfortunately, the ubiquitous bottom strap is hooked around the stanchion, and must be unhooked before deploying the ring. Strobe lights are mounted just under the after lip of the cockpit in self-launching holders. A disadvantage of this installation is that the light must go under the lower lifeline when launched, in order to follow the path of the horseshoe ring. Once again, panic could complicate the launch.

For sloop-rigged boats without transom tubes, the man-overboard pole is usually mounted on the backstay. The PVC-pipe bottom fitting is seized to the bottom of the backstay. The bottom of the tube is left open, with a small stainless steel machine screw across the bottom opening to keep the pole from falling through. The upper fitting, secured to the backstay with tape, is another length of PVC pipe. To launch the pole, it is first lifted up to clear the bottom socket. Then, the pole is pulled down to free the upper end of the pole from its holder.

The flag should be completely contained inside the pipe to keep it from fading or becoming tattered. In addition, if the upper pipe is long, and the lower pipe short, the flag will still be contained within the upper pipe when the bottom of the pole is cleared from its holder, eliminating the possibility of the flag hanging up as it is dragged down through the pipe.

An unusual solution to many of the problems associated with conventional rigid man-overboard gear is the Pier Six Personal Recovery System. This system includes an inflatable man-overboard pole, which is lower in height than a conventional pole, but according to the manufacturer will stand more upright when deployed than the normal fiberglass man-overboard pole. The system also includes an inflatable horseshoe ring with a pouch which could be used for flares, dye markers, and so forth. The whole set is contained in a compact fabric-covered case which mounts to the stern rail and is quickly deployed by a pull on the handle. The case has room inside for a strobe light, which is not included. The whole rig can be removed from the lifelines and put below when in port, out of the sight of thieves.

All this careful equipment stowage won't help a bit, if your crew doesn't know the setup and how it works, or if the crew can't get an injured or exhausted crewmember back aboard once the boat returns to him. The only way to know for sure that your system works is to try it. You may never need to use it, but knowing the man-overboard system will work without a hitch is one of the keys to confident offshore and coastwise sailing.

A Man-Overboard Retrieval System That Works

Locating and returning to a crewmember in the water is a serious problem. Even more serious, however, can be the problem of getting the person in the water back aboard the boat once he is located. The more shorthanded the crew, the more the problem is compounded.

ORC racing regulations require safety harnesses, the use of which in most conditions would help solve the problem. Still, harnesses are not widely used, and there is no realistic way to require crews to wear them. For cruising boats there aren't even any regulations requiring that harnesses be aboard, let alone any outside inducement that they be worn.

Although much has been done in devising methods for lifting victims from the water to the deck of a boat, there is nothing that makes that task easy. If you think for a moment how difficult it can be to hoist a small outboard motor or a good-sized fish into the cockpit, the problems involved in pulling a semiconscious 150-pound man aboard become obvious. Without outside assistance—either mechanical, human, or divine—a person in the water may never reach the deck of the average sailboat. When we learned of a device developed specifically for retrieving a victim from the water onto a sailboat, the Lifesling, we ordered one from its non-profit developer, The Sailing Foundation, and tried it.

It works. In fact, it seems the most practical system we have seen for getting at least a conscious person back aboard a boat, even when there is only one person left aboard. We repeated the retrieval of a 170-pound man three times, twice by a woman, once by a man, in each case working strictly alone on a 34-foot sloop in winds ranging from 10 to 15 knots. The average time from overboard to back aboard was 12 to 15 minutes, with no part of the system rigged beforehand. That time included deploying the Lifesling and tether from the stern rail, circling under sail until the victim could reach the tether and pull the sling to him, pulling the sling with victim to the side of the boat, rigging a tackle, and lifting him over the lifelines to the deck.

The principle behind getting the sling to the victim is the same as that used by ski-boat operators to let the skier retrieve the tow line. The sling at the end of a tether is towed behind a circling boat until either the tether or the sling reaches the person in the water inside the circle (see **Figures 7-4** and **7-5**).

The circling can be accomplished equally well under sail or power, assuming conditions permit a reasonable amount of maneuverability. Clearly, sail is preferred to power in that there is no danger to the person in the water from the spinning propeller and there is less risk of tangling the crucial tether around the prop or shaft.

It is important to stop the boat as soon as the sling is within

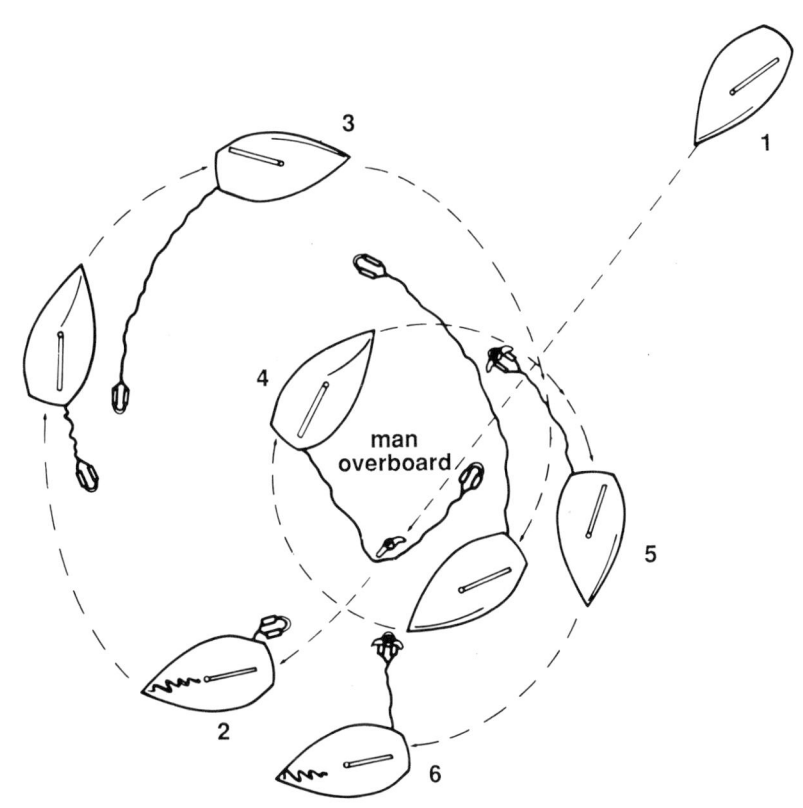

Figure 7-4. The procedure for getting the sling to the victim.

reach of the victim. Speed can pull it away from him or, worse, tow him under once he is in it. The logical step is for the crew to immediately cast off all halyards and get the sails down; even a boat drifting with flogging sails can make enough speed to make it difficult for the victim.

Our experience suggests trying to bring the victim alongside the windward side of the boat. On that side he may be thrown against the topsides by broadside waves, but the boat has no tendency to push him under as it makes leeway. However, which side of the boat he is on seems less important than getting him close to the boat as soon as possible and tying the tether up short to keep him there.

The tackle to hoist the victim is attached to any convenient halyard. We used the main halyard, pre-marked so that the tip

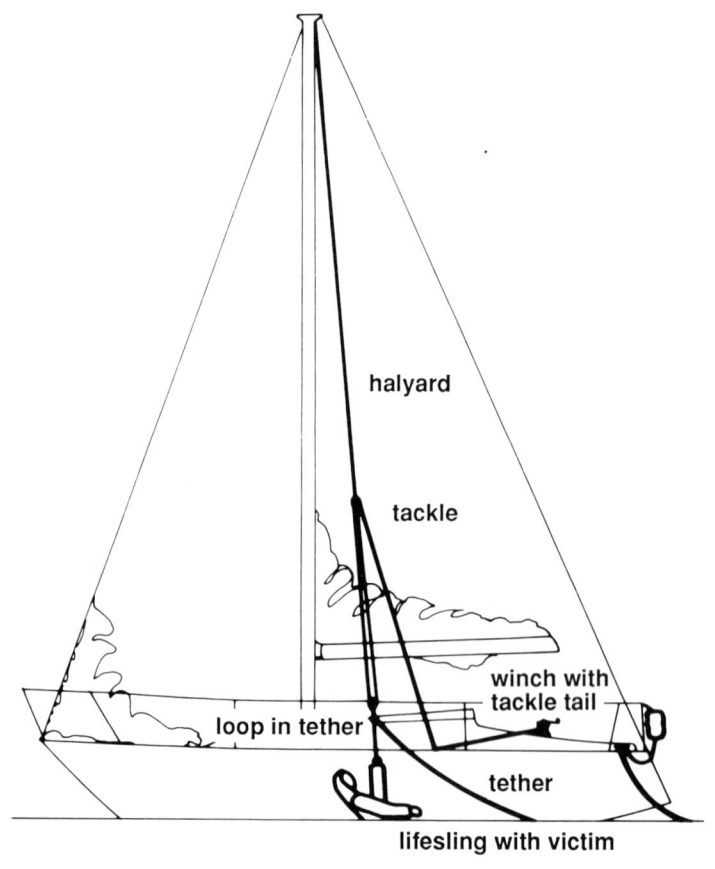

Figure 7-5. The system set up for hoisting aboard.

of the tackle was at least 10 feet above the deck. A three-power tackle with the tail run through a block on the rail and to a self-tailing sheet winch proved perfectly adequate to lift 170 pounds aboard. Had we been able to run the halyard tail with a fair lead to the winch, we could have done away with the tackle and still managed to bring our victim aboard more quickly, since there would have been less rope to wind up and no need to rig the tackle. Nevertheless, the tackle should remain part of the system, unless circumstances prevent its use.

The lower block of the tackle shackles into the loop in the sling tether. The tail is wrapped around the most convenient winch (it need not be the biggest) and the victim hoisted clear of the water. Assuming he is conscious and functioning, he should be able to help himself as soon as his feet get to the rail, although in all our tests the "victim" remained limp and "helpless" throughout the hoisting.

The effective use of the Lifesling presupposes that the victim is conscious and rational. He has to be able to grab the sling or its tether when is comes close to him and then put the sling over his head and under his arms. From that point on, he can be rescued without further effort on his part. Although it is desirable that the victim be able to help himself, we think the Lifesling still has promise in retrieving an unconscious person. We noted in our tests that with some judicious boathandling and a measure of luck, the tether could literally be wound a turn or two around the victim, if he remained floating upright with his head and shoulders above water (such as while wearing a life jacket or float coat). With a turn or two it should be possible to pull him to the boat where his arms can be held upright and the sling dropped over them without anyone having to go over the side.

We are leery of a crew flinging himself into the water to go after an unconscious victim. A reasonable answer, however, is for the rescuer to don the sling as a sure method of remaining attached to the boat and of being retrieved with the victim. In short, one of the decided advantages of the concept is its possible usefulness in the retrieval of an unconscious victim, by far the most frightening prospect of a man-overboard catastrophe.

The crew left aboard to handle the boat and the retrieval must be calm and skilled with both the boat and the system. There is little room for panic or lack of confidence. The Lifesling is not a safety device for which one can read directions in mid-winter to be used to save someone in mid-summer. The whole procedure must be understood and then practiced in less than ideal sailing conditions to gain both the knowledge and the confidence.

At the same time, the system does seem to leave considerable room for errors, foul-ups, sloppiness, and improvisation and still effect a rescue. What is imperative is that the boat be capable of circling the victim, even at a fairly wide radius; that the boat be able to be stopped quickly and surely; that the sails be readily released; and that the block and tackle be at hand without the delays of hunting or assembly. Except in extremely cold conditions when hypothermia is a concern, once the victim is in the sling, retrieval can be done slowly enough to avoid mistakes of haste or excitement.

While it is desirable not to injure the victim, it is more important that he not drown or be lost due to over-caution. In heavy seas, we cannot imagine the victim not being wave-thrown against the topsides or a stanchion while being hoisted on deck. Also keep in mind that this system seems both surer and easier on the victim than hastily improvised rope slings or man-handling under or over the lifelines.

The patented Lifesling lists for just over $100.00, a price that includes the buoyant sling, polypropylene tether, a pouch for the tether and a bag with printed instructions that hangs on the stern rail to hold both the sling and the tether bag. Regardless of the price, we believe that the system (combined with a crew that can deploy it) is cheap insurance, and should be considered essential safety gear along with good safety harnesses, man-overboard gear, and life jackets.

Certainly it will not get someone back on board as easily as he went overboard. But it does seem to give a more than reasonable chance of recovering an overboard victim, even for a shorthanded boat. That is more than we can say about other devices and schemes sailors may be relying upon.

MARINE DISTRESS SIGNALS

Coast Guard regulation 33 CFR Part 175, which requires the carrying of visual distress signals by pleasure boats, went into effect on January 1, 1981. The regulations require that any boat carrying six or fewer passengers for hire, and any pleasure boat 16 feet or more in length, carry approved day and night visual distress signals when operating on the Great Lakes or coastal waters of the United States. These coastal waters include bays and sounds which open onto the territorial sea, and the mouths of some of the larger rivers.

Vessels under 16 feet operating in these waters at night are also required to carry approved night distress signals. Only boats participating in parades, races, and regattas, and rowboats and completely open sailboats under 26 feet long are excluded from the requirements.

The distress signal requirements may be met in two ways: with pyrotechnics, or with non-pyrotechnic devices. Pyrotechnics include flares and smoke signals. Non-pyrotechnic devices include specially marked distress flags and automatic, battery-powered signal lanterns.

Hand-Held Flares

The cheapest and simplest way to meet the new signalling requirements is to carry three, Coast Guard-approved hand-held red flares. The major suppliers of distress signals for pleasure boats market a package of three hand-held flares as a minimum compliance kit. At a retail price of about $18 to $30, and typical discount prices of $12 to $20, meeting the letter of the law can hardly be deemed expensive. Since the flares must be replaced every 42 months, minimum annual compliance will cost less than $10.

Hand-held flares received last-minute Coast Guard approval for use aboard pleasure boats. Objections have been raised to their use due to the hot slag that is a combustion by-product of some hand-held flares, posing a potential hazard to both the user and the boat. This danger is most easily seen in the case of a gasoline leak or on a wooden boat, when the slag could set the boat on fire, or could ignite gasoline vapors.

If hand-held flares are used for distress signalling, it is imperative that they be held over the leeward rail, as far away from both the user and the boat as is possible. If gloves are aboard, they should certainly be worn when holding burning flares. It is also advisable not to look directly at the flares while they are burning.

Hand-held flares have other disadvantages. Since they are held only a few feet above the water, they are visible at a distance of only three to five miles under ideal conditions. They burn for only two minutes—long by pyrotechnic standards, short when you are trying to attract the attention of a rescuer. In an emergency situation, it is probably useless to light a hand-held flare unless a potential rescuer is in sight.

Red hand-held flares carrying Coast Guard type-approval number 160.021 may be used to meet both the day and night distress signalling requirements. Because of their limitations, they should be considered as the primary signals only aboard boats sailed in well-travelled waters.

Smoke Signals

Orange smoke signals carrying type-approval numbers 160.022 (floating) and 160.037 (hand-held) are approved for daytime signalling only. Hand-held smoke signals are cheaper than floating signals, and are most likely to be used by small boats. Smoke signals cost about the same as hand-held flares.

Smoke signals have the advantage of being seen from a greater distance than hand-held flares on a calm day. During daylight, they are also more visible to aircraft than hand-held flares. Under gale condition, smoke signals may be practically useless. Since they do not emit light, they are not suitable for night use.

Aerial Flares

Projected pyrotechnics cost more than the hand-held variety, but they can also be more useful in attracting the attention of rescuers, since they can be seen from a greater distance. Projected signals include pistol-fired and hand-launched meteors and parachutes flares.

There is a tremendous variety of aerial signals available. Hand-launched pyrotechnics vary from tiny meteors such as the Sigma Scientific "Skyblazers" which cost about $6 each, to the Olin 25-millimeter meteors and parachute flares which cost $15 to $30 each, to the Solas hand-launched parachute flares which cost nearly $50. Which type you choose depends on how and where you use your boat, and how prepared for distress signalling you wish to be.

METEORS. Approved meteor flares carry Coast Guard type-number 160.066. They include both hand-launched and pistol-launched signals. Approved meteors may be used for both day and night signalling.

Most meteors project to a height of about 250 feet, burn with a high intensity for about six seconds, and then extinguish themselves while falling back to the surface. Obviously, a flare 250 feet above the surface can be seen much further than one six feet above the surface. Typically, a flare 250 feet above the earth's surface can be seen 21 miles away, in good visibility conditions. At that range, the meteor would be visible only briefly, before it fell below the horizon.

PARACHUTE FLARES. Parachutes flares reach a higher altitude (above 1000 feet), burn longer (at least 30 seconds), burn brighter, and cost more than meteors.

Parachute flares have many advantages. At an altitude of 1000 feet, a flare can be seen at a distance of 40 miles by an observer at sea level. The longer burn time and slower rate of descent make parachutes visible for a longer period of time than meteors. Their high candlepower makes them more likely to be seen in condition of limited visibility. Aside from cost, the primary disadvantage of parachute flares is that in high winds, they may not reach maximum altitude, and may be blown well away from the distressed vessel. It is worthwhile to note that in the 1979 Fastnet Race, boats reported that their parachute flares were almost instantly blown away by the gale-force winds.

LAUNCHING DEVICES. Pistol-launched flares are generally cheaper than self-launching flares. To fire a pistol-launched flare, however, you must have the proper flare pistol. Flare pistols used in small boats are usually 12-gauge or 25-millimeter bore, The larger 25-millimeter flares are more expensive than 12-gauge flares, but they generally project higher and burn brighter and longer. Only meteors are available in 12-gauge. Because of the bulk of the parachute packing, parachutes are available only in 25 and the larger 37-millimeter diameters.

Like flares, pistols vary tremendously in price. Approved pistols carry type-number 160.028. Pistols cost as little as $10.00 for a plastic 12-gauge unit to well over $100.00 for a high-quality 25- or 37-millimeter pistol. The metal-framed Olin 25-millimeter rapid-loader pistol costs about $40.00.

We have found that American-made 25-millimeter pistol flares are too big in diameter for some European pistols with a nominal bore of 25 millimeters. It is imperative that you check flares and pistols for compatibility.

Non-Pyrotechnic Signalling

The alternatives to pyrotechnic devices are a special orange distress flag for day use, and an automatic signalling lamp for night use. Non-pyrotechnic devices might be safer in use (by small children, for example) but have limited visual range. Their primary advantage is that they are not "one-shot," their signal is long-lasting, and they may be reused.

Approved orange distress flags carry Coast Guard type-approval number 160.072. They must be at least three feet square, and consist of a black ball shape and a black square on an international orange field. The best flag we have seen is made by the Safety Flag Company of America, and retails for about $14. This flag carries the Underwriters Laboratories marine classification in addition to Coast Guard type-approval.

Automatic distress signal lanterns, the only non-pyrotechnic devices approved for night signalling, are relatively expensive. The light must float, and must send an automatic Morse SOS signal for at least six hours. Both Guest and Olin make approved automatic signal lanterns. Each light is also available in an emergency kit which includes a distress flag. Automatic signalling lanterns carry approval number 161.013.

The Cost of Compliance

The daysailer will obviously carry a smaller range of signals than the ocean-going cruiser or racer. Minimum compliance may be adequate for a dinghy. Yes, dinghies used at night must meet the standards for night signalling when operating in the waters covered by the law.

The coastal cruiser will certainly carry one of the more elaborate signalling kits, which usually contains the entire range of pyrotechnic devices in varying quantities. Ideally, these kits should be supplemented with extra smoke signals and flares.

Ocean-going cruisers should consider carrying no less than the Category One requirements listed in the Offshore Racing Council's Special Regulations. Compliance with these regulations will cost about $300. A bit steep, you say? Just how much is your life worth?

Distress signals must be stored in a dry and readily accessible section of the boat. They are legally required to be stored in a watertight container. (Surplus ammunition boxes make good storage containers for pyrotechnics.) Everyone aboard should know where they are, and know how to use them. The locker, drawer, or container where the signals are stored should be clearly identified. At the same time, if small children are aboard the boat, the flare locker should probably be locked. The key must be instantly available, however.

As a final note, remember that pyrotechnic signalling devises have to be replaced every 3-1/2 years, and be sure that any new distress signals you purchase carry Coast Guard-approval numbers. There are devices presently on the market that do not meet Coast Guard standards.

EPIRBs

The concept of the EPIRB (an acronym for "Emergency Position-Indicating Radio Beacon") is fetching: a self-contained emergency radio transmitter to notify the Coast Guard that you and your boat are in a life-threatening situation. Unfortunately, uneven performance and proposed changes in the system make choosing an EPIRB difficult right now.

There are currently three classes of EPIRB, A, B, and C, the electronic characteristics of which are set by the Federal Communications Commission. Originally developed for use by aircraft, Class A and B EPIRBs have been available in the pleasure boat marketplace for more than ten years. They are electronically similar, but Class A EPIRBs are required in Coast Guard-approved commercial installations and are built to more stringent specifications. Class A EPIRBs must float free of a sinking vessel and turn on automatically; they have to be self-righting within one second and must float with the antenna base at least 2 inches out of the water; they have to have a test switch; and a test unit has to perform to specifications after being dropped three times into the water from a height of 60 feet.

Class C EPIRBs, developed for use on marine VHF channels 15 and 16, were not generally available on the market until 1984, and consequently don't have an extensive track record. They are required on commercial vessels only on the Great Lakes.

Class A & B EPIRBs

Class A and B EPIRBs broadcast an emergency signal—a wailing or downward swooping tone—on two VHF frequencies used in international aviation, 121.5 and 243 MegaHertz. These frequencies, the aircraft equivalent of marine channel 16, are supposedly monitored by commercial and military aircraft except during landing approaches, so that when an EPIRB begins broadcasting, any airplane within line of sight should receive the signal and should report it to the Federal Aviation Administration for relay to the Coast Guard.

"Should" is obviously a loaded word. The situation is best summarized by the following quotation from one company's EPIRB manual: "This unit is not to be relied upon as an alerting device, because the monitoring of distress frequencies by commercial or government aircraft is mainly voluntary. Any alerting function is strictly an extra which is not guaranteed by this company." (Thanks alot.)

Partly because of this, in 1982, the U.S. and Russian governments agreed to have satellites tune in on the aviation frequencies. The American "SARSAT" and Russian "COSPAS" satellite tracking systems have obviously increased the line-of-sight area in which Class A & B EPIRBs can be received. Also, the coverage of the satellites is round-the-clock, not dependent on the timing of aircraft passing overhead. The Russians and Americans have agreed to keep the system operating through 1990, and currently Canada, France, Britain, Norway, and Sweden are involved in the international agreement by virtue of earth stations that receive and relay signals from the satellites.

It all sounds sophisticated and hi-tech, but unfortunately it isn't. The proposals to upgrade the current system clouds the choices for sailors right now. The problem is that Class A and B EPIRBs were designed from the beginning as low-power "homing" transmitters, and not really as broadcasting machines

Safety Equipment

to be involved in a satellite system. While the satellite system has worked with current EPIRBs, the whole system can best be described as jury-rigged engineering, something with which high-tech types are not comfortable. Thus comes the proposal for a whole new EPIRB system with the potential for putting the current Class A and B EPIRBs out of business.

The proposed EPIRB system, developed by NASA engineers, would work on a different frequency already on the satellites (406 MHz). Since the system will be designed primarily for satellite operation, the expectation is that it could eventually make current EPIRBs obsolete.

There would be two major advantages to the new system. First, position locating would be much more precise. Current EPIRBs turn on and stay on, as you would want in a homing device. But if there are two on at once, a satellite can make little sense of the location of either. Also, the continuous signal makes it hard for the satellite to lock on and to measure the "Doppler" shift in frequency caused by the motion of the satellite relative to the earth. It is by measuring the Doppler shift that precise position finding is achieved, such as occurs with SatNav. In the new EPIRBs with a "pulsed" rather than a continuous signal, the shift could be measured much more precisely.

Second, in a new system designed for satellite use, every EPIRB could transmit an individualized signal with encoded information so that, for example, the name of the boat or the EPIRB's owner could be known immediately. With this information, search-and-rescue operations could be more effective. In addition, identifying the transmitter would help solve the major problem plaguing the current system—false alarms from accidentally triggered EPIRBs.

It all sounds very good for the future. But exactly when the future will occur is questionable, especially considering that there are a couple of unfriendly governments involved, a number of unwieldy bureaucracies (besides NASA, there's NOAA, the FAA, the FCC, all the military air units, and the Coast Guard who have to test, approve, and make rules), and a marine electronics industry which has to wait for the governments' and bureaucracies' specifications before they can begin designing or making the new EPIRBs.

Class C EPIRBs

With all this happening to Class A & B EPIRBs, why not a Class C? The Class C is a more recent design directed at boats rather than airplanes. By FCC specifications, when a Class C EPIRB is activated, it broadcasts a 24-hour series of signals in a specified sequence controlled by a microprocessor chip; first an emergency wail on the marine calling and distress frequency, Channel 16, then a longer "homing" signal on Channel 15. The wail is the distinctive "wheee-whaah" sound of a European ambulance—an unusual enough sound on marine bands that anyone monitoring Channel 16 should take note.

Boater acceptance of Class C EPIRBs, however, has been a problem, probably because Class C units have received none of the publicity that has accompanied successes with Class A and B units. And there has been some skepticism about Class C. The question with Class C devices is range: how far will a VHF signal carry when transmitted from a 17-inch antenna at sea level? "Up to 30 (or 25, or 20) miles" are the ranges used in advertisements. Simple calculations show that normal line-of-sight distance for VHF transmission is about what the ads say, depending on the antenna height.

From an EPIRB floating in flat water, VHF range is approximately 17.5 nautical miles to a 200-foot-tall Coast Guard or marine operator antenna on shore. The same Class C EPIRB would reach a sailboat's masthead antenna 40 feet above sea level up to 8.5 nautical miles away, and would reach a 15-foot-high antenna on a Coast Guard search-and-rescue vessel up to 5.5 nautical miles away.

We tested two Class C units with the cooperation of the Castle Hill Coast Guard station in Newport, and found these distances to be reasonable expectations. We floated the two EPIRBs and turned them on when we were about 8 miles offshore. We got a loud-and-clear "hit," not only at Castle Hill but also at the Block Island station, about 13.5 miles away.

One consideration is that, in large enough waves, a floating EPIRB will be momentarily blanketed (thus, silent) when in the trough, but in practice we found that this is not a serious problem. The unit floats on the crests of waves long enough and frequently enough that the signal is heard.

Considering the proposed changes in the system, and the likelihood that the hardware will eventually become outdated, you may think "Why bother with an EPIRB at this time, if indeed at all?" The fact is that an EPIRB is a proven safety device which has worked for sailors in catastrophic situations. Moreover, an EPIRB is one of the few things that will work in the ultimate emergency—when you lose your boat and, with it, your means of getting to safety. With Class C EPIRBs discounted to less than $100, and the Class B devices available for less than $200, they are cheap insurance indeed.

MASTHEAD STROBE LIGHTS

Masthead strobes have become a hot selling item in recent years. Since they were introduced as collision-avoidance lights a number of years ago, the rationale has been that they put a sure attention-getting device at the level of a ship's bridge. This concept sounds better in advertising than in reality. When the masthead appears at the level of a freighter's bridge, it's usually a little too late to worry about collision-avoidance.

A better, more logical reason for placing the strobe at the masthead is that it will not blind the crew in the cockpit. It also can be seen from a greater distance.

Whatever the case, the original purpose of the strobe was to simply call attention to the presence of the boat in an unmistakable manner on the high seas. Unfortunately, however, the strobe has been misused, notably by fishing boats that activated it when the crew turned in. Similarly, some misguided sailboat owners have activated them before going ashore for the evening, using the flash to find their boat when they returned later in the evening (and annoying everyone on nearby boats in the interim).

Now the strobe is no longer legal as an attention-getting device. It *is* legal as a *distress* signal. One might argue that the prospect of being run down at sea by a ship constitutes a distress situation, but that would be an extra-legal argument.

If you use a strobe light, you should be prepared to explain your distress to those who respond. And conversely, if you see a strobe, it is only proper that you respond. Remember, it may not be at a masthead of a boat with a nervous skipper; it may be a man-overboard light floating near a helpless victim.

We believe that one or two man-overboard lights within instant reach of the helmsman should be adequate for those (hopefully) rare instances when emergency circumstances warrant such a light. But if you do opt to install a masthead strobe, remember its purpose—distress.

Incidentally, for getting attention in a sailboat there is hardly anything more eye catching than a powerful flashlight moved back and forth on the sails. Not only is it clearly visible on both sides of the sail, but it immediately identifies the craft as a sailboat and gives the viewer a notion of the direction it is heading. Moreover, if the light is readily at hand; it needs merely to be picked up and switched on.

INFLATABLE LIFE RAFTS

"Why should I spend $2500 for a life raft when I can buy one for under $1000?" "Is there really that much difference between life rafts?" These are among the most common questions sailors ask. The deaths of more than a dozen sailors in the 1979 Fastnet finally moved safety issues out of the closet. The growing concern over offshore safety—the realization that sailing can entail certain risks—has been healthy for the sport, encouraging the development of better safety gear and emergency procedures.

Unfortunately, few guidelines exist to help in the choice of safety equipment. You can still buy a $15 safety harness of dubious quality. You can still buy man-overboard strobes that leak, radar reflectors that barely reflect, and life rafts more suitable for use as wading pools than for survival in the open ocean.

Although it stands to reason that the sailor crossing an ocean needs better safety equipment than the inland sailor, safety equipment is a poor place to start to cut corners. Would a mountaineer leave his best rope and carabiners at home because he was only climbing a small cliff?

For some safety equipment, there is absolutely no argument in favor of buying less expensive gear. The best safety harness is a bargain whether you're sailing on the Great Lakes or the Atlantic ocean.

Life rafts, however, are another story. Or are they? "I can get an aircraft life raft for $800. Since I only cruise between Florida and the Bahamas, isn't that raft good enough?" If you're lucky, maybe. If you're unlucky, no.

Because weight is critical aboard an airplane, aircraft life rafts are as lightly constructed as possible. This means that the fabric is less rugged, more prone both to damage and environmental deterioration than a raft designed for offshore marine use. A life raft carried aboard an airplane is a short-term survival craft. In the inhospitable marine environment, it is likely to have a sharply limited lifespan and minimum serviceability.

Remember, bad weather is not necessarily a factor in an aircraft ditching, so an aircraft life raft is not designed to be a seaworthy craft in heavy weather. Most boats that sink, however, do so in heavy weather; the life raft must prove more seaworthy than the mother ship. A lightweight aircraft life raft simply doesn't fill the need.

We define a life raft as an aircraft type if it has a single layer of buoyancy tubes, independent of whether it consists of a single buoyancy chamber or a number of chambers. We also consider any raft without a self-erecting canopy (a raft without an overhead inflatable arch tube) to be an aircraft raft.

If a raft has only a single layer of buoyancy tubes (that is, it looks like a single rubber doughnut instead of two doughnuts stacked on top of each other) it is unsuited for use as a sailboat life raft. Loss of buoyancy in one chamber will cause a portion of the raft to sink, flooding the raft and exposing its occupants to the water. With a single layer of buoyancy tubes, the raft's freeboard is likely to be so low that waves constantly slop over the sides, soaking the occupants. Even in the warmest tropical waters, the likelihood of hypothermia is greatly increased, as the heat exchange between your body and water is much greater than between your body and air of the same temperature.

Aircraft-type life rafts are widely sold as marine life rafts, and are available through most of the marine mailorder outlets. If your boat sank in good weather, surrounded by other boats which were looking for you, an aircraft raft might be adequate.

Unfortunately, you rarely get to choose when, where, and in what conditions you sink.

"Is it alright to buy a secondhand life raft?" Possibly. Never buy a secondhand life raft without having it inspected and repacked, even if the inspection certificate is current. All the components of the life raft package—fabric, emergency gear, inflation system, container—should be carefully examined by an authorized repacking station before purchase. If it's in good condition, a secondhand raft can be a good value, even with the extra $125 to have it inspected and repacked.

"What about renting a life raft?" For many sailors, renting a life raft makes a lot of sense. Unless you're making an offshore passage every year, renting is probably the cheaper way to go. Some life raft agents have rental rafts and there are agencies that specialize in the rental of safety equipment for those who rarely go offshore.

Renting is fairly expensive, however. One agency's rental charge for a six-man Avon Mark III valise raft is $320 for a week, $680 for a month, $870 for a seven-month season, and about $950 for a year. Short-term rentals are proportionately more expensive because the raft should be repacked after every rental. If you need a raft for one month every year, you can probably rent for about five years before exceeding the cost of owning a life raft.

"What do you look for in a life raft?" Unfortunately, it's far easier to define a poor life raft than it is to describe a good one. All kinds of rafts have saved lives. Of the rafts which failed, of course, we have no record. It seems likely that no matter how rugged the condition for which a raft is designed—wind, sea, burning oil, overloading and so on—that worse conditions can occur in which the raft will be lost. It can never be buoyant enough, strong enough and well enough equipped to guarantee that he who buys one will be saved.

Our primary concern here is to point out the features that in our opinion automatically eliminate a raft from consideration for offshore use. Choosing the best raft involves complex subjective considerations as well as engineering and construction questions. The choice is made more difficult by the fact that the expensive rafts are invariably better than the cheaper ones. Each boatowner must decide for himself how to weigh the cost of

Safety Equipment

survival gear against the odds of needing it, and against the value of a human life.

FIRST AID KITS

While we tend to place a high priority on life rafts, man-overboard gear, and emergency communications equipment, first aid kits are the kind of thing we all tend to ignore when outfitting a boat. We ignore them at least, until we actually need them. When is the last time you looked inside your kit?

In the typical kit, the aspirin has congealed into a solid mass; the medications are long since outdated; the Band-Aids are soggy; the scissors are rusted shut, and only a few inches of adhesive tape are left.

If you haven't done so already, now is the time to consider the problems you might encounter on your boat, and how you would deal with them. You should evaluate your own kit, and your first aid training. After such an inspection, many sailors will find themselves in the market for a new first aid kit.

The marine mailorder houses offer the sailor a bewildering array of price and complexity. Some are genuine junk, others are both useful and well worth the price. Your choice will depend both on the type of sailing you do, and the ability of you and your crew to administer the first aid that the kit provides.

Most first aid kits are simply that—the *first* treatment of simple problems, rather than the treatment of real emergencies. Some kits, however, are capable of treating serious injuries or emergencies, as long as a member of the crew is trained to use the equipment in the kit. A good example is suturing equipment—it takes skill to sew up a wound.

If your boating is limited to daysailing and coastal cruising, you'll rarely be far from medical care. All you should need is a simple kit to manage problems for the few hours it may take to reach trained medical help. For offshore cruising, however, a more extensive kit is required. You need to be able to manage a medical problem for several days or more. To handle the needs of the offshore cruiser, and as a suggested option for the daysailor, several authorities recommend that *two* kits be carried—one kept for serious injuries, and another for minor injuries and non-emergency medications. If only one "super" kit is carried, it won't be long before the crew has raided it for every minor problem, leaving it inadequately stocked when needed for a real emergency.

Several of the kits on the market are Coast Guard-approved. The Coast Guard recommends, but does not require, first aid kits on pleasure craft. It *requires* approved kits in life boats and life rafts. To receive Coast Guard approval, kits are tested for watertightness and impact resistance. The kit's contents must be packaged in special sized boxes. Every aspect of the kit's assembly is specific. Meeting the Coast Guard's standards is expensive. So is the constant testing required to ensure those standards; one out of every 100 kits produced must be tested by an independent laboratory. It's hard to justify the cost of a Coast Guard-approved kit; all you're really getting is a more sophisticated container.

Here are the most common medical problems that every coastal cruiser, and the prudent daysailor, should consider. The offshore sailor needs to be prepared for some of the less common problems, as he often may find himself several days away from professional care.

Common Marine Medical Problems
- minor trauma - *cuts and bruises*
- minor burns - *including sunburn*
- allergic reaction
- headache
- foreign bodies - *in eyes; as well as splinters*
- heat exhaustion
- hypothermia
- motion sickness

Less Common Marine Medical Problems
- major trauma - *gaping wound, fracture, dislocation, concussion*
- major burns - *large second-degree, or any size third-degree burn, especially on hands or face*
- medical problems - *asthma attack, anaphylactic reactions, skin infection*

Items to Look for in a Basic Kit
• dressings - *gauze pads, non-adhering pads (Telfa)*
• bandages - *adhesive strips (Band-Aids), stretch bandages (Kling), triangular bandages, adhesive tape, Steri-strips*
• anti-bacterial solutions - *either as a solution and/or on pre-soaked pads (alcohol or Prevodenelodine)*
• sterile solution - *for flushing wounds and eyes*
• burn cream
• aspirin or acetaminophen (Tylenol) - *for mild pain*
• sunscreen - *with sun protection factor (SPF) of 15 or better*
• antihistamines - *for mild allergic reactions and seasickness*
• accessories - *emergency blanket, emergency light, cold pack, and splinter forceps*

Additions for the Offshore Sailor
• thermometer - *including one with a scale that goes as low as 95 degrees or below*
• scalpel
• suturing kit
• anaphylactic kit - *for severe allergic reactions*
• antibiotics
• prescription pain medication

When shopping for a first aid kit, it is helpful to remember that most marine medical problems are similar to those encountered at home. Some kits lack the basic necessities, while others may be overstocked with equipment that no crewmember is trained enough to use.

Training, in fact, is the key to successful first aid. All cruising yachts should carry an emergency first aid manual, and hopefully will have at least one crewmember schooled in emergency first aid and CPR.

8

The Ship's Tender

A dinghy is the simplest of boats. Choosing a dinghy is not the simplest of tasks, however, considering the hundreds of models available. Many sailors don't think twice about their dinghy—as long as it gets them to shore and back, and occupies the kids for a few quiet hours. It's only after owning several dinghies that it becomes painfully obvious that some are decidedly better than others. With today's prices for an 8-foot sailing dink running from $500 to $1500, a practical sailor can no longer afford to make a poor choice. Toward that end, we'll take a look at the options in the design of "hard" dinghies, followed by inflatable dinghies later in this chapter.

Hull Shape

The shape of the modern dinghy is quite different than that of the "yacht tender" of 50 years ago. Tenders were rowing boats; they were long and slender with curved bilges and narrow ends.

Today's dinghies, like the yachts to which they belong, are short and fat with flatter bottoms and fuller ends. Compared to the boats of yesteryear, today's dinghies row and sail like bathtubs, but they hold more for their length, are lighter, and take up less space. The wide stern of the modern dinghy is necessary to support the weight of an outboard and driver, something the old yacht tender never had to contend with.

The modern dinghy, commonly 8 feet long, needs its fuller bilge and flatter bottom for stability. However, no bottom should be completely flat. If it has no deadrise (if it is flat athwartships), any water that gets into the boat will slosh from one chine to the other and invite a capsize. A slight "V" to the bottom helps keep any water in the center of the boat. As a precaution, never set foot in a dinghy without a bailer at hand. A Clorox bottle with the bottom cut out works well; always tie it into the boat so it won't float away if you swamp.

If a dinghy has no rocker (if the bottom is flat fore and aft), the bow will partially submerge even when the boat is lightly loaded. This problem is accentuated in a square-bowed pram; without substantial rocker, rowing a pram is like rowing a wooden crate.

A hard chine dinghy usually has a greater beam at its waterline and hence is more stable. But a chine hull is often more prone to flexing, gelcoat cracking and breakdown of the fiberglass laminate. Flared topsides are more stable than plumb topsides.

The hull shape of any dinghy is a compromise. Generally, the more capacity it has for people, gear and engines, the poorer it rows and sails.

Capacity

On the stern of every new production dinghy is a plate stating the maximum recommended outboard horsepower, the maximum weight of the crew, and the total capacity of crew and gear. The total capacity is determined by a U.S. Coast Guard test performed by the manufacturer, and is a fraction of the weight required to completely submerge the dinghy. This capacity is what the Coast Guard considers safe. You can overload it, but if you have an accident it could nullify an insurance claim.

The horsepower rating is a function of the dinghy's flotation.

To be rated for an outboard larger than two horsepower, the boat must remain upright and level when swamped, and still support 50 percent of the maximum crew-weight capacity. This lets the crew sit in the boat with the water at about waist level. Most dinghy builders rate their boats for outboards of two horsepower or smaller, because Coast Guard rules for this category are less strict. A boat with this rating must support only two-fifteenths of the maximum crew capacity when swamped, and remain upright and level with the crew outside the boat hanging on to the gunwales.

The Coast Guard requires that all foam flotation be encapsulated or be immune to corrosive chemicals such as gasoline. Most dinghies have the flotation in compartments in the bow and stern. Some also have foam along the chines running fore and aft. If the boat should begin to swamp, this longitudinal flotation keeps the water in the center of the bilge to add stability. It also adds to the hull rigidity and makes a comfortable seat when sailing to windward.

Interior volume is important in a 8-foot boat. Prams have more space for a given length, but without the traditional "V" to their bow, they don't track through the water as well as a conventional boat. High freeboard affords more volume, and more protection in choppy water, but it also adds windage, a significant factor when rowing in a strong breeze.

Construction

Production dinghies are almost universally built of a relatively thin laminate of fiberglass. Thin laminates tend to be flexible, which often makes a dinghy "mushy" to row and sail. If you can see the gunwale flex as you row or sit on it while sailing to windward, your dinghy is soft. Soft dinghies often develop extensive gelcoat crazing, especially if the gelcoat, which is inherently brittle, is sprayed on too thick.

Aside from the weight and quality of the laminate, there are several other things that support a dinghy's structure. The size of the gunwales is important. A wide, heavy, rolled fiberglass gunwale not only adds stiffness, but it also provides a comfortable handhold. Wooden strips lining either side of the gunwale serve the same purpose, but require more maintenance.

Thwarts are essential for structural rigidity. Every dinghy should have one amidships, and either a thwart or glassed-in flotation in both ends. Thwarts have a tendency to break loose from the hull, so they must be fastened securely. The woodwork on most dinghies is mahogany. For reduced maintenance, however, teak is preferred. Oiled teak is also less slippery than varnished mahogany.

A skeg and bottom strakes not only protect the hull, but also help prevent bottom flexing. The skeg should be substantial enough to help the dinghy to track straight while rowed or towed. To protect the boat as it is dragged across a dock or a beach, the skeg must be straight so it bears evenly from where it begins on the stern to where it fairs into the hull at the point of maximum rocker (maximum hull depth). Skegs that are molded into the floor of the boat to form a shallow sump are nice; they collect water which helps keep the bottom of the boat dry. However, beware of hollow skegs which cannot be repaired from inside the boat. Molded fiberglass skegs and strakes are sturdier than bolted or screwed-on wooden ones. Without any holes drilled in the hull, they are also less likely to leak.

Every dinghy needs a rubrail on the gunwale. Most come with white or black vinyl rubrails. While the vinyl itself is almost indestructible, the usual pop rivets that fasten it to the rail are good for a couple of seasons at best. Glued-on rubrails are just as bad. The best way to permanently attach a plastic rubrail to a rolled fiberglass gunwale is to bolt it on with small machine screws, lock washers, and cap nuts. There are also vinyl rails that come in two parts; a base that is riveted on and a snap-in cover to hide the rivets. Wooden gunwales are sometimes protected by neoprene rubber molding covered with canvas. These are good for a few years before the canvas rots or the securing staples fall out. If the canvas is held on by screws with finishing washers it will last longer.

Rowing and Towing

As we said earlier, the short, fat dinghy is not a graceful rowing machine, but there are several things that make rowing bearable. The most important is a good set of oars. Oars are commonly 5 to 5-1/2 feet in length and made of ash. They are too short and too heavy for relaxed rowing. Consider spending the extra money for a pair of 6-foot spruce oars; the difference is remarkable. Because they are softer, spruce oars must be copper-tipped and have a leather collar to prevent chafe at the oarlock. Spoonblade oars are fine for racing shells, but the expense is unwarranted for the average dinghy.

If possible, try to row a dinghy before buying it. In calm water, pull three or four strokes and stop to see if the boat tracks straight. Going across the seas, the boat should not bob so much that you have to time your strokes between waves. Going into seas, the boat should never ship water with only one person aboard. When rowing alone, make sure you can extend your legs and brace them against the stern or stern seat comfortably. Check to see if the boat has two rowing stations, a desirable feature. As you pull the oars, watch the oarlocks—are they, or the gunwale itself, working? Both are a sign of weakness. Finally, see if the oar is chafing against the rubrail as you pull.

Bronze oarlocks and sockets are stronger than those cast of pot metal. Pot metal sockets must have plastic bushings to protect them; these bushings can come out. Oarlocks and sockets made completely of plastic work smoothly until they are heavily stressed; then they tend to break. Closed oarlocks can be kept on the oars with rubber collars. Open oarlocks must stay on the boat and are too often the victim of theft.

When towing, you should be able to stow the oars on the floor of the boat under the center thwart. A good dinghy will tow straight with its bow clear of the water. If the towing eye is too high, or if the boat has too little rocker, the bow will submerge and the boat will weave back and forth on its tow line (and perhaps capsize). The towing eye should be through-bolted to a backing plate near the waterline to raise the bow, and the tow line should be adjusted to keep the dinghy riding on the stern wave of the mother vessel.

Sailing Gear

Do you want a sailing dinghy? This is something you should decide before buying the boat. The sailing option usually adds from $300 to $500 to the price of the dinghy. Buying the sailing gear later could be considerably more expensive, particularly if the boat was not equipped with a daggerboard trunk, and a step and partner for the mast.

If you decide to buy a sailing dinghy, be sure to check its rig carefully. Dinghies come with a variety of rig types. Although it has been many years since racing and cruising sailors abandoned the gunter, lug, sprit and lateen rigs for the higher performance of the marconi rig, many dinghy manufacturers continue to opt for these less efficient systems. The old rigs really aren't any faster to set up, and with the advent of the two-piece mast, the taller marconi rig is just as easy to store.

The system we prefer is an unstayed two-piece mast, held together by a sleeve, with a grooved track and an external halyard. The Laser-type luff-sleeved marconi sail, which slides over a spar without a halyard is cumbersome because it cannot be lowered without unstepping the mast.

Dinghy sails are, for the most part, shapeless. The sail for an 8-foot dinghy is usually 35 to 40 square feet, of a cheap 3-ounce Dacron or 4-ounce nylon, and has a short service life even with careful use. When set in light air, it is characterized by a deep pocket next to the mast because the only shaping it has is luff curve. The best dinghy sail would be made of 3.8 ounce Dacron and have a curve cut into the length of most panels (broadseam) to give it a smooth, even camber. The battens are commonly sewn into their batten pockets. The best battens have a hole drilled through the aft end and are seized to the sail.

Rudders and daggerboards are often shapeless half-inch plywood. They should be rounded on the leading edge, and taper from just ahead of the middle to a fairly sharp trailing edge. Daggerboards should be deep and fit tightly in the trunk. The trunk should be fiberglass, not wood, and be rigidly attached to the center thwart. To keep water out of the boat while towing or rowing, the trunk must have a separate cap.

Finally, with an unstayed mast, check the mast partner and step. Both are subject to heavy loading. Before you buy a sailing dinghy, insert the mast to make sure it fits snugly. The greater the height of the partner above the step, the more support it will give the mast. The boat should also have a line to hold the rig in the boat should it capsize (the downhaul works nicely), for if the mast comes out of the step, it will often break the partner.

Nothing beats a small boat for learning the basics of sailing, because it is more responsive than a larger, heavier boat. Even if you already own a cruising sailboat, your children should have a small boat to learn on. A sailing dinghy doesn't make as good a trainer for small children as a "board boat," such as the Sunfish. Dinghies are tender and are not self-rescuing, so when they capsize they are difficult to bail out and sail away. However, if you cruise with your children, a sailing dinghy does makes a great "babysitter."

INFLATABLE DINGHIES

Perhaps the most important consideration when purchasing an inflatable boat is the quality of the fabric. Poor fabrics invariably mean decreased performance, and often reduced hull life. Detecting poor fabrics is not always easy. Manufacturers of boats made of less durable materials are understandably not very specific on the subject.

A variety of materials are currently being used for hull fabrics, but they can be divided into two main classifications: those which are reinforced with some kind of cloth material, and those which are not.

Unreinforced Hull Fabrics

Unreinforced fabrics are almost invariably made of a compound of polyvinyl chloride (PVC) plastic, and boats made of this material are generally of fairly simple design to permit mass production. Since PVC material is not especially expensive (when compared to Hypalon/neoprene compounds) boats can be produced and sold at relatively low prices. PVC, however, is not noted for its long life, and an unreinforced PVC hull will usually become unserviceable within two to four years. Reinforced PVC hulls generally remain useful for a somewhat longer time, but you can expect the material to stiffen and the hull to become difficult to deflate and stow.

By way of explanation it should be noted that polyvinyl chloride is a petroleum-derived product, and that in its pure form is stiff and hard, which is one reason why it is used in the construction of pipe. In order to use PVC as a fabric, it must be thinned with a plasticizer so that it becomes flexible. Aging in PVC fabrics occurs mostly because of the gradual evaporation of the plasticizer. As evaporation proceeds, the basic PVC characteristics return, and the fabric becomes stiff and brittle. In unreinforced hulls, the usual manifestation of this is the failure of a seam. Seams, especially those in the tubes which must hold air pressure, are extremely difficult to repair and the boat must usually be relegated to the scrap heap.

How can you extend the life of a PVC hull? The four main reasons why the plasticizer evaporates are friction, microorganisms, chemicals, and heat. Since all of these causative factors are difficult to avoid in normal use, the trick is to minimize the boat's exposure to them. Towing a dinghy behind a larger boat for extended periods creates friction. As an alternative bring your dinghy aboard between ports of call. This will not only help to preserve the inflatable, but will save fuel costs if running under power and increase speed if under sail. Microorganisms are found in sea water, especially in warm climates, and will cause brown spots to appear on the PVC when they begin working. Hose your boat off when not in use and don't permit it to sit alongside in the slip for weeks on end.

Gasoline spills will also quickly harden the fabric. If you don't believe this, take a piece of fresh hull repair material and soak it in gasoline for 24 hours. The fabric will become stiff enough to use as a spoon. Flush off gasoline spills quickly to avoid the chemical interaction which leeches out the plasticizer. Finally, to minimize heat damage, it is best to deflate and stow your boat when it will not be used for extended periods. Continuous exposure to the sun can be damaging and expensive.

Now, having said all of the above, should you buy an unreinforced PVC boat? Certainly, if you stick to one of good quality, and if the price is reasonable. In addition, there are some other facts which you should consider when contemplating the purchase of an unreinforced PVC hull. The biggest single disadvantage to these boats is that new unreinforced PVC materials tend to be soft and prone to stretch, especially when warm. Because of this, the boats are always a bit mushy and floppy when inflated. This softness often precludes the use of large outboard motors, since the hull has too much flex (unless special strengthening rods are installed) and will bend when power is applied. The latter point may be quite important if you already have an engine which you plan to use.

As a rule, the quality of an unreinforced vinyl boat will depend first on the design; second, on the thickness and quality of the fabric; and third, on the strength of the seams.

The worst design flaw is the failure to provide proper chambering. Too often, in poorly made boats, the hull consists of a single undivided oval tube which, if punctured, will lose air and deposit the passengers in the drink. The easiest way to discover if a boat is chambered or not is to count the number of filler holes, or valves, which it has. If the main buoyancy tube has two chambers, then it will have two points of inflation. When making this count, don't count floor or deck chambers. Even though these float, it is unlikely that they will keep you from taking a bath if a main unchambered tube goes.

As mentioned earlier, boats made of unreinforced PVC material will stretch considerably when internal pressure is applied. This tendency becomes more pronounced as material thickness is sacrificed to profit. More importantly, thin material also means weaker seams with a greater tendency to split, even under light pressure loads.

Often fabric quality and seam construction can be determined by a careful inspection. Begin by feeling the fabric. Boats made of good fabric *feel* tough. Even when uninflated, the fabric feels heavy and remains reasonably stiff. Notice whether the fabric looks or feels excessively oily. Cheap PVC fabrics often have an oily look and feel to them, probably because of incomplete polymerization.

Closely examine the seams. These are almost always made by heating and welding the two sheets of material together with a bonding machine. On poorly made boats, the machine often overmelts the vinyl to the point where the remaining material in the seam in thinner than either of the original sheets. A correct weld will be almost as thick as the combined original material.

The final test is to look at the warranty. See if the manufacturer has enough faith and confidence in his own product to warrant it against defects for at least one year. Find out when the warranty begins. Sometimes it begins on the date the merchandise leaves the factory, rather than on the date of purchase. If the boat has been in the supply channel for any length of time, the warranty could have already expired.

A good quality boat made of unreinforced PVC material will always be less expensive than a similar quality boat made of reinforced fabric. If you understand the overall shortcomings of unreinforced materials, that even the best electronically welded seaming is inherently weaker than the lapped seams found on more sophisticated and expensive inflatables, then perhaps one of these boats is for you. However, if operating conditions include the probability of heavy use, and if you require absolute reliability and long-term durability, then you will be better served by a more expensive boat made of reinforced fabric.

Reinforced Hull Fabrics

Reinforced fabrics for inflatable boats are made by impregnating or coating some form of cloth material with a suitable substance to prevent the passage of air. Unprotected natural fibers and coatings, like cotton and natural rubber, are not sufficiently durable to withstand the weathering and the normal abuse expected in boating. This is not true with modern synthetics like nylon, polyester, Kevlar, neoprene, Hypalon, and even PVC (subject to the caveats previously listed). All are relatively long-lasting synthetics now being used in the construction of inflatable boats.

Of the fabrics, nylon is the most frequent choice because of its lower cost, greater strength, and resistance to deterioration. Occasionally polyester (Dacron, or its European counterparts) is selected because of its low stretch and higher melting point, which permits stronger hot vulcanization of the seams. Kevlar is also beginning to appear because of its very great strength to weight ratio.

The coatings which are applied to these fabrics are normally some form of synthetic rubber, like neoprene or Hypalon, or some mixture of polyvinyl chloride. Natural rubber is still occasionally used, but to be of any lasting value it must be coated on the exposed side with a synthetic coating, like Hypalon.

In inflatable boat literature, the DuPont trademark *Hypalon* is the word most frequently seen. By definition, Hypalon is a chlorosulfonated polyethylene; a synthetic rubber made by reacting polyethylene with chlorine and sulphur. Hypalon, when properly compounded, is truly amazing stuff. Extensive tests and actual experience have proven that Hypalon is unusually resistant to damage from sunlight, ozone, flame, petroleum products, mildew, most acids, abrasion, flexing, and low temperature. The result is an almost indestructible material ideally suited for use in inflatable boats. Trouble is, Hypalon, in its pure form is not easily bonded with normal adhesives. For this reason, in most applications it is either mixed with neoprene synthetic rubber, or used as an outer protective coating over the more vulnerable neoprene. Pure Hypalon outer coatings have a way of wearing or chafing off and exposing the more fragile material below. For this reason, the neoprene/Hypalon mixture seems the best solution since, if properly compounded, it will approach the qualities of pure Hypalon for durability.

Polyvinyl chloride is the other primary fabric-coating substance which is now being used by a number of inflatable boat manufacturers. While PVC does not have the extended lasting qualities of neoprene/Hypalon, its lower cost and much greater ease of manufacture have brought it to the marketplace. PVC-coated fabrics can be electronically welded by machine which results in great savings in labor costs. Further, if the vinyl-coated material is abraded, it can easily be recoated by the owner so long as the fabric base material is intact. Recoating a chafed neoprene/Hypalon boat is a good deal more time consuming.

Fabric Color

The best strengthening material for neoprene rubber is carbon black, consequently all of the earlier neoprene inflatables were either black or very dark grey. Dark boats suffer from two big disadvantages: they absorb heat from the sun which makes them uncomfortable to sit on; and they change pressure quite noticeably from day to night for the same reason. The introduction of Hypalon and vinyl has changed that, and now good quality inflatable boats are able to be produced in much lighter grays and a variety of colors.

Coating the Fabric

The technique used in coating, or proofing, the fabric is as important as the material used. If the impregnating substance is not properly bonded to the base it will tend to separate under pressure, especially at stress points like fold and seams.

Knife-coating and calendering are the basic ways in which fabric is coated. In knife-coating, the impregnating material is spread on the base fiber with a device similar to a long, rigid knife blade or spatula. The proofing material is thinned with a solvent so that it will flow easily, and then it is layered on, one thickness at a time, until eight to ten coats have been applied. Rubberized materials made in this way are almost always poorly bonded between layers because of the porosity imparted by the thinning solvent, and subsequent separation of the individual layers is common. Vinyl material which is knife-coated does not suffer from this defect because a different chemistry is involved.

The calendering process is the very best way to coat rubberized fabrics. In this process, the base material is run between two extremely heavy rollers (a calender), which compresses the proofing substance deeply into the cloth fibers, and essentially welds the materials together.

Equipment costs for buying and maintaining calendering equipment are high, and material fabricated in this way is always more expensive. For this reason it is rarely used to make low-cost boats.

Recoating Deteriorated Fabric

When boats made of natural rubber or a poor grade of neoprene begin to deteriorate, the skin develops an overall pattern of fine cracks, which permits air to seep through. Can a boat in this condition be recoated and brought back to usable condition? Maybe. If the problem is detected quickly, there are products on the market which can seal seepage holes in deteriorating fabric. Whether the effort will be worth the time and cost is doubtful. The problem is that cheaply made boats are exactly that, and if the fabric is deteriorating you can expect to find other related problems. As mentioned earlier, cheaply made boats always use inexpensive rubberized fabrics made by the knife coating process. This means that, in addition to the pattern of cracking, you

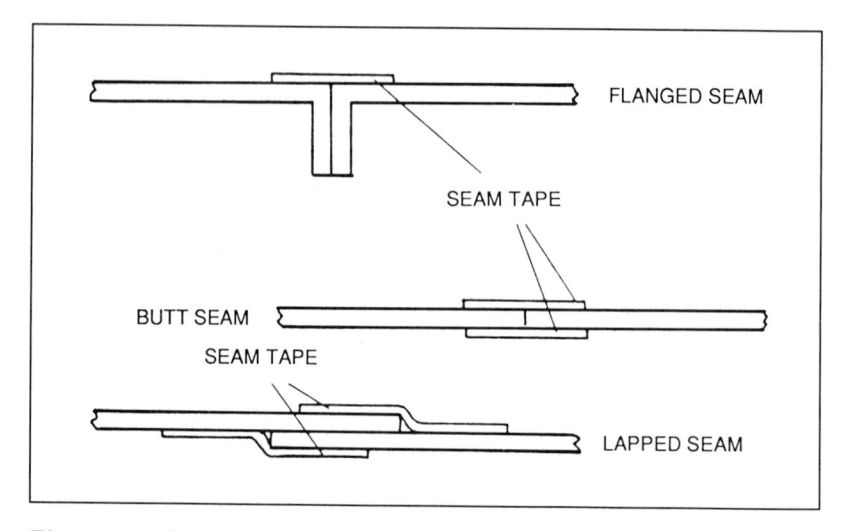

Figure 8.1. Three types of seams used in inflatable boats.

will probably discover some degree of layer separation, usually at points where the fabric has also begun to deteriorate in the seams, where the recoat will not reach. The seam area will remain weak, and this may lead to early failure.

Recoating is an "iffy" proposition, with no guarantees. If the boat is new, and the seepage is minor, then a new skin may prolong its life. On the other hand, you may recoat today, and have a split seam tomorrow. There is no way to know.

Seam Types

There are three different ways in which the seams of inflatable craft can be constructed. On quality boats, the preferred method is to lap the seam, one piece over the other, with a minimum overlap of one inch. With seams of this type, the exposed outer edge should face aft to prevent lifting as the boat moves through the water. The edges of the seam may or may not be taped, but if they are not, the inner edge is often sealed with a bead of silicon, or similar flexible material, to help retard wicking.

The butt seam is often the seam of choice when boats are fabricated out of PVC-coated materials. A butt seam which has been electronically welded is perhaps as airtight and strong as a seam can be made. Flanged seams are the least attractive of the three types, and must be reinforced on the inside with tape to prevent separation under pressure (Taping is not necessary on the flanged seams used on heat-sealed unreinforced vinyl inflatable boats.)

Wicking

It is a fact that even on the best boats there will be some pressure loss if the hull sits inflated for any length of time. This is because air escapes, very gradually, by flowing along the strands of the base fabric, until it is finally released along some exposed cut edge. This process is called wicking, and it is normal.

What is important, is that the boat should not soften to the touch in less than five or six days.

Chambering

Multiple chambers are to the inflatable what built-in flotation is to the hard boat. Chambering is essential to safety, and any inflatable boat which does not incorporate this feature should not be considered for purchase.

In the larger sportboats, and in many dinghies, chambering is most often achieved by the creation of internal bulkheads at intervals along the tube. These bulkheads are not flat walls. As a rule they are either cones or hemispheres. This design makes it far easier to achieve and maintain equal pressure in adjacent tube sections without repeated checks with a gauge. This is possible because the cone or dome will float fore and aft as pressure in one side or the other varies. With a flat bulkhead there would be no way to compensate for pressure differences, and the bulkhead would be under constant strain.

Since most people do not understand this fact about bulkhead design, they often worry needlessly when they begin to deflate their boat. They release pressure in one chamber, and notice a pressure loss in the chamber alongside as the divider shifts to the deflated side. Depending on the distance that the bulkhead has shifted, the pressure loss in the inflated side can be quite noticeable. To the uninitiated, this suggests that a leak has occurred in the bulkhead and the safety of the boat has been compromised, but this is not true.

Valves

Air is introduced and removed from inflatable boats by means of valves. How efficiently this is done is very much dependent on valve design. The valve must be sufficiently large to permit rapid air movement in and out, yet small enough to be unobtrusive when the boat is in use. Other requirements in a good valve include high resistance to corrosion, low potential for damage, and simplicity and aesthetic appeal.

One of the most functional valve designs now in use, consists of a threaded base, permanently attached to the hull, which accepts an insert (frequently made of plastic) to which the hose end connects. The bottom of the insert has a rubber diaphragm which opens and closes as the pump is operated. The diaphragm permits the operator to stop pumping, or even disconnect the pump hose, without loss of air pressure. A cap provides the final seal over the pump connection point once the hose is disconnected. The advantage of the valve insert is that it can be removed, leaving a much larger port for rapid deflation.

Keels

Flat, sloppy bottoms are acceptable on dinghies which move slowly through the water, but at speed, the flat bottom pounds badly, and directional stability is difficult to maintain.

The inflatable keel compensates for these problems. The all-inflatable dinghy rarely has a keel as standard equipment, but these are sometimes added by owners of boats which have floorboards. Even though dinghies are inherently slow creatures, tightening up the bottom fabric can add a knot or two under power, and the keel does provide some additional directional stability. The easy solution is to force small-diameter boat fenders between the floorboard and the bottom fabric.

Floorboards

When floorboards are used in dinghies, the primary function is to provide some substance to the otherwise floppy bottom. Without a solid decking, the dinghy bottom resembles an under-filled water bed, and many passengers find this distasteful and bothersome, especially if water has gotten into the dinghy and pools around their ankles when they stand.

Varnish or clear polyurethane seem to be the favorite finishes for floorboards. These materials are transparent, and when they are scratched the wood below absorbs water and becomes discolored. It would be more practical, and probably less expensive, to finish the floorboards with a few coats of a high-grade marine paint. Unlike varnish, paint can be touched up in minutes and still look good.

Air Pumps

Air is the primary ingredient in an inflatable boat, and a good pump is an essential item. Despite their seeming simplicity, there is a lot of variation in both the efficiency and quality of pumps, and many of them are totally unsuited for use with inflatable boats. Bicycle and automobile pumps, for example, are very inefficient for this purpose, since they are designed to deliver a lot of pressure but very little volume.

A large-diameter foot pump, or bellows, is the best choice for an inflatable boat. The bellows expand to a large size between strokes, which means that it will deliver a lot of volume each time it is compressed. Further, it is actuated by the weight of the body, rather than by back and arm muscles, an important point when you consider that it may take 20 to 25 minutes of pumping to inflate one of the larger sportboats.

It is almost impossible to overinflate a good inflatable boat using a foot bellows. The pressure which any pump can deliver is a function of the piston size versus the force of compression. The piston size of a standard inflatable-boat foot pump is large enough so that even the weight of a heavy person will be insufficient to cause pressure problems. This is not true in the case of some hand pumps which can easily achieve pressures of over ten pounds with very little effort.

There are ways to check pumps, and it is a good idea to test before you buy. Be on the lookout for any of the following deficiencies: Recycling spring too weak for fast recovery after each stroke; fabric pump skirt not tightly secured to the bellows and leaking air; pump skirt of flimsy material which will disintegrate after a few uses; air intake valve not closing properly resulting in loss of air on compression; pump hose too short, too narrow, or so thin and flexible that it kinks. Of course, if you want to make life easy on yourself, buy a small electrically operated pump to do most of your inflating work.

What about inflating a boat at a gas station, or by using high pressure air from a scuba tank? These sources can be used, but *only with great caution*, and only to the point where the boat is inflated, but still soft.

Once a boat has been inflated to the point of hardness, the difference between three pounds and fifteen pounds of pressure is hard to detect, and it becomes a simple matter to blow out every seam in the boat. This has happened more than once, and the lesson is expensive.

Carrying Bags

One of the attractive features of inflatable dinghies is the ability to deflate and store the boat when it is not in use. To do this properly, the boat must not only deflate and disassemble easily, but must reduce in size sufficiently to fit its storage bags. With properly designed bags, this is not a great chore, but this is not always the case. Too often bags have been designed to fit boats when they leave the factory with all of the air vacuumed out. No thought has been given to the poor guy who will be pushing, prodding, and kneading the thing, trying to restuff it into a bag that is too small. Look the bag over when the boat comes out of its box. Correctly fitted bags will have some excess room in them when they come from the factory, and any straps or ties will have sufficient extra length to allow room for expansion.

Aside from fit, check the bags for fabric quality and strength. The material and the seams must be strong enough to withstand years of heavy use. Chafing can be a problem as boats are loaded and unloaded and moved about in transit. Mildew will blossom on untreated canvas when someone forgets to thoroughly dry the hull before putting it in storage. Any bag will have a short life under those conditions.

As with the boats themselves, the best materials for carrying bags are the synthetics, such as nylon. They are better still if they have received a waterproof coating of some sort. With a quality inflatable, the bags are important because they are protecting a large investment. Make certain that the bags are of good quality and have a proper fit, and be sure to use them whenever the boat is deflated and stored.

* * *

The first step in choosing a ship's tender is to determine whether you will be shopping for a hard dinghy or an inflatable. For the daysailor who will occasionally tow the dink, but will usually leave it tied to the mooring, a hard dink is probably the best alternative. For the coastal cruiser and the bluewater sailor, the choice is often made based on what type of tender is easiest to carry onboard. For the larger boat, a hard dinghy stowed either on deck or on davits is the logical choice. On the smaller cruiser, an inflatable may be the only practical solution.

Once you have decided on the type of tender you will purchase, then you can begin to look at the features of individual models. Don't believe everything you read when you are shopping for a dinghy. Every dinghy, of course, according to the manufacturer, offers the highest quality workmanship in a durable and attractive dinghy that will row, tow, sail and motor to beat the band. And few will mention maintenance unless it is to say that none is required.

The fact is that in small boats, the compromises are large, and the smaller the boat, the greater the compromises. No dinghy will row, tow, sail, and motor with equal effectiveness. Your second task then, is to define your priorities. Then find a dinghy designed for the priority at the top of your list. If you get some other good features in the bargain, you're that much ahead.

Index

Anchor Rodes 101-104
   Chain Size 102-103
   Rope Size 103-104
Anchor Selection 93-101
   Secondary Anchors 99
   Storm Anchor 99
Anchor Wells 112-114
Anchor Windlasses 104-111
   Electric 109-110
   Hydraulic 110
   Manual 107-108
Anchors
   CQR, Bruce, and Northhill 95
   FOB 95
   Kedge and Babbit 95
   Lightweight 93-94
Boom, Stow-away 60-61
Bow Rollers 115-117
Canvas
   Natural Fiber 80
   Synthetics 80-82
Canvaswork 79-91
   Design 85-86
   Fabrics 80-82
   Fasteners 86-90
Compasses
   Bulkhead 122-127
   Digital Magnetic 127-128
   Fluxgate 128-132
   Pedestal 119-122
Dinghies
   Capacity 223-224
   Construction 224-225
   Hull Shape 222-223
   Rowing and Towing 225-226
   Sailing Gear 226-227
Distress Signals 206-211
   Aerial Flares 209
   Hand-Held Flares 207-208
   Non-Pyrotechnic Devices 210
   Smoke Signals 208

EPIRBs 211-215
First Aid Kits 219-221
Global Positioning System (GPS) 132-134
Ground Tackle 92-104
Ham Radio 178-185
Hand-held VHF Radios 177-178
Inflatable Dinghies 228-238
   Air Pumps 237
   Carrying Bags 238
   Floorboards 236
   Keels 236
   Recoating Deteriorated Fabric 233-234
   Reinforced Hull Fabrics 231-232
   Unreinforced Hull Fabrics 228-231
   Valves 236
Inflatable Life Rafts 216-219
Integrated Instruments 160-166
Lifesling 201-206
Loran-C 136-143
   Interference 140-141
   Radio Wave Inaccuracies 140
Luff Grove Devices 31-33
Mainsheet Traveler 74-78
Man-Overboard Gear 196-206
Masthead Strobe Lights 215-216
Personal Flotation Devices 186-196
   Type I: "Mae West" PFDs 192-193
   Type II: "Yoke" PFDs 191-192
   Type III: "Vest" PFDs 191
   Type V: Semi-Inflatables 193-194
Radar 149-159
   Installation 157-158
   Licensing 158
   Safety 159-160
Radio Direction Finders 143-144

Reefing
    Continuous 41-44
    Roller 40
    Slab 41
Roller Furling
    Headsails 12-13, 44-54
    Mainsails 54-60
Rope 67-73
    Braided 69
    Breaking Strength 71-72
    Laid 68-69
Sail Inventory 11-21
Sailcloth 22-25
Sailmaker, Choosing 21-22
Sails
    Construction 14-15
    Downwind 19-21
    Headsails 16-17

Mainsails 17-19
Mylar 30-31
Racing 28-30
Tips on ordering 25-27
SatNav 134-135
Sextants 145-148
Single Sideband Radios 178-185
Spinnaker Pole 34-37
Telltales 37-39
VHF Radios 167-177
    Antennas 176-177
    Receivers 170-172
    Transmitters 168-170
Whisker Pole 34-37
Winches 62-67
    Friction 64-65
    Power Ratio 65-67
    Sheet Loading 62-64